Daily Inspiration
For Conscious Living

WIDE AWAKE.
EVERY DAY.

DEDICATED TO YOU

DEAR READER

WIDE AWAKE. EVERY DAY.

DAILY INSPIRATION FOR CONSCIOUS LIVING

To contact the author: http://outwriteliving.com

Author: Starla J. King
Cover photo: Starla J. King
Author photo: Gabrielle Fox of Gabrielle Fox Photography
Book and cover design: Roslyn Nelson

ISBN: 978-0-9892822-2-2
Library of Congress Control Number: 2013951744

Publisher: Little Big Bay LLC
littlebigbay.com

DAILY INSPIRATION
FOR CONSCIOUS LIVING

WIDE AWAKE.
EVERY DAY.

STARLA J. KING

"Let the beauty we love be what we do.
There are hundreds of ways to kneel and kiss the ground."

RUMI

ACKNOWLEDGMENTS

I would like to offer a heartfelt "Thank you" to each and every person who sparked or fanned the flames of this writing dream over the years. I do believe that we are all part of each other in some way, and I am forever grateful for that divine alchemy.

Thank you to the great spiritual beings and organizations whose teachings deeply influenced my thinking, beliefs, and life approach:
Gurumayi Chidvilasananda,
Pema Chodron,
Don Miguel Ruiz,
Shunryu Suzuki,
the Siddha Yoga Foundation,
The Center for Right Relationship,
the Coaches Training Institute,
the Creativity Coaching Association,
and my parents, Aaron M. and Betty D. King.

Thank you to Coleman Barks for permission to use his translation of Rumi's words, as quoted at the beginning of this book. Those words have for years been a beacon for my growth in living an awake life.

Thank you to my eight brilliant, delightful, and wonderfully off-kilter siblings — Michael, Jewel, Robert, Steve, Angela, Marty, Noël, and Heidi — for teaching your baby sister how to play with life.

Thank you to Nancy J. Duncan, my business and life coach, for lighting my inner kindling and keeping it burning for over six years by supporting a profound journey to my truest, most inspired, and most awake self, and to this book.

Thank you to Lorin Beller for providing foundational tools for my growth and learning at a pivotal time in my work life.

Thank you to Rebecca Cohen for being a safe space.

Thank you to Ushi Patel for giving my words courage through the inspiration in her book of poems, *Brave the Unknown*.

Thank you to my coaching clients, who (likely unknowingly) gave me incentive to keep going on this project.

Thank you to each beautiful being who allowed me to share their gift of words in this book:
Lorin Beller,
Tina Burkholder,
Rebecca P. Cohen,
Nancy J. Duncan,
Laurie Foley,
Eileen Kennedy,
Joan King,
Marty King,
Sandy Manne,
Margaret Gibbs McCain,
Anna G. Penning,
Pamela Slim,
Jo Steele,
Cheryl Peachey Stoner,
Ellen Stoune,
Angel Sullivan,
Tererai Trent, and
Steven Wiebe-King.

Thank you to my early readers, Joan King and Kristy King, who held my heart in their hands with gentleness and honesty.

Thank you to my publisher Ros Nelson of Little Big Bay for taking my pages of words and sculpting them skillfully and gracefully into tangible beauty. Clearly, the book gods heard my request.

Thank you to my feline office mates, Jazzy and Gitter, for their constant company and companionship.

And finally, to my wife Sandra A. Manne, aka "Toonces," thank you for offering me your heart in which to place a newly-awakened love 17 years ago. How appropriate that it all started one day at a bookstore! Thank you also for honoring the essential place that writing holds in my life, and shoring me up from every angle on this project. I love you now and always.

TABLE OF CONTENTS

INTRODUCTION

In July of 2009, my business and life coach sent an email to me that became a never-fading torch which has lit the way for the direction of this book.

"I was wondering how you might be able to simply, with few words, create impact on the reader that has them leaning into their lives — and this precious moment — in a new, profound take-your-breath-away way."

This book is my answer to that challenge.

We can skim through life on the surface, with our eyes half closed as our souls remain restless and obscured behind our mind's ongoing ramblings, or we can engage with a richness of living that goes deeper, with both eyes open and our minds pausing regularly to sit in the lap of our vibrant souls.

We can choose to experience only the small sliver of a sleepy life, or we can choose to step into the dynamic, full spectrum of a conscious life and be *wide awake, every day.*

This book has nothing to do with a huge, complicated process; it's all about the simplicity of paying close enough attention to finally see what's already there waiting to wake us up.

In our Mennonite family of nine children, growing up in Cuba, Mexico, and then rural Virginia, living simply (and simply living) was both a spiritual and physical requirement in our daily lives. I was steeped in Bible teachings, nature, the work of my hands, music, play, and community, yet I longed for something more. I lived fully within the parameters of learned belief and life systems, yet I yearned for freedoms I didn't know then that I could choose.

Little by little, fueled by an intense need for authentic self-expression, and supported by therapists, coaches, and all manner of introspective exercises, I dared test the waters of those childhood boundaries. As I grew, so did my courage, inspiration, and delight in this incredible gift called life.

I now know the power of choice, and the inspirations in this book are the result of many years of choosing my own version of living as broadly, deeply, reverently, and completely as I know how.

Although filtered through my own perspective and experience, *Wide Awake. Every Day.* combines wisdom from many who have come before me and others who walk beside me. My teachers have shown up in the form of artists, coaches, spiritual leaders from Eastern and Western religions, soul-friends, nature (including animals), and the words from my own pen, and they have gathered together here to offer you this book.

You will find seeming contradictions from one page to the next: recommendations for rest followed by a nudge to test the edge of exhaustion; suggestions toward laser focus followed by an urging toward expanded attention; encouragement to move toward relief followed by a gentle challenge to stay with the discomfort. Different facets of life benefit from different approaches on any given day in any given situation.

Also, you will notice these pages are not grouped by theme or category; life does not unfold in neat groupings, so neither does this book. Consider it a real-life practice in discovering and responding to the varied gems that each day holds.

Each day includes a *Bring It To Life!* exercise and questions for contemplation to help you integrate each day's learning into your own life in a more personal way.

This book is a tool kit offering, not a lesson plan, so soak in what speaks to you and step around what doesn't — *you get to choose.*

I'll conclude with a poem by a soul-friend, written after she came back from a perspective-shifting walk in the woods. "I seriously woke up," she reports. This (facing page), dear readers, is what it looks, feels, and sounds like to be *wide awake, every day.*

They say you should write the book you wanted to see on the shelves and couldn't find. This is that book for me. May it also be the book you've been looking for. Let's stay wide awake, every day, together. *Starting now.*   – Starla J. King

Growth Spurt

Rebecca P. Cohen

Prickly-twisted branches along an uneven, pitted path
poke my web of thoughts, but do not bleed.
Their invisible scars weigh heavy as I stumble
and scout and search for a beautiful vista
until I give up looking
and stop.
The once-distant, thunderous sound
crashes along my rocky shore
and crashes and floods and breaks
louder and louder until
the lines rusted over lifetimes run
clean with the fresh, gently flowing river water
running pure,
and I awake
in warm rays of golden sparkles
outstretched on the undulating bright green moss
holding hands in connected threads
at the base of the Tree of Life
with eternal, sacred knowing.

JANUARY

"Let each moment open your eyes."

SJK

AWAKE

Build your heat
through the fires
of attention,
flames licking your eyelids
kissing them apart to
melt the icy fear holding
your heart
at bay
and with each blink
you spark into
life and
Awake.
Awake.
Awake.

BRING IT TO LIFE!

Today, open your heart to noticing the details of each experience you have.
Let each moment open your eyes, increase your attention, and expand your gratitude.

How does this exercise impact your day?

I felt happy and did not once dwell on the bad in my life.

"The past quickly goes stale even as the future lures us with hopeful promise,
but the present — the right now — is where real life happens."

SJK

IN THE MOMENT

Sitting at an outdoor café, I watched a precious little girl dancing on a tiny piece of mulch. Her bright pink barrettes (matching her entire outfit) had a life of their own, bouncing in a slightly delayed rhythm, accentuating her determination of each jump step so carefully aimed at that one piece of mulch. The plaza was bustling around her, but she was oblivious to anything except her dance and that shred of wood. ✎   As adults, we often lose this single-minded fascinated focus. The big picture, that thing that happened yesterday, and the next thing on our list arrests our attention, and we overlook the magic of the present, the delight in right now. Like the cool breeze at dusk, the lingering touch of a friend, the flavor complexities of a single, savored bite of food. ✎   The past quickly goes stale even as the future lures us with hopeful promise, but the present — the right now — is where real life happens. The present is where the embodiment of joy dances on a piece of mulch.

✎

BRING IT TO LIFE!

As you go through your day today, notice the young children.

What captures their attention?

What does their body language tell you when they're focused on activity?

How might you bring that full-focused, present-moment enthusiasm to your own life?

Children never dwell on something big, their attention is often drawn towards the little things, whether good or bad. Their body language often shows determination. By focusing on the present, not the future which may contain stress.

"The sweet nectar of life is offered to each of us in so many ways;
it's simply up to us to pause, notice, and receive it."

SJK

SWEET NECTAR OF LIFE

As a child living in rural Virginia, I spent many hours outdoors. Late spring days would find me roaming nearby dirt roads, indulging in the sensory abundance of the wild honeysuckle that scrambled along fences and coughed in the dust at the side of the road. ⌒ I don't remember who taught me this, but I learned that there's a single, exquisite drop of sweet nectar at the base of each honeysuckle flower, surprisingly easy to access. I would pop the base of a flower off, gently draw the stamen out of the resulting hole, and each time marvel at the shimmering drop of liquid candy that came with it. Whole afternoons disappeared into timeless joy as I sucked those delicate nectar drops off living threads while enveloped in what I imagined must be the sweet smell of heaven. Those honeysuckle moments were — and still are — intoxicating, nourishing, delightful, and a multi-layered treat to the senses. ⌒ The sweet nectar of life is offered to each of us in so many ways; it's simply up to us to pause, notice, and receive it.

⌒

BRING IT TO LIFE!

Look today for anything that seems like a potential experience
of the sweet nectar of life, and receive it.
At the end of the day, write a list of those experiences.

How did this focus impact your day? I enjoyed time with my dog.

"If I am here and nobody sees me, do I truly exist?
If someone looks at me, but doesn't SEE me, do I truly exist?"

SJK

I SEE YOU

In South Africa, the Zulu greeting is *Sawubona* (I see you), with the response *Sikhona* (I am here). A person is a person because of other people. I exist because of you; you exist because of me.  Think about the experience of someone catching your eye and the instant pulse of connection you feel. That is the feeling of being seen. Have you ever had someone look softly into your eyes while lightly touching their fingertips to your chest or arm for a moment? That pure, liquid gold feeling of a feathery touch of connection — literally, figuratively, and spiritually — that is the feeling of being seen. How often do we take that extra step, that extra bit of energy to see — really, truly see — the other people in our lives?

BRING IT TO LIFE!

Today, stretch beyond just looking at people, and take the extra time to see them
(loved ones and strangers alike). One way to do this is to notice each person's eye color,
for eyes are indeed the windows to the soul.
What was different for you when you saw someone instead of just looking at them?
How might this change your interactions in the future?

I can't put into words what was different, I felt that the person may have felt seen. Eye contact is very important, I may try to make eye contact more, I often don't like it because I feel invaded, but I can still make ey contact without letting myself feel invaded.

"When open to the healing powers of darkness,
I am often met by a darkness so soft that all my edges fade."

SJK

A DARKNESS SO SOFT

So often we think of darkness as the absence of light or hope. It's the thing we fear, the feeling we avoid, and the state we fill with monsters and malevolence. ✑ Yet, recently I've discovered that when open to the healing powers of darkness, I am often met by a darkness so soft that all my edges fade, and from this soft space of comfort, I begin to understand how we might all be interconnected parts of a global divine energy. ✑ In a darkness so soft, let's wait a few moments before rushing to the glare of the light.

BRING IT TO LIFE!

In the darkness before dawn or after sunset, step outside
and feel the soft cashmere of darkness around you.
How might your emotional dark times change
if you remember this physical darkness so soft?

"Close the books, flip the switch — enough.
Breathe, clear, dive in to self."
NANCY J. DUNCAN

STEP AWAY

Sometimes work needs to take a back seat. It's almost sacrilegious to say that in this largely work-focused American society. We get gold stars for working late and sacrificing "me time," and being in a crazy rush all the time is more likely to get a double-thumbs-up than if we push back our desk chair and say, "I'm outta here — taking a break!" I find that it's usually on the days we most strongly feel we can't possibly afford to take time for ourselves that we most need to do so. Like tonight when I need to write a blog post and it's already getting late and I'm tired and I just … need … rest. So that's exactly what I'm going to do. I'll stop writing so you can stop reading and we can all step away from our computers, books, and work, then step toward our families, our hobbies, and our internal quiet. Go now … rest.

BRING IT TO LIFE!

At your most over-extended moment today, step away for 10 minutes and take a full rest.
If that time is at the end of your scheduled workday, step away for the rest of the evening.
Notice what changes during the time you are away, including what you feel in your body,
what your thoughts are, what activities you choose to engage in (or not!).
How might stepping away more regularly impact your life?

JANUARY 7

"Feel more. Hide less."

SJK

NOTE TO SELF

Love more. Eat less.
Feel more. Hide less.
Write more. Panic less.
Allow more. Judge less.
Grin more. Grouch less.
Intuit more. Resist less.
Plan more. Plan less.
Sing more. Think less.
Delight more. Despair less.
Cry more. Avoid less.
Step in more. Drift less.
Unpack more. Tidy up less.
Heart more. Gremlin less.
Create more. Doubt less.
Believe more. Believe more.
– All my love, Me (You)

BRING IT TO LIFE!

Write a note to self using this "more and less" format. Carry it with you, and add to it
during the day. Encourage someone else to share their "more and less" ideas.

"What if our natural state bears an uncanny resemblance
to the divine?"

SJK

OUR NATURAL STATE

So many of our learned messages (religious and other) tell us that we are sinful, broken, and lacking, and that we need to spend our whole lives making up for these inherent shortcomings and failures. ✐ I used to subscribe fully to that belief, prayerfully apologizing to the God who I believed I had disappointed simply by being alive in this world, while at the same time some part of me fought that idea. My open heart in church would regularly close in protection as I was frequently asked to confess my sinful nature. ✐ On the day I began work with my professional life coach, she noted her belief that we are all "creative, resourceful, and whole." I felt that truth in the depths of my core, and it immediately began to erase the nameless self-apology I'd carried around with me for years. ✐ What if we live as though our natural state is wholeness? What if we always are and have enough? What if we have nothing to make up for, no sinful nature to apologize for, and no inherent failures born in us from our first breaths? ✐ What if our natural state bears an uncanny resemblance to the divine?

BRING IT TO LIFE!

Today, suspend disbelief, and live and believe as though every part of you is whole,
healed, and a reflection of pure love and light. Set a timer for 10 minutes, and describe
what that might feel and look like today, getting as specific as possible.
Then go live from that place of wholeness.
How does this impact the way you think about yourself and interact with others?

"We all deserve to be treated like royalty,
no matter our capabilities, capacities, or achievements."

SJK

LIKE ROYALTY

He was pedaling slowly, taking some effort to pull the covered cart attached to his bicycle. I first noticed how the grin on his face contrasted with the impersonal feel of the city sidewalk grunge, then my eye was drawn to the cart itself. It was built like a Nativity scene, open in the front, with the three wooden sides, top, and bottom all covered with an exquisite silky cloth, patterned as if made for royalty. Inside this carrier, sharing the grin of the man providing her travel, sat a physically challenged girl, riding with the air of a princess in full delight of her court. We all deserve to be treated like royalty, no matter our capabilities, capacities, or achievements. We all deserve to be treated like royalty.

BRING IT TO LIFE!

Today, start by treating yourself like royalty.
Then carry that feeling out to the world around you, treating all you come in contact
with today as utterly deserving royalty.
How does this impact your day?

"Clear the clutter of yesterday's complexities,
and apprentice yourself to today's fresh understandings."

SJK

BEGINNER'S MIND

A foundational Zen concept is that of beginner's mind — an open, innocent frame of mind and way of being that allows us to see and experience ourselves and our world anew. In a society so often striving for expertise, beginner's mind can be quite a stretch. ✎ It makes sense, though, that the way to new insights and understanding is to approach each moment with the wonder of newness. How is this possible? — we ask of nature's candy-scented, floral artwork. Who am I really? — we ask of the mirror, meditation mat, or prayer space. What is possible here? — we ask in each new experience. ✎ Beginner's mind: a testament to the profound power of simplicity. Clear the clutter of yesterday's complexities, and apprentice yourself to today's fresh understandings.

BRING IT TO LIFE!

Take a beginner's mind approach to your day today.
Pick an object near you, and observe it as though you've never seen it
(or anything like it) before.
What questions would you ask about it?
What new understanding or discovery do you find when you show up with a beginner's mind?
How does this perspective impact your day?

JANUARY 11

"You can find peace even in the dirtiest and soggiest places."

ANNA G. PENNING

EVEN THERE

It was a low-light photo of a barren sidewalk, taken at an angle providing just enough tilt that it looked as if the two small birds were in danger of sliding out of our view. A light sheen from what must have been a rainy day highlighted the scattered bits of browning blooms and dirty, yellow construction paint. It wasn't pretty by any means, yet, as the photographer noted in the caption, it felt like peace. She's right; we can find peace even in the dirtiest and soggiest places. In the murky water stagnating underneath a bridge, in the crumbling ruins of an abandoned building, and in the overcrowded, disarrayed shelves of our minds, yes, even there, we can find peace when we look with our hearts.

BRING IT TO LIFE!

Today, look for peace, especially in the dirtiest and soggiest places.
At the end of the day, take five minutes to write a list of all the places in which
you found peace, and share this list with someone.
How did this exercise impact your day?

"Give your heart to the branches."

SJK

COME TO YOUR SENSES

Give your heart to the branches.
Drape your love through the leaves
as they whisper sweet nothings
in the seductive breeze
and urge you to
come
to your senses
and
drink.

BRING IT TO LIFE!

Today, take five minutes to surrender your senses to nature.
How does this impact your mood and perspective?

JANUARY 13

"Three simple little letters can change everything."

SJK

AND

We have an "AND" on our wall: a little wooden block that simply says in a plain typewriter font: AND.   Why? To always point us toward abundance. AND is the word of possibility, collaboration, adding to, connecting, and seeing beyond.   Three simple little letters can change everything.

BRING IT TO LIFE!

Write "AND" on a sticky-note, and carry it with you today.
How does this impact your thinking and interactions today?

"There's something magical
about what shows through the state of exhaustion."

NANCY J. DUNCAN

FULL ENGAGEMENT

I recently realized I often hold back, wanting the security of knowing I have something left in reserves. It's an understandable approach, this very human desire to finish strong, combined with a natural act of self-preservation. But finishing strong doesn't make up for the mediocrity of under-pacing the entire rest of the journey. In this holding back, is it possible that we shortchange ourselves, never getting to see what we can really do when we *fully* commit and engage to *fully* experience the capacity of our talents, skills, gifts, faith, and trust? Maybe it's in that place near the bottom of our reserves where our greatest creative potential awaits. Maybe that's where something magical shows through.

BRING IT TO LIFE!

Pick one activity today that feels important to you, and give it more energy
and effort than you usually would.
Then give it a little more, until you are fully engaged.
What do you notice?
Is this a way you might want to approach your life more often?

"And the sky never disappoints, does it?"

TINA BURKHOLDER

BEHOLD THE SKY

We live so much of each day in our heads: thinking, planning, strategizing, trying to figure out, wondering, guessing, questioning, deciding, worrying, and hoping. "All brain" leaves little room for heart, and we become "lost in thought." Lost to the richness of life that waits in the intersection of mind, heart, body, and soul. ⌐ We can find ourselves — every single time — by beholding the sky: taking the magnificent expanse in through the eyes, barely touching the mind, and settling it right into the heart where your soul can sip from it through-out the day. ⌐ Whatever you're facing today, behold the sky ... because the sky never disap-points, does it?

BRING IT TO LIFE!

Make yourself a note to "Behold the sky."
Use a sticky-note, or set a reminder on your phone,
or write a washable ink tattoo on the inside of your wrist;
whatever will prompt you throughout the day to internalize the sky.
How does this impact your day?

"Maybe real = beautiful. Period."

SJK

REAL BEAUTY

It's like a treasure hunt every day here in the city, looking for the flashes of beauty in the raw realness of the urban environment. You'd think my treasure chest would be nearly empty, with just a withered leaf or broken liquor bottle to show for my hunt, with the chill of the previous night's senseless murders and the darkness of poverty still clinging tightly. But no, it's not that at all. My urban beauty treasure chest is crammed so full that the lid no longer shuts. The emerald color of a weed contrasting with the red brick of a crumbling building takes my breath away. A spent flower petal on the sidewalk becomes a Georgia O'Keefe painting in my mind's eye. The morning sun kissing a broken warehouse window melts my heart. Maybe it's the scarcity that enhances my experience of beauty here in the city. Maybe it's the sense of hope as nature muscles its way through the cracks of abandoned buildings. Maybe it's a fear-fueled need to see beauty, no matter what or where, to keep my soul alive. Or maybe it's just that the joys and pains in the light and shadow facets of real life are inherently gorgeous. Maybe real = beautiful. Period.

BRING IT TO LIFE!

Look around you for something you naturally label as "ugly" (or at least not beautiful).
Take a few minutes to look closely at the object or scene until you find beauty
in some part of it. Repeat this exercise three times today.
What do you notice about your definition of beauty?
How might you find more beauty in the less pleasing views in your life?

"Heed the voice that begs for a break,
pay attention to the whispers of your body as it pleads for stillness,
and listen to the tears for their message of rest."

SJK

HEED THE VOICE

It was a big deal, our decision to skip the normal exercise routine this morning. I was worn out, and my exercise buddy (my wife) was dragging, so we called it a "no go," luxuriating over that cup of coffee instead of sweating it out at the gym. I'm a firm believer in regular exercise, keeping our bodies active to boost our full-self health. Yet, when every cell is tired, when your mind cries out for a break, and when resistance to effort is so strong that it brings tears, heed the voice within. Heed the voice that begs for a break, pay attention to the whispers of your body as it pleads for stillness, and listen to the tears for their message of rest. Heed the voice, and honor its requests.

BRING IT TO LIFE!

Take 10 minutes today to sit quietly and listen to that still small voice within.
Is your body aching? Is your brain tired? Is your heart running dry?
Or — on the other end --are your reserves overflowing?
Heed the voice and honor its requests by changing your behavior accordingly today.
How does this impact your day and your interactions with yourself and others?

"Give the whispers of your own daring spirit the space to be heard."

SJK

CLEAN WINDOWS

Each spring as the sun starts shining more brightly through the house windows, I am highly motivated to wash windows so none of that precious light is blocked from coming in, nor my view blocked from seeing out. We look through dirty windows so often in our lives and wonder why we can't see out. We struggle for clarity, for self-respect, to make our place in this world, and to understand who and why we are. In our struggle, we pack our schedules and our minds so full that we don't get to (or have to) hear the silence and receive the messages therein. We keep our emotional windows dirty. If we give ourselves silence, we can hear the whispers of our own daring spirit, the inner wisdom that nudges us to our next step along life's path. If we clean our windows, we clear our view and let the sunshine light our way. Give your whispers the space to be heard. It's so much easier to see through clean windows.

BRING IT TO LIFE!

Take the time today to carefully clean the window in your home that provides the most powerful access for sunlight. Notice how your body feels inside as the window gets cleaner. Notice how the light more brightly shines when the window is clean, and how much easier and more pleasing it is to see out. When the window is clean, take 10 minutes to sit in comfortable silence, breathing deeply, and listening easily to your thoughts as they pass by. At the end of 10 minutes, notice any insights that may have come up. Pay attention to insights that show up throughout your day.

"It's about the love … in anything … and everything … always."

SJK

IT'S ABOUT THE LOVE

It's not about the differences in each other that we don't understand.
It's not about gay or straight or both or neither.
It's not about my right and your wrong.
It's not about dogma … or catma.
It's not about my God vs. your God … or no God.
It's not about fear or hate or better or worse.
No.
It's about the Love … in anything … and everything … always.

BRING IT TO LIFE!

Today, as you become aware of differences between you and others,
notice where your mind goes and what it tells you.
Then notice where your heart goes and what it tells you.
What does it mean to you in each situation — to make it about the love?
Practice this daily, and notice the impact on you and those you interact with.

"When we empathize, we are connected through compassion to ourselves,
to others, and to the divine within and around us all."

SJK

WHY BOTHER?

Why bother making the effort to live an awake life? Why bother noticing the details, paying attention through all our senses, and doing the work to open our hearts to all experiences of life, even those of pain and discomfort? ᦑ Because when we notice, we see. When we see, we feel. When we feel, we experience. When we experience, we begin to empathize. And when we empathize, we are connected through compassion to ourselves, to others, and to the divine within and around us all. ᦑ So why bother? Because awake = alive to the fullest degree possible, and in the end isn't that what enhances the life of this world?

ᦑ

BRING IT TO LIFE!

Practice being wide awake today.
Write a list of reasons to pay attention to as much of your life as possible.
Make your reasons personal, and if it resonates with you, add global reasons as well.
At the end of the day, re-read your list of reasons,
and add any more that came to you through your experiences today.

*"We can live so vibrantly, so completely, and so fully
that we pour ourselves into every moment, to the very last drop."*

SJK

RUN OUT OF INK

I've had to increase my backup stash of pens, as I've been writing so much and so often that I keep running out of ink. There's an odd sort of pleasure in each empty pen stroke, something about the knowledge that in that empty pen is evidence that I've poured myself out through the very last drop of ink. We don't have to be writers to pour ourselves out. We can live so vibrantly, so completely, so fully that we pour ourselves into every moment. We can love, rejoice, cry, yearn, believe, and question to the very last drop. And then pick up the next pen and keep writing, keep pouring, keep living so passionately that, again, we run out of ink.

BRING IT TO LIFE!

Take 10 minutes to write how it would look and feel for you to pour yourself into every
moment of life. Today, experiment with putting that imagining into action.
See how much of yourself you can passionately pour out today.
At the end of the day, reflect on your experience.
What pouring out felt more like filling up? What pouring out drained you?
How long until you would run out of ink? One last, and important, question:
what is your version of having another full pen ready to go? Put that in place.

"In all of those circumstances,
we have someone who knows our name, who knows us.
And so we live."

SJK

SOMEONE WHO KNOWS YOUR NAME

I've been reading Lawrence Hill's intense novel, *Someone Knows My Name,* a disturbing and uplifting story of slavery and human resilience in the face of unimaginably dire circumstances. I've only been able to read it in small sips, to allow my sensitive soul to recover between readings, yet I've not been willing to fully step away from the book. I keep being drawn back to the story's examples of the things that allowed the captives to feel human in situations that tried to shred their every last ounce of dignity and hope, the most striking of these being the use of each other's names. Slaves chained together with dead and dying others, lying in months' worth of human waste muck, gave each other the knowledge of their names. As the main character, Amanita, describes it, "In the darkness, men repeated my name and called out their own as I passed. They wanted me to know them. Who they were. Their names." Each of our lives have their unique flavors of hardship; we are each "chained" to particular struggles and challenges. Yet, in all of those circumstances, we have someone who knows our name, who knows us. And so we live.

BRING IT TO LIFE!

Today, take five minutes to record a list of people who know your name.
Write them all down. You are known.
As you go through the day today, offer others the gift of hearing their names.

"Maybe it's time to put your nose prints on a window."

SJK

NOSE PRINTS ON THE WINDOW

Sunlight streaming through our French door reveals a smattering of tiny, triangular nose prints along the bottom glass panels, just high enough to match the nose height of curious felines watching the patio activity from inside our kitchen. Every time I see those sweet little nose prints, I'm reminded of the cats' total attention to the curiosities of their lives. A leaf moves, and the cats' entire bodies notice, ears perked up as they focus laser stares to gather information. A fly becomes an excuse for a free-for-all, whole-being frolic. Birds on the wire incite an all-cells, all-senses alert. What might we discover if we approached life with that same all-in sense of curiosity and wonder? Maybe it's time to put your own nose prints on a window.

BRING IT TO LIFE!

Sit or stand at a window in your home today for five minutes and pay attention
to everything you can possibly take in with all of your senses on high alert.
What do you notice about your energy during and after those five minutes?
Take that "nose to the window" approach with you today, and notice how it impacts your day.

"Once in a while, we get the incredible experience of realizing
that our spirits are all collaborating all the time."

SJK

INFINITE COLLABORATION

After meditation this morning, I realized that on days when I have a phone call scheduled with a deeply spiritual colleague, I more easily slip into a deeper meditation, followed by a more inspired writing time — even before I've spoken with that person. It seems the connection to some people is an open door to profound spiritual energy; a doorway I can easily step through to access that divine energy more fully within myself. In this human life, we are little, self-contained human bodies moving around our world, sometimes touching each other, often not. Then once in a while, we get the incredible experience of realizing that our spirits are all collaborating all the time. Some call it God, some call it art, or creativity, the divine, universal energy, a higher power, or relationship — whatever we call it, it's an infinite collaboration of spirits, worthy of attention and cultivation.

BRING IT TO LIFE!

Think back to a time when you felt especially connected to another human being.
Then think and feel beyond that to the connection with their spirit.
Take that focus with you today, and look to connect spirits with those around you.
How does this exercise impact the way you interact with people?

"Nourishment is there, all the time, waiting for you to cup your hands in its bounty
like drinking from a crystal clear spring of icy, pure water."

SJK

WILL YOU DRINK?

Our world is overflowing with nourishment. ⤶ Eye contact with someone else's heart. ⤶ Dew-drops quivering in early morning sunshine. ⤶ The call of birds planning their day. ⤶ Soul-carrying notes of a favorite song. ⤶ A full raindrop splashing on your nose like a chuckle from God. ⤶ Vibrant colors cheering from a corner of graffiti art. ⤶ The gentle hum inside your heart when love steps in. ⤶ It's all there, all the time, waiting for you to cup your hands in its bounty like drinking from a crystal clear spring of icy, pure water. ⤶ Will you drink?

BRING IT TO LIFE!

Take five minutes to sit quietly and imagine dipping your hands into a cold rushing stream
on a hot day, then drinking deeply from the refreshing liquid.
Feel the cool nourishment travel from stream to hands to lips to mouth,
then throughout your body as you swallow.
As you go through your day today, take that image and those feelings with you.
Drink in all the sensory nourishment you can find, taking care to drink deeply
of the most healing and pure experiences.
At the end of the day, write a list of all that you drank in today.
How did this perspective impact your day?

"To be fully awake requires an open heart."

SJK

FULLY AWAKE

Some days I resist being fully awake. The 5:10 a.m. alarm feels harsh, even though it's just quiet music. Stepping outside feels like a painful cracking of my protective shell, the gentle breeze on my arms like an invasion of privacy and the light of sunrise a flame too bright for my tender eyes. ✑ On those days — awake on the outside while stubbornly asleep on the inside — I feel sensation and potential beauty as scrapes against my closed heart, leaving a scratch here and a bruise there as they try to gain entry. ✑ To be fully awake requires an open heart. It requires courage and determination to let the surface become intimate and the closed become open. It stretches our faith to be vulnerable to the sensory and soulful experiences of everyday life. ✑ And oh, is it ever worth it.

BRING IT TO LIFE!

Notice right now how open your heart seems to be by how deep or shallow your breaths are.
Pause to take three long, deep breaths as you visualize your heart area opening.
Open both eyes wide, as if you are absolutely wide awake.
Are you able to hold that feeling of openness, of being fully awake?
Practice it throughout the day, and notice how it impacts you.

"What is it that turns your hamster wheel of daily life
into an inspired path of purpose?"

SJK

WHAT DO YOU WANT?

I mean truly deep-down, soul-bursting longing yearning desiring cellular-level core-of-your-being want. ➣ What. Do. You. Want? ➣ I clearly remember the day a few years ago when my professional life coach asked me that question so sincerely, earnestly, and compassionately, "Starla, what do you want?" that my heart melted, and my immediate answer was tears, not words. ➣ We all need and deserve to have someone give us the gift of asking, soul to soul, "[your name here], what do you want?" That question, asked earnestly, honors the deepest parts of our existence, the parts that spend so much time waiting to be seen, heard, felt, and noticed. ➣ We spend so much of our time striving, reaching, accomplishing, and going for that holy grail of … what, exactly? Enough money to pay the bills? Sure, but beyond that, what? What is it that turns your hamster wheel of daily life into an inspired path of purpose?

BRING IT TO LIFE!

Set aside 10 minutes today for writing time. Before you start writing, take a deep breath and become aware of your heart. As soon as you feel your heart (whatever that means to you), write at the top of your page, "What do I want?" followed by, "I want … "
Complete that phrase over and over with whatever comes to mind, not stopping until the 10 minutes are up. *What do you notice about what you really want?*
How can you take one step toward that today?

"What might be asking you to surrender today?"

SJK

SWEET SURRENDER

Open
my heart wide, Beloved.
Place me
within the pulsing beat
of your love
surrounding me
in a rhythm so deep that
I have no choice but
surrender.
Sweet
sweet
surrender.

BRING IT TO LIFE!

What might be asking you to surrender today?
Take a step in that direction, and see where it leads you.

"Stop. Leave some space."

SJK

LEAVE SOME SPACE

It's in our nature to squeeze something into every nook and cranny of time. Finish a meeting 10 minutes early, and you have time to dash off a few email replies, edit a document, fold some laundry, finish one To-Do list and create another one. Motor through it all, nose to grindstone, can't let up or you'll get (even more) behind. Stop. Leave some space. Take those 10 minutes, and refuse to fill them with work. Fill them instead with space: space to play, to breathe, to regroup, to step away from the computer screen. Ten minutes to add stress ... or remove it? You get to choose.

BRING IT TO LIFE!

Give yourself 10 minutes of space today (schedule it on your calendar
to ensure you reserve that time).
Listen to music, read poems, watch water drip off a roof, or anything else
that feels like "space" to you — the choice is yours.
Experiment daily. Rinse. Repeat.

"Just a brown paper bag to one person,
but a lifetime of love and belonging to another."

SJK

LUNCH IN A BROWN PAPER BAG

I read an article once about a woman who offered to provide lunches for a neglected child, and the child requested the lunch in a brown paper bag, because, he explained, when the other kids see that paper bag, they know someone cares about you. Just a brown paper bag to one person, but a lifetime of love and belonging to another. Simple. Powerful. Profound.

BRING IT TO LIFE!

What evidence do you see throughout your day that someone cares about you?
Is there enough caring left over for you to provide someone else a metaphorical
"brown paper bag lunch" tomorrow?

"Language is a full-experience expression with a life of its own,
richly textured in all the senses, and worthy of rapt attention at all times."

SJK

THE LIFE IN LANGUAGE

Hearing the French language makes my knees weak. I was in a local coffee shop writing when I heard several people speaking the unmistakable sounds of French. I put down my pen and, trying not to dash over to stand in the center of their group for better hearing, I listened with delight as they unknowingly dipped me into a quiet bliss. The round, sensual fullness of every word, accented with crisp consonants and voluptuous vowels of the French language, takes my breath away. I somehow feel the sounds on my tongue, their shapes melting to the back of my throat as I swallow their cadence like a river of warm, liquid chocolate. Those few minutes remind me that language is not simply dead letters put in a row to form words and sentences. Language is a full-experience expression with a life of its own, richly textured in all the senses, and worthy of rapt attention at all times.

BRING IT TO LIFE!

As you go through your day today, listen — really listen — to the language people
are speaking around you.
Even if it's your native language, hear it as though it's new to you.
What treasures of experience did you find?

FEBRUARY

"Shadows and light: a match made in heaven,
to be noticed on earth."

SJK

SHADOWS

As the early morning sun whispered its love across the gingko leaves blown to the ground from yesterday's spring storms, I noticed a striking clarity in the leaf shapes. Apparently the low sun angles accentuated the shadows, which in turn accentuated the depth of shape and contrasting intensity of color. Bright overhead sunshine, however, removes the shadow, visually flattening the shape and washing out the color. Our lives are richest when the light and shadows play off each other. The depths of the down times provide a contrasting backdrop that enhances the vibrancy of the up times. Conversely, the gentle light of joyful times turns black to gray and one step closer to color. Shadows and light: a match made in heaven, to be noticed on earth.

BRING IT TO LIFE!

Today, notice the effect of shadows in your environment at different times of day,
particularly the contrast between midday and morning or evening.
Pay close enough attention so that you can remember this beauty of shadow and light
contrasts, and use it as a comfort next time you face a trying time.

"My waterproof skin is a powerful reminder
that Someone or Something cared enough to seamlessly craft function and beauty
into one incredible package: me."

SJK

WATERPROOF

I clearly remember the moment I became aware of the incredible miracle of the human body. I was about nine years old, rinsing soap off my arms near the end of my shower when it hit me: my skin is waterproof! Here I have all these tiny little holes (pores), and even though I've been standing in pouring water for a good 10 minutes, I'm not water-logged! I was amazed. So amazed that close to 40 years later, I still remember my heart expanding and my eyes widening as I realized that this creative feat meant there must be a phenomenal Something (or Someone?) paying attention to us. We so often take our human bodies for granted, yet, in times when I'm grasping for faith, my waterproof skin is a powerful reminder that Someone or Something cared enough to seamlessly (literally!) craft function and beauty into one incredible package: me. We are each a waterproof miracle.

BRING IT TO LIFE!

Next time you wash your hands, wash them as though you have never seen them before. Notice your skin, the way the knuckles wrinkle and expand in little creases, how each finger ends in a precious little segment of nail and how the water runs off because the skin is waterproof. Hold this information close, and when your faith is low, remember the miracle of your waterproof skin.

"We're not that different. Unique?
Oh yes. But different? Not so much."

SJK

WE'RE NOT THAT DIFFERENT

On the subway, I watched a cherubic, burqa-draped baby grinning at me, her mom's eyes sparkling at me through their cloth frame ... as she adjusted her white iPod earbuds. Across from her, a golden-clothed woman with exquisite Mediterranean cheekbones stared carefully ahead as two pale-skinned man-boys with buzz cuts fought sleep, nodding against the dirty window pane. ⬟ For those few minutes, all of us were united in a physical space with the common quest to get somewhere else. ⬟ In our stories of daily life, we're really not that different beneath the exterior. Unique, yes, but different? Not so much.

BRING IT TO LIFE!

Today, be aware of people you would typically note as "different" from you,
and find a commonality of any sort. Pretend they own the same breed of dog you do,
or that their favorite book is the same as yours (even if in a different language),
or that you both share the same sky.
How does this exercise impact your perspective in relation to that person?
How might you find more commonalities in people
whose seeming differences would normally distance you?

"Don't you love it when the connection to source is so sweet and THERE.
All that love ... is just there, waiting for us to say yes."

ELLEN STOUNE

EXTRA-ORDINARY

The other morning I had my day planned out as usual: an ordinary day led by a full To-Do list. Ordinary, that is, until I took a walk in the snow, and everything changed.  It was blustery: the cold wind burning my cheeks, my coat collar scraping my chin, precipitation blowing into my eyes, my nose running, and my hands too cold to activate the touch screen on my iPhone. But I didn't care one wit. I was too arrested by how the slight dusting of snow was turning everything ordinary into extra-ordinary.  Instead of feeling the wind, I saw the shapes of the bare trees, the geometric composition of pipes and fences, the flaming color of a red twig dog-wood shrub, the snow-specked fur of a black dog racing in exuberant circles in the park, and the random mosaic on an otherwise nondescript wall, reminding me of the splash of beauty my mosaically-inclined niece adds to my life.  My heart immediately filled with gratitude for all my nieces and nephews, and the richness of relationships in my life ... and suddenly nothing mattered except the delicious profundity of the extra-ordinary moments of my day.  May you be likewise blessed on this extra-ordinary day.

BRING IT TO LIFE!

Where can you find extra-ordinary in your day today? Let yourself get deliciously derailed for some small (or large!) part of your day. At the end of the day, reflect on what happened and how it happened. *Is this something you might want to do more often?*

"Wringing a dry sponge tighter won't produce water."

SJK

FILL YOUR WELL

We push, we pull, we wrangle, we struggle, and we scrape the bottom of our dehydrated spirits in a maddening attempt to create something with nothing. But wringing a dry sponge tighter won't produce water. Insistence won't produce inspiration. Empty needs our help to become full. When the words you need to write just aren't coming out, take a walk. When the equation you need to solve just won't fall into place, go to an art museum. When the project plan timeline refuses to gel and the essay just won't flow and your metaphorical paints are all dried up, relax your internal sponge, and go fill your well. Read what makes your mind spin; listen to the songs that make your heart dance; let your senses out to play in the sun, the rain, the mud, the city, the country. Take it all in, soak it all up until your sponge is dripping with life, and when your well is full, drink that vibrant water, then offer a drink to those around you.

BRING IT TO LIFE!

Write a list of activities that fill your well.
Choose one of those to do today for 10 minutes, and notice how
the level of inspiration in your "well" changes after that time.
Keep your list of well-fillers handy for any time your well begins to run dry.

"After a rain, the colors are achingly intense,
almost defiant in their stance of shining beauty through a blanket of gray."
SJK

AFTER THE RAIN

Some of the most amazing photographs I've ever seen weren't taken in bright sunshine on a tropical island, or at sunrise or sunset over a city skyline — they were taken after a strong rain, while the sky was still heavy with dark clouds and water puddled anyplace willing to hold it. ⟿ After a rain, the colors are achingly intense, almost defiant in their stance of shining beauty through a blanket of gray. ⟿ We see the same thing happen after an internal rain of emotions pouring down through a torrent of tears. As teardrops quiver on our eyelashes, even with additional rains still threatening, our inner light refracts differently, and we can start to see the rich color in our situation. The line between beauty and pain is so very thin, and the release of teardrops can be what carries us from the side of pain into the depths of beauty.

BRING IT TO LIFE!

Next time it rains, look (or go) outside, and pay close attention to the colors.
Notice how vibrant they seem, even in a post-rain, cloudy, damp grayness.
Take five minutes to focus completely on the beauty of the colors
so you can remember this feeling next time your internal rain storms appear.

"I'd love to bathe in kittens."

MARTIN G. KING

BATHING IN KITTENS

"I'd love to bathe in kittens," my brother Marty said. "Imagine it: you're lying on the floor, with about a hundred tiny kittens tumbling and climbing all over you and each other, their soft little bodies covering you, and some of them stopping to stare in your eyes. Wouldn't that just be amazing?" This from a 49-year-old man. We all have the capacity to imagine our most soul-soothing scenarios, to set them up in our minds with so many specific details that our bodies begin to believe they're real. Bathing in kittens? My heart opens with a huge smile, my muscles relax, my breathing deepens, and the cares of my world disappear in the sensation of joyous bundles of playful fur soothing me. Our minds can create a powerful experience for our bodies, so why not use that incredible capacity intentionally?

BRING IT TO LIFE!

What is your "bathing in kittens" scenario?

Take five minutes to imagine every detail of a deeply soothing experience.

Then take another five minutes to write it down so that you can revisit it at other times.

Notice how the feeling in your body changes by the end of this exercise.

"Get curious ... and get un-everything-else."

SJK

MUTUALLY EXCLUSIVE

It occurs to me that there are several mutually exclusive states of mind/heart/soul:

Curiosity and Fear

Curiosity and Anger

Curiosity and Despair

Curiosity and Hate

Curiosity and Hopelessness.

Deep curiosity — the kind where you really want to explore, question, discover, and know — draws our full attention so completely that other emotions don't stand a chance. Get curious ... and get un-everything-else.

BRING IT TO LIFE!

Today, pay close attention to your emotions and reactions to various situations,
experimenting with applying curiosity to each situation.
What do you notice about curiosity?
Is this a practice you'd like to use more often in your life?

"If we choose to apply reverence to any act of eating, can't it become a sacred moment,
a reminder of the life and grace we receive with each bite of nourishment?"

SJK

DO THIS IN REMEMBRANCE

Sitting in the sunshine on our patio at lunchtime, I drink a fully-natural, green smoothie and savor the mix of fresh fruit, vegetables, and coconut water. The burst of pure freshness with each sip evokes a clear mental image of farmlands that birthed these items, and I feel an immediate gratitude for the intimate connection of ingesting nature. These fruits and vegetables literally become part of me, giving me life and health. I'm reminded of the sacred act of communion, the symbolic receiving of bread and wine (or juice or water) as a life-giving, grace-invoking ritual, accompanied with the words of Christ, "Do this in remembrance of me." No matter our religious affiliation, or lack thereof, if we choose to apply reverence to an act of eating, can't it, too, become a sacred moment, a reminder of the life and grace we receive with each bite? Choose to taste colors, smell the newly-tilled soil, see the farmers' scratched, weathered hands dropping seeds into the garden rows, and realize the miracle in each edible element sprouting from our earth. Do this in remembrance ...

BRING IT TO LIFE!

Today, set aside five minutes to savor a fruit or vegetable. If you have a local market, purchase it there! Taste the rich red of a tomato, and smell the sun-warmed vine.
Feel the weight of the fruit in the hand of the person who picked it.
Smell the winey air of a vineyard as your teeth break the skin of a grape.
Appreciate the infusion of life into each cell as you swallow this gift from the earth.

"The expression of genuine gratitude is not a contained pipeline;
it's an expanse of free energy that allows
all within its range to benefit."

SJK

THE GRATITUDE EFFECT

Buying groceries in the self-checkout lines at the local Super Fresh, I overheard an interaction between the attendant and a customer who was perplexed by the instructions on the checkout screen. The attendant cheerfully walked the customer through several steps to successful completion of her grocery purchase. As she gathered her bags, the customer thanked the attendant, adding, "I so appreciate you!" and re-iterated the positive ways the attendant had provided her support. ✎ She could have just said a quiet "Thank you" and walked out, but she took the time to show deep appreciation, and with the phrase, "I appreciate you," she made it personal. ✎ I walked out of that store with my heart glowing from that exchange — one that I had no part in except as someone fortunate enough to overhear a friendly, helpful, and gracious interaction between strangers. Let's not forget that the expression of genuine gratitude is not a contained pipeline; it's an expanse of free energy that allows all within its range to benefit.

BRING IT TO LIFE!

Find and express your gratitude throughout your day today. In three or more situations,
make it personal (about the person, not just the deed), starting with yourself as that first person.
At the end of your day, write down the gratitude experience you remember most clearly,
including ways others may have been indirectly positively impacted by your gratitude.

"Nature knows how to support us, inspire us, and love us."

SJK

NATURE KNOWS

We all have days (or weeks, or months) of feeling as though nobody (ourselves included) knows how to support us, inspire us, or love us in the ways we long for. ✎ But nature knows. ✎ Nature knows how to caress our hair with a gentle breeze, warm our hearts with tender sun kisses along our neck, and offer us a decadent tray of sweet, rich wildflowers along a meadow's edge. Nature knows how to sing our hearts to peace through a bird's verses, rock our minds to quiet through the ocean's soothing rhythms, and show us tangible hope in the blood-red new growth on the tips of a photinia shrub. ✎ Next time you find your needs un-met, step outside and discover just what it is that nature knows.

BRING IT TO LIFE!

Take a 15-minute nature break today — time outside in a park or a garden,
or just lean against a building, breathing the outdoor air.
Notice everything that nature offers, from a breeze to bird song, to the color and tenacity
of weeds, to carefully crafted flower petals.
How does this awareness impact your perspective today?

"Dance to the rhythms of life."

SJK

THE DANCE

Today my Beloved
I step into your arms and dance
to the rhythms
of pure
sweet
Life.

BRING IT TO LIFE!

Who or what is your "dance partner" today
– the collaborator and support in the experiences of your day?
What do you need to do to feel that connection today? Do that.

*"What if expressing the deep-down truth of who we are
is the most beautifully and bravely creative, self-actualizing act we can do?"*

SJK

TOO MUCH

When we struggle with the idea that we're not _____ enough [fill in the blank: talented, smart, creative, compassionate, selfless, etc.], we can find all sorts of support: self-help books, blog posts on self-esteem, confidence-boosting workshops, skills training classes, and on and on.   But how do we deal with the idea that we're too much? That we're too _____ [intense, deep, trusting, intellectual, emotional, enthusiastic, etc.]? The support there fades, leaving us with one pervasive message: BE LESS OF THAT. We do ourselves a huge disservice when we squelch the most abundant parts of ourselves. What if whatever we fear we're too much of is exactly what the world around us needs most? What if our (perceived) "too much" is exactly the right size to collaborate perfectly with someone else's (perceived) "not enough"? What if expressing the deep-down truth of who we are is the most beautifully and bravely creative, self-actualizing act we can do?

BRING IT TO LIFE!

What is your "too much"?
Express that action two or more times today, and affirm that same action in others.
How did those actions impact your day?
Write down your observations.

FEBRUARY 14

"What you believe is what you create;
isn't that worth a considerable amount of attention?"

SJK

WHAT DO YOU BELIEVE?

We tend to race through each day, one task to the next, reacting, adapting, and catapulting ourselves through to the next challenge that shows up in front of us. How often, though, do we pay attention to the messages we whisper to ourselves as we choose the next action, the next thought, the next task? How often do we actually stop to check in with our inner world long enough to clarify what we believe? What do you believe about the world around you? How much kindness vs. ill will? How much compassion vs. hate? How much possibility vs. helplessness? What do you believe about your self? How much beauty, how much capacity to love and be loved, how much value do you intrinsically hold within you? Since what you believe is what you create, isn't that worth a considerable amount of attention?

BRING IT TO LIFE!

Take 10 minutes to write your answers to the questions about what you believe.
Do those beliefs support your growth and serve you well?
Are there any beliefs you'd like to shift?
If so, write down the new belief you'd like to have, and cross out the corresponding old one.
Keep that new desired belief near you over the next few weeks, and notice any changes.

"We can choose, at any time of day or night, to let it go."

SJK

LET IT GO

In the gentle light of morning
Let it go.
In the deepest dark of night
Let it go.
In the ruthless glare of day
Let it go.
In the dawning, the evening, the bright, the black
Let it go.

We can choose, at any time of day or night, to let it go: the anger, the pain, the grief, the confusion, the grasping, the gripping, the hoping, the fearing. At any moment, we can choose to let it go.

BRING IT TO LIFE!

What do you need to let go of today?
At each natural segment of the day (morning, noon, night, or set a repeat timer for regular intervals), remind yourself with a deep breath in to Let It Go, and with a deep breath out, release it. Letting go takes practice, and often many times of letting go, until we are actually able to release completely.
What do you need to let go of today?

"It turns out that what we're really looking for is our own selves."

SJK

THE LONGING FOR SELF

In a world dominated by fairy tale love stories in movies and romance novels, we learn to believe that deep connection is only to be found in relationship with someone else. Time spent alone is equated with being lonely, and connecting with the inner mysteries of ourselves is devalued in favor of finding satisfaction and fulfillment in the arms of someone else. When we long for connection, we naturally assume we long for external relationships, but it turns out that what we're really looking for is our own selves.

Longing to connect,
I reach for my heart in you,
missing my own gems.

BRING IT TO LIFE!

Set aside 10 minutes today for a date with yourself.
Whatever you choose to do during those 10 minutes is up to you,
as long as you focus your attention inward. If you choose to take a walk, notice
how your heart feels as you take in your surroundings.
If you choose to sit quietly, take a pen and notebook with you, and ask yourself,
"What do you want me to know about you?" Jot down quickly whatever comes to mind.
How might your self-awareness change if you do this exercise regularly?

"We could get by on skill and expertise,
but add the element of joy, and we have the chance to transform anyone in our sphere,
including ourselves."

SJK

THE WAY WE DO IT

Watching a video of a performance by a cello-piano-violin trio, the *Ahn Sisters*, I was mesmerized from the very first note. Yes, the music itself was stunning, but what really caught my attention was the smiles they let shine through as they began playing. Those smiles played through their bodies into their instruments, and I felt as though I was listening as much to joy as to music. After the performance, after I had already written the previous paragraph of this page, the violinist, Angella, spoke of the importance of playing music from the heart. It came through, their music from the heart, so very clearly. The way we do what we do best matters. We could get by on skill and expertise, but add the element of joy and we have the chance to transform anyone in our sphere, including ourselves. It's not just about what we do, it's about the way we do it.

BRING IT TO LIFE!

If you have access to the Internet, look up an *Ahn Sisters* performance video
and watch them play. Notice and hear the joy and heart in their music and performance.
Today, pay close attention to the way you do whatever you do,
especially what you're particularly skilled at.
Is your heart there? If so, enjoy it. If not, what might help bring your heart to your tasks?

FEBRUARY 18

"Clouds at the beach? Who cares! I've got a perfect, teeny shell!"

SJK

WHAT CATCHES YOUR EYE

It was a February vacation day, and I was walking on the beach in Florida, bummed at the cloudy, chilly weather at a time I was so longing for sunshine to thaw the Northern winter from my bones. Sure, the aqua water was pretty, and the rhythmic sound of waves dashing up the shoreline was appealing, but without sunshine, it felt more like a tease than a generous offering.   Then something caught my eye: a tiny flash of deep coral-orange in the otherwise beige, brown, and black sand mix. Bending down to look more closely, I realized it was a perfect, tiny, flame-colored shell! I've always had a soft spot for perfection in miniature, so this little discovery perked me right up. Clouds at the beach? Who cares! I've got a perfect, teeny shell! Imperfect vacation? Who cares! I've got a perfect, teeny shell! Three hours later, I was sitting outside shivering under the cloud cover, and smiling, because sitting on my Kindle beside me was what? A perfect, teeny shell! Yes, it really can be that simple.

BRING IT TO LIFE!

As you go through your day today,
notice what catches your eye in a way that brings you joy.

"The cats remind me that the purpose of meditation is to provide a strong undercurrent
of peace, compassion, and gratitude throughout the distracting realities of life."

SJK

THE UNDERCURRENT FOR LIFE

Most mornings I spend about 30 minutes in silence, sitting on my meditation mat facing the window that gradually feeds me the sunrise as I repeat the mantra, *Om Namah Shivaya* (honoring the divine within me), and practice letting go of thoughts as my heart gets priority. Recently, while sitting peacefully in that heart space, the quiet was broken by the sound of intense chewing and swallowing, followed by a wet sneeze: my cat on the windowsill, wholeheartedly snacking on a plant. Eyes still closed, I felt my other cat's soft paws kneading my calf, interspersed with painful pricks as her claws dug in. Then the deep, rumbling purring began, followed by her burrowing under the blanket draped over my legs. Yes, I could banish the cats during meditation, but they remind me of the purpose of meditation — to provide a strong undercurrent of peace, compassion, and gratitude throughout the distractions of life. They remind me to find my center and allow life to go on powerfully around me as I choose where to put my attention and when to allow my energy to get swept along with life's current.

BRING IT TO LIFE!

Do you have a daily practice that gives you a strong undercurrent for life –
ways to keep the peace, compassion, and gratitude flowing as a foundation supporting
all of your life's movements? If so, pay special attention to that practice today.
If not, what might you do each day to create a positive undercurrent of your choosing?

"Musical dissonance, at its essence, is the contrasting beauty and pain
of a transition period. Rather like life, isn't it?"

SJK

DISSONANCE

Every once in a while, I am drawn back to the hymns and choir music of my earlier years, steeping myself in a blend of nostalgic memories and rich voices. I usually listen to the overall blend of sound, but recently I've been focusing more on specific sounds — those of dissonance. Unlike the soothing, harmonious combination of notes we most often hear and appreciate, dissonant chords have a tension in their note combinations that sounds harsh or somehow unresolved to many of us. ✎ Although those dissonant sounds don't sit easily in my ears or on my heart, they are the source of some of my greatest listening pleasure. Musical dissonance can put us on the near edge of relief and release, place us in the sweet center of discomfort, and provide a touch of blissful almost-pain through the promise of deep resolution to perfectly aligned harmony. ✎ Musical dissonance, at its essence, is the contrasting beauty and pain of a transition period. ✎ Rather like life, isn't it?

BRING IT TO LIFE!

Listen to a few songs today, and listen particularly for that sound of dissonance.
Notice how you feel as you hear the unresolved chords, then the resolution.
How might you apply this understanding to a transition period in your life?

"With malice toward none, with charity for all."

ABRAHAM LINCOLN

WITH CHARITY FOR ALL

People's Progression for Equality, one of the more than 3,000 incredible public murals in Philadelphia, depicts workers building a huge statue of Abraham Lincoln, with his words etched above: "With malice toward none, with charity for all." That quote stops me every time I pass the mural, urging me to reflect on the tall order of that message. It's one thing to remove malice; it's quite another thing to also replace it with charity! I'm allowing that if we can't find the strength to remove malice in an exchange with someone, we can start instead by adding charity. Genuine charity applied in even the smallest dose has the power to melt malice away. It's no coincidence that the man who freed the slaves spoke of malice toward none, charity for all. Perhaps with Lincoln's same guidance, we can equally free ourselves.

BRING IT TO LIFE!

Think of someone in your life who evokes in you feelings of malice.
Then think of someone who evokes in you feelings of charity.
Holding onto the feeling of charity, take a deep breath and return to the first person
you thought of. *Were you able for even a moment to feel charity for the person
who more often evokes malice in you?
How might your view of and interactions with this person change
if you practice this exercise daily?*

"Soak in the comfort of dusk."

SJK

RELIEF

I watched the leaves
fall
with my tears of the past
and I heard the wind
sigh
with tomorrow's unknown.
Then I felt the sun
set
gently warm through my soul
as dusk softly lingered
and I tasted
sweet
life.

BRING IT TO LIFE!

Schedule a date with yourself today to watch dusk arrive (and, if feasible, watch the sunset!).
Imagine the past fading away and the future merely a warm glow as you soak in
the comfort of the light and feeling of dusk.
What did you notice in that present-moment focus on dusk?

"What if everything within and around you
is exactly as it was intended?"

SJK

RIGHT NOW

What if
who you are right now
what you believe right now
who you love right now
what you don't have right now
what you don't know right now
what you don't understand right now
is exactly right, right now?
What if everything within and around you
is exactly as it was intended, at least for right now?

BRING IT TO LIFE!

Is there something in yourself or your life that you're pushing against
right now, wishing it were different?
What might it mean to you if that something is exactly right, right now?

"How might our worlds change
if we responded first to the God in others?"

SJK

THE GOD IN OTHERS

Gurumayi Chidvilasananda in her book, *Enthusiasm*, suggests that one reason to use gentleness in our everyday actions is to not disturb the God in others.   I love this image of gentleness, not as a weak or subservient way of being, but as a powerful show of compassion and reverent worship — a deep honoring of the divinity in those around us.   How might our worlds change if we responded first to the God (or spirit, divinity, higher power, etc.) in others and let that guide our interactions? How might it feel if others first responded to the God in you?   Let's experiment, both ways!

BRING IT TO LIFE!

Today, decide to respond to the God (or other benevolent life force) in others,
choosing gentleness first.
As you do this, be conscious of allowing them to likewise experience
the natural divinity in you.
Write down in detail at least one interaction that resulted from this experiment today.
Is this exercise something you want to do more often?

*"Is it possible that human weathering from life's experiences
is what creates an increase in our beauty and value?"*

SJK

PATINA

When copper experiences extended contact with weather, it typically oxidizes, eventually taking on a green or brown film. I see this effect all around the city, often on spires atop gorgeous historical cathedrals and on statues around the parks and buildings. What strikes me is that architects tend to value this weathered patina effect more than the bright, shiny newness of copper. So, from at least their perspective, the corrosion and chemical impacts of the wear and tear of time are actually preferred. Is it possible that in the same way, human weathering from life's experiences is what creates an increase in our beauty and value? Is it possible that our imperfections actually provide our most cherished results and impacts?

BRING IT TO LIFE!

Set aside 10 minutes in a quiet space with no distractions.
Write down some of the key experiences that have created a valuable "patina" in your life.
As you go through your day today, notice any copper elements,
from bright, shiny new to weathered, greenish patina,
and consider the value of each state.

"What if … we start using the words
miracle, magical, *and* mystical *again?"*

SJK

WHAT IF … ?

What if … we decide that satisfaction matters more than money?
What if … we find something to celebrate about ourselves each day?
What if … we step through the fear to show exactly who we are?
What if … we allow tears to hold the same beauty as a smile?
What if … we do business from the heart as much as from the head?
What if … we marvel daily at the live artwork in every leaf, flower, branch, and blade of grass?
What if … we start using the words *miracle, magical,* and *mystical* again?
What if … ?

BRING IT TO LIFE!

Take a deep breath in, then a deep breath out.
On your next breath in, say to yourself, "What if" and on your breath out, finish that sentence
with whatever first comes to mind. Write that sentence down.
Repeat this exercise for five minutes.
How does this change your perspective on the day ahead?

"Care about others, about yourself,
about anything in your path."

SJK

CARE

A cashier at the coffee shop has C A R E tattooed on her fingers just below her knuckles, facing outward — a message to the rest of us as much as to herself. ⮌ Care. Care about others, about yourself, about anything in your path. Care.

⮌

BRING IT TO LIFE!

How will you care today?

*"Because we are human, we can think and feel and express and interact and connect
and love and hope and move and, well, live."*

SJK

BECAUSE WE ARE HUMAN

As I get older, I realize how much I've taken my body's capabilities for granted. Sure, I have appreciated how many years of basketball-playing delight it has given me, and how many soul-nurturing miles on the runner's road it has supported, but I've overlooked some other physical miracles. Because we are human, we have senses to take in the world around us, internal body systems to process those experiences, and all manner of physical ways to then express those internal goings-on. Because we are human, we can think and feel and express and interact and connect and love and hope and move and, well, live. Let's honor, cherish, and take the utmost care of this gift of body we've been given, simply because we are human.

BRING IT TO LIFE!

Write a gratitude list for your body, starting each sentence with
"I thank you, body, for _____."
No matter how difficult, commit to finding five or more things
you appreciate about your body.
Think of an action you can take to more fully honor your body,
and do that today.

MARCH

MARCH 1

"Mother Ocean's love is boundless, and the sky is a cape of possibility!"

TINA BURKHOLDER

OCEAN OF CONSCIOUSNESS

As I headed off to a writing retreat at the beach, my coach sent me an email starting with, "Before you head off into your ocean of consciousness," and it struck me that consciousness is exactly what Mother Ocean offers us. ≈ In the rhythm of her waves, we hear our own breathing. ≈ In the ebb and flow of the tide, we feel our own natural rhythms. ≈ In the expanse of the horizon, we feel our delicate smallness. ≈ In the minutia of each grain of sand, we realize our own greatness. ≈ In the crash of the waves and taste of the salt, we are reminded that even the fearful and distasteful experiences of our lives are soaked in beauty. ≈ Mother Ocean awaits, with boundless love and the sky's cape ready to wrap gently around our hearts.

BRING IT TO LIFE!

Set a timer for 10 uninterrupted minutes to spend time with Mother Ocean.
If you're near an ocean, fantastic — go visit her! If you're not, simply spend virtual time with her; the Internet is great for this. Listen to an audio recording or video of waves, look at photos of ocean scenes, write a description of a past or imagined interaction with the love of Mother Ocean, etc.
After the 10 minutes, notice how you feel inside: your breathing, your heartbeat, your thoughts.
Is this an exercise you might find helpful on other days?

"What if everything we're striving to become, we already are?"

SJK

WE ALREADY ARE

What if everything we're striving to become, we already are? What if the wisdom we look for in everyone else is already bubbling up from our own selves? What if the compassion we try to grow is already filling our every cell? What if the meaning we search for is already sitting in our lap? What if the love we long for is already burning in a deep fire of our own souls? Numerous spiritual and life beliefs include the idea that we already have everything we need within us; we've simply forgotten it over time. So, what if, instead of striving to become who we might be, we start simply remembering who we already are?

BRING IT TO LIFE!

Take five minutes to write a list of things (attributes, characteristics, etc.)
that you feel you're striving to bring forward in yourself.
Take that list with you today, and note evidence of you already
being those things on the list.
How might you mirror someone to their forgotten selves in a similar way?

"What does your God ask of you?"

SJK

DO YOU NEED A NEW GOD?

Does your God ask for your fear or your love? Does your God ask for judgment or compassion? Does your God urge you to grow, or command you to shrink? If your God asks for fear, judgment, or confinement, perhaps you need a new God.

BRING IT TO LIFE!

Write down the qualities of the God (spirit, divine, energy, universal guidance,
inner knowing, higher power, whatever you wish to call it) you believe in
– or don't believe in.
Is it a belief that inspires and encourages you?
If not, what tweaks might you make to provide yourself
a positive source of deep strength?

"There in the whisper of sunlight through shimmery leaves,
I find myself."

SJK

THIRSTY

Thirsty
for a glimpse of myself
I drink the rich juice of memories
so sweet but followed as always
by a depleting sugar crash.
So I go instead
to the tree waiting so patiently just
beyond my doorstep, and there
in the rough protection of the patterned bark,
the whisper of sunlight through shimmery leaves
promising of solid growth,
I find myself.

BRING IT TO LIFE!

Studies have shown that patients who have a view of trees outside their window
heal more quickly than those who don't.
How can nature heal you today?

"Humor is a creative expression
that speaks magically across our differences."

SJK

THE HUMOR BRIDGE

I've realized that one of the first things I do when meeting someone for the first time is to try to tease out their laugh. I used to think I do that to put myself at ease, but, even more these days, I'm naturally drawn to shared laughter because it puts us on common ground.

When we can laugh together, who cares how much money we each have in the bank,
or whether we live in the city or suburbs,
or whether we're cat people, dog people, neither, or both,
or what color we are (or aren't),
or what God we believe in (or don't),
or whether we prefer tea over coffee,
or what sexual orientation we are (or aren't),
or whether we love or hate social media (or both or neither),
or what language we speak?
Humor is a bridge we can build on any land, in any conversation, in any situation.

BRING IT TO LIFE!

Today, initiate sharing a laugh with someone different than yourself (in any of the categories above or one of your own definition). *Could you feel humor as a bridge?*
How might you use humor to walk to the side of someone you're currently distant from?

"Maybe 'unraveled' is actually our place of power."

SJK

UNRAVELED

We tend to think of "unraveled" as a loss and something to avoid, or at least to repair, as if there's an unquestionable security in instead being tied up into a big bundle. But what about the times we get emotionally tied in knots? Isn't unraveled exactly the state that can loosen us up and free us from restrictions we've wrapped so tightly around ourselves? What if, when the knots threaten our growth, we take Rumi's advice and allow ourselves to follow the pull of what we really love ... and let that thread-pull gently (even if painfully) unravel our preconceived ideas, our fears, and our resistance? Maybe "unraveled" is actually our place of power.

BRING IT TO LIFE!

Picture the end of a colorful thread tied lightly to something you love,
tugging gently for you to follow it.
Imagine moving in that direction and the thread spooling out freely
as you take a few deep breaths.
How does it feel to follow that thread?
Next time you feel resistance or an internal knot forming,
allow yourself to "unravel" through this visualization exercise.

"Our lives carry evidence of the workings of a supportive universe.
The evidence is there; are you looking for it?"

SJK

EVIDENCE

I often wake up to cat toys scattered around the bedroom — in places they were not when I went to sleep — or a random, fuzzy toy mouse half-hidden under a bunched up blanket on the couch, or a curly-cue or crinkle toy tucked into the cat bed on my desk. These discoveries always amuse me, as they're such sweet evidence of feline activities that have gone on without my knowledge. While perhaps not as immediately clear as the appearance of cat toys around the house, our lives carry evidence of the workings of a supportive universe. The contact from a friend at exactly the right time; the new client who teaches you exactly what you need to grow in your business and as a person; the dog who nuzzles your hand when you cry; and the cashier at the grocery store who looks you in the eye and smiles at you with a sincerity that shows you your own value. The evidence is there; are you looking for it?

BRING IT TO LIFE!

Today, look for as much evidence as possible to show you that you have support in this world.
If feasible, create a running list that you add to throughout the day.
Or, at the end of the day, write down all the day's support evidence that you remember.
How might your days be impacted if you looked for supportive evidence each day?

MARCH 8

"The To-Be list — for the art of life."

SJK

THE TO-BE LIST

Many of us are quite skilled at creating and maintaining To-Do lists. We pay attention to them throughout each day, go to bed with them on our minds, dream about them, then wake up with our minds chomping on them, itching to get doing again. ⟨ But what about our To-Be lists? ⟨ How do we want to be each day? How do we want to interact with our world today? How do we want to emotionally and spiritually approach each task? What sorts of choices do we intend to make today? ⟨ The To-Be list — for the art of life.

BRING IT TO LIFE!

How do you want to be today? Write it down in present tense (for example,
"I am at peace today. I consciously make healthy choices today.")
Carry your To-Be list with you today.
At the end of the day reflect on how your intentions (your To-Be's) played out.

MARCH 9

"Make your deepest desires known to the universe
in whatever way works for you."

SJK

IN WHATEVER WAY

A colleague emailed me a photo of her "grandchild on a rainy day" — a precious-faced bear cub, quite close up, with its damp little body looking rather out of place against a human-built, wooden deck floor. This little guy is just one of a family of bears who hang out on her property and are now in their third generation of incredible connection with her. ᕤ They came to her because she asked them to in a very specific, meaningful-to-her way: "I made a poem once, wrapped each tiny line of paper in suet, and fed it to four bears. Asked them to take me into their lives as part of their family. Seems to have worked." ᕤ She requested her heart's deep desire through a poem in suet, while others offer whispered prayers. I've floated heartfelt letters down a stream, while others offer fruit and flowers at an altar. All different, all valid, all personal and powerful. ᕤ Make your deepest desires known to the universe in whatever way works for you.

BRING IT TO LIFE!

What is one of your deepest desires? Write it down.
How might you offer a personalized request to the universe about that deep desire?
Do that, today.

"Our bodies are tied powerfully to our emotions,
connected in a two-way exchange of information."

SJK

LAY IT DOWN

One of our exercises in a relationship systems coach training course included the act of taking a roll of tape — representing a conflict in relationship — and, together with our coaching role playing partner, placing it ahead of us on the floor, gently laying it down and stepping back to our chairs. ✍ I was surprised (and admittedly embarrassed) when I released that roll of tape and tears flowed down my cheeks as a sob escaped. That physical and emotional act of laying down something meaningful transported me for a few seconds to the graveside of my mother, where just two months earlier, I had used that same motion to place a glow-in-the-dark star in her grave. ✍ Our bodies are tied powerfully to our emotions, connected in a two-way exchange of information. Body language provides us clues to our emotional state, and we can impact our emotional state by using our bodies intentionally. ✍ Want to lay some inner struggle or sensation down? Make the motion of placing an object on the ground in front of you, and feel the release. ✍ Lay it down. Simply lay it down.

BRING IT TO LIFE!

Are you ready to lay down a conflict, self-criticism, grief, confusion, an issue you're grappling with? Choose a place where you'd like to release it: your meditation mat, the base of a tree, into the wind, into your journal, your prayer beads, any place that resonates with you.
Cup your hands as if you're holding the thing you're ready to lay down.
Bend down, open your hands, palms up, and lay that burden down.

"Perhaps if we get better at 'I'm proud of you' with others,
we'll learn how to bring it home to ourselves."

SJK

SO PROUD OF YOU

"I am so proud of you!" said one of my sisters to another in an email this morning, and I got teary. ∽ I probably wouldn't have gotten so melty if she had just said, "Great job!" or "You're amazing!" or "I'm so happy for you!" It was something about the phrase "I'm proud of you." ∽ Something like this: I acknowledge the effort it took you to get to this place. Your success means something to me. I gently claim an interconnection with you and honor who you are (including and beyond your accomplishments). ∽ We could benefit by hearing a sincere "I'm proud of you" more often in this culture. We so easily praise end-result accomplishments and tend to overlook the intricate maneuvers of the process going on — which sometimes includes an almost complete reshaping of the person. ∽ Perhaps if we get better at "I'm proud of you" with others, we'll learn how to bring it home to ourselves.

BRING IT TO LIFE!

Look for one situation today in which you can genuinely and graciously say,
"I'm so proud of you!" to someone.
Whether or not you find that situation, write a list for yourself entitled "I'm proud of you, [your name] for … " Add to that list over the days, weeks, and months
as you discover more things you're proud of in yourself.

"Perhaps it's not only the little ones who need
emotional nightlight comfort."

SJK

NIGHTLIGHT

With each new toddler and young child in my family, I'm reminded of the importance of the always-on nightlight — that beacon in the vast darkness of a little one's imagination. Perhaps it's not only the little ones who need that emotional nightlight comfort, as I often do on the dark nights of the soul, discovering time and time again that I have an internal source of light, always on. Always.

Nightlight

Find Me
here inside
you
nightlight always on
soft orange glow
gentle steady beacon
of true, warm, safe.

BRING IT TO LIFE!

Is it possible that you have an always-on internal source of light?
What might that look like, feel like?
Take 10 minutes to write down your thoughts.

"I'm in awe of the gift of the connection we are each given as we read these same words,
dear reader, on the same day across time,
as part of one shared Heart."

SJK

IN AWE

I often sit outside in my back yard in the early morning hours to ease my heart into the day. ✎ On one particular fall morning, as I watched steam dance off my coffee in the cool morning air, my mind wandered to the blessedness of life, and I was filled with an overwhelming sense of amazement and wonder — an all-encompassing feeling of awe. It was a feeling so strong that it eclipsed my litany of inner grumblings, anxieties, and concerns about the upcoming day, and poured itself out into the following "In Awe Of" list. ✎ The generosity of my friends and colleagues as they offer invaluable support for my work and life. ✎ The miracle of life unfolding in the body, heart, mind, and soul of my great-nephew. ✎ The unfathomable speed of a hummingbird's tiny wings as it sips sweet nectar from flowers in my garden. ✎ The out-door sounds blending into a symphony of musical magic expressing the rich collaborations of nature. ✎ The unbelievable orange-red brightness of a cardinal posing as a late summer flower on the neighbor's black wrought iron arbor. ✎ And most of all? I'm in awe of the gift of connection we are each given as we read these same words, dear reader, on the same day, as part of one shared Heart. Thank you.

BRING IT TO LIFE!

Write your own "In Awe Of" list, and whisper a thank you for each item on the list.
Ask someone else today what are three things on their "In Awe Of" list.

"Common is more lovely than we may realize."

SJK

IN FAIRNESS TO AZALEAS

I've been unfair to azaleas as a whole, especially during my few years as a landscape designer. I've turned my nose up at these lovely flowering shrubs because they have been so common in my surroundings, often used as a default planting around new construction, public buildings, front yards, back yards, and side yards. They bloom boldly but briefly, leaving a typically unremarkable clump of greenery on nondescript stems for the majority of the year, so they didn't earn spots in my planting designs. Then I moved to the city and started noticing breathtaking displays of stunning color showcased in planters along the sidewalks, with sunlight catching raucous waves of fuchsia in one pot and divine purple in another, and I realized, "Good heavens, those are azaleas!" I apologized out loud to one of those incredible shrubs, confessing my oversight with a fervently whispered, "I've not been fair to you, gorgeous plant. I've not been fair." So I take my own lesson from the azalea to remind us that common is more lovely than we may realize.

BRING IT TO LIFE!

Take the time to look carefully at something that you've grown so familiar with
that it seems "common" to you.
What new beauty or interest can you find there?
How might this approach impact other areas of your life?

"Today, I'm going to look for angels."

JOAN K. KING

LOOKING FOR ANGELS

One day a while back, my sister-in-law Joan announced, "Today, I'm going to look for angels." That evening, she reported that she had indeed seen angels: in the warm smile of the man on the train; in the friend who met her for lunch and connecting conversation; and in the conference attendee who shared her vision for the work she is doing in this world. This wasn't the first time she'd found angels, and it wouldn't be the last. ⟜ I think often of Joan's example, and with each remembering, I announce to myself, "Today, I'm going to look for angels." I've experienced angels in ideal clients showing up out of seemingly nowhere, and the child in the coffee shop who wouldn't relax until her mother let her come over to tell me "Hi," and the deep rumbling purr of my cat as I (attempt to) meditate. ⟜ Never ever stop looking for angels.

BRING IT TO LIFE!

Right now, announce to yourself, "Today, I'm going to look for angels."
Never mind if you actually believe in angels. Just for today, suspend your disbelief.
At the end of the day, take 10 minutes to think back through your day.
and remind yourself of all the possible angels you saw.
Write a list of these angel sightings, and keep it handy for days
when you can't seem to find something to believe in.

"Our inner wisdom loves a good metaphor."

SJK

METAPHORICAL MOMENTS

Our inner wisdom loves a good metaphor. Like a shorter version of the parables included in sacred texts of various religions, a metaphor provides deeper meaning by connecting two or more seemingly unrelated things. To create your own new, deeper, more profound understanding of the universe teasing out your inner wisdom, look for metaphorical moments each day: a broom sitting outside a house might prompt the question, "What am I ready to sweep up in my life?" The dried leaf hanging onto a lifeless branch might have you asking, "What lifeless thing do I need to let go of?" There is magic in these meaningful metaphorical moments; why not make the most of them?

BRING IT TO LIFE!

Look for metaphorical meaning throughout your day today.
At the end of the day, list all the metaphors you remember and the meaning
you want to carry with you this week.
How might your days change if you keep noticing metaphors?

*"We run the risk of putting our heart to sleep
if we let the regular become invisible."*

SJK

WHAT WE GET USED TO

Sharp, little blue-green chunks of broken car window lying scattered on the sidewalk used to disturb me. Whose car is that? Is everyone okay? How could anyone do such a thing? Did anything get stolen? Will that car owner ever feel safe again? Now, after two years of city living, I barely notice the glass, my thoughts unbroken by the sharp edges among the fallen leaves and someone's discarded french fries from the night before. ✍ We quickly get used to the things we see or experience regularly, letting them fade into familiarity, our senses dulling to the already-known. Although at times we need rest from that which is too much and too intense in our world, we run the risk of putting our heart to sleep if we let the regular become invisible. ✍ What if we get-used-to less often and rediscover the familiar more often?

BRING IT TO LIFE!

Go through today as if everything were new and unfamiliar.
What do you notice that had faded into the background?
What does this exercise awaken in you and those around you?

"The offering of our spoken or written names to each other
can be a powerful gift of presence, calling us forth to be exactly who we are."

SJK

CALLED BY NAME

In a crowded room loud with the noise of various conversations, someone quietly says our name to the person across from them — and we hear it. It's the same for me when someone says my name in conversation; other words and everything around me fades for an instant as I lean toward that gift of direct connection through my spoken name. I notice, too, when I'm addressed by my name in emails that my heart whispers a quiet "Thank you." Perhaps this deep appreciation for being called by name comes from being the youngest of nine children, wanting so badly to be seen as a unique, valued individual with my own bright identity. Or perhaps it's a natural part of each of our lives as one human in a world of billions. No matter what the reason, offering our names to each other, spoken or written, can be a powerful gift of presence, calling us forth to be exactly who we are. With compassion, with attention, with love — let's call each other by name.

BRING IT TO LIFE!

As you go through your day today, address each person by name,
focusing on them completely as you speak their name.
Also listen for your own name, and notice how you feel and what you think
when someone speaks or writes your name.

"We all wear a uniform in some way,
whether it's our facial expression, our emotions, our intentions,
or even, yes, our clothes."

SJK

IN UNIFORM

I live in an urban area surrounded by hospitals, so I regularly see people walking around in health care scrubs. Although I know nothing about most of those people, I assume simply because of their uniforms that they must be kind, helpful — and most likely tired — people. It actually feels safer and more loving to me here because of the qualities I associate with those medical uniforms. ➹ We all wear a uniform in some way, whether it's our facial expression, our emotions, our intentions, or yes, our clothes. ➹ What uniform do you wear in public?

BRING IT TO LIFE!

Take five minutes to write a description of the uniform you most typically wear in public.
What do your emotions, facial expressions, thoughts, and actions suggest about your inner
state and your consideration of those around you?
Is this the uniform you want to be wearing?
If so, appreciate your inner and outer alignment!
If not, write a description of your desired uniform,
and take one step today toward that change.

"Imagine if all of your breaks were treated as golden."

SJK

KINTSUGI

Crack my heart wide open.
Hold my hand
as the wound pours out pretense
til even the sediment is gone
and I have endless space
for boundless love.
Seal me then lightly, so very lightly
with your glue of precious gold,
a molten river flowing
rich with the reminder
of that beautiful break.

Kintsugi (golden joinery) is a Japanese art of repairing broken pottery with an adhesive mixed with gold dust, highlighting the beauty of the break. Imagine if all of your breaks were golden.

BRING IT TO LIFE!

Set aside time today to look up photos of *kintsugi*, paying close attention to how
the gold-infused adhesive turns a break into a key ingredient in a work of art.
What break in your life have you been seeing as less-than-beautiful?
How might it transform you to see those broken edges rimmed with gold?

"Sometimes we need to prioritize our health over our work."

SJK

SICK DAYS

It always surprises me how we applaud the new retiree who "worked for 43 years and didn't take even one sick day!" What a great work ethic! What strength and fortitude!   It's that sentiment that keeps me at my desk typing lethargically, while I cough and sneeze, trying to force productivity out of a body that's operating at half mast ... and wringing myself bone dry in the process. ⪍ Sometimes we need to prioritize our health over our work and just stop and rest to give healing a fighting chance.

⪍

BRING IT TO LIFE!

Write a note that says, "Don't forget sick days," and put it near your desk.
Let it remind you to listen to your body and to have the strength
and courage to say, "Enough is enough."
Just take the sick day!

*"Beholding is a deep, sacred witness of the very essence
of who we are; an embrace of the divine within us."*

SJK

BEHOLDING

In her book *Eastern Body, Western Mind*, Anodea Judith speaks of the importance of knowing the person we are inside. Thomas Moore echoes her words, stating that befriending ourselves is the "basis of all relationship." Oscar Wilde also describes our relationship with self as "the beginning of a lifelong romance." What is it here that gives such power to our self-awareness? It is, as Judith calls it, the act of beholding. Beholding is not a simple seeing; it's a deep, sacred witness of the very essence of who we are, an embrace of the divine within us. No judgment, no fixing, no anything except a fully open welcome and honoring of all we witness in ourselves. It's in this beholding that we find a lasting relationship with ourselves, the foundation for real healing, strength, and growth.

BRING IT TO LIFE!

Behold yourself today.
Witness everything within you, and as much as possible, allow it to be exactly what it is.
Simply witness and embrace whatever shows up.
How might you give yourself this deep attention regularly?
And how might it expand to others?

"When we make it a point to literally see the other side,
it can remind us to open up a whole new world
of different perspectives."

SJK

THE OTHER DIRECTION

A friend shared photos she had taken on her morning commute to work — notable on that day simply because she had taken a different route. Later, I found myself fully engrossed in the delights of my own walk to the train — notable simply because I had used the other side of the street. ⌒ When we make it a point to literally see the other side or come from the other direction, it can remind us to open up a whole new world of different opinions, fresh perspectives, and new chances for empathetic understanding.

⌒

BRING IT TO LIFE!

Take a different direction or use the other side of the street or hallway
as you walk to a destination today.
What new things do you notice?
How does this impact your perspective?
How might you expand this experience into other areas of your life?

"Some times we need to lose our leaves, cleanse the past we hold within us,
and drop all those things that no longer serve us."

SJK

LOSE YOUR LEAVES

The dearest miniature Angel Wing Begonia sits on a windowsill in the stairwell leading up to my office. I say hello to it each time I walk by, stopping to admire its wavy, red-trimmed leaves and hot pink, heart-shaped flowers. That little plant grew vivaciously for months, sending out new stems and clumps of lush flowers week after week, and I grew quite fond of its showy display. ⟲ Then one day a leaf fell off ... and another ... and another, then the next day, still more. This continued until only three leaves remained. My heart ached as I'd climb those stairs and see tired, brown stems and those three ... then two ... struggling leaves. ⟲ Then one day I saw new, bright green growth peeking through near the base of one stem. The next day, there was new growth partway up another stem, and a tiny new nub pushing its way into daylight on yet another stem. Within two weeks, that plant had come back to life, flaunting its red-trimmed leaves once again in all their vibrant glory. ⟲ Sometimes we need to lose our leaves, cleanse the past we hold within us, drop all those things that no longer serve us, and give ourselves a new, vigorous zeal for not just surviving, but for thriving.

BRING IT TO LIFE!

What might you be wanting to "lose" right now
in order to more fully step into growth and thriving? Take one step in that direction today.

MARCH 25

"Let's always be awake to the possibilities."

SJK

CLONED KITTIES

A few years back, the news outlets were all abuzz about the first successfully cloned kitten. They named her CC! We're a cat-loving household, so while the science was interesting, we were honestly much more enthralled by the cuteness of that little bundle of precious. I had been having a particularly rough life-is-too-big-for-me patch when I got a mid-morning email from my wife that said simply, "I'd like two cloned kitties pleece." No greeting, no closing, just an adorable, phonetically spelled request for not one, but two cloned kitties. Such a small gesture of connection, but in that moment, it was exactly what my heart needed in order to stretch into hope. Some of life's most precious moments come in the smallest, most unexpected ways. Let's always be awake to the possibilities.

BRING IT TO LIFE!

Today, if you have the energy for it, reach out to someone
in a small gesture of connection.
If you're too weary, then commit to staying open to noticing
the small gestures of connection offered to you from others.
At the end of the day, recall your most meaningful small moment from the day.
What made it meaningful to you? To others around you?
Is this a practice you'd like to continue?

"We all need a call to worship — sometimes a gentle one,
sometimes the loud clanging one that won't be ignored.
And we need to answer that call willingly, graciously, and completely."

SJK

CALL TO WORSHIP

I live a block away from a majestic Catholic parish, and every day, every 15 minutes, the church bells chime the time. It's a soothing, joyful sound, adding a certain comfort to the rhythms of each day. Until, that is, it's time for Mass. I was rather stunned the first time I heard that call to worship, not expecting the drastic change from a gentle chiming to jarring, clanging bells loudly insisting we all pay attention as they called us and called us and called us to their time of worship. Even though those bells don't lure me to the cathedral, they always call me to moments of worship. They break through whatever thoughts and experience I'm having at the moment and ask loudly, "Have you been feeding your soul?" Have I been reading the books that inspire me, spending time in meditation and quiet, communing with those I enjoy on the deepest levels, allowing joy as much as pain, and remembering the miracle of every ounce of nature? We all need a call to worship — sometimes a gentle one, sometimes a loud, clanging one that won't be ignored. And we need to answer that call willingly, graciously, and completely.

BRING IT TO LIFE!

Write a list of everything that acts as a call to worship in your life, and list ways you engage in worship, whatever that means to you. *Are there any changes you'd like to make? A louder call? A gentler call?* If so, take one step toward that change today.
If not, offer gratitude to that call for bringing your attention to worship.

MARCH 27

"It may feel safer and easier to keep our boldest parts hidden,
but it's when we spread our wings
that the rest of the world gets to see our full, stunning beauty."

SJK

OPEN WINGS

We have a surprising number of birds who regularly visit our urban backyard patio. Rooftops and electrical wires interspersed with treetops and determinedly tall shrubs are apparently enticing a mix of Mourning Doves, finches, sparrows, and an occasional cardinal pair to hang out there.  Although the gentle coo of the Mourning Dove stirs my heart, my attention is more easily drawn to the patterns and colors on the other birds ... until, that is, I see the full spread of the dove's wings as they glide in for a landing. In flight, their pointed tails are framed in white, utterly striking against gray-brown wings with a dash of bold, black spots in the center. It may feel safer and easier to keep our boldest parts hidden, but it's when we spread our wings that the rest of the world gets to see our full, stunning beauty.

BRING IT TO LIFE!

Today, find photos of a Mourning Dove (a library or the Internet are great sources).
Notice the difference in their colors and patterns when the wings are open or closed.
What might be an area in your life where you are ready to spread your wings
and show a bit more of your beauty?

"Sometimes it takes a physical effort
to let the emotions break free and loosen their grip."

SJK

BREAK FREE

I had known all week that something was brewing. Restlessness kept chewing away at my inspiration, little emotional bite marks scattered through each day. I'd sit down each morning to meditate, willing myself to release whatever was going on. I tried to space myself out, write myself out, think my way out … all to no avail. Then that Friday morning, my physical trainer had me work my muscles to fatigue. With the final pull of exercise bands, my mind let go and the tears came through — suddenly, insistently, and beautifully. My dear trainer simply responded with a gentle, "Ah … it's been awhile." Apparently I had been holding my feelings deep in my muscles: grief, fear, doubt, resistance, and self-sabotage all came through when my body was finally too tired to cling to those emotions. That mind-heart-body connection is so very powerful. Sometimes it takes a physical effort to let emotions break free and loosen their grip. So next time you're stuck — emotionally, mentally, intellectually, or spiritually — get moving, literally, and give yourself a chance to break free.

BRING IT TO LIFE!

Think of something in your life that is concerning you.
Take that concern on a brief walk with you, and focus on the movement of your body.
At the end of your walk, notice any shift in your emotions
or how you're thinking about what was initially concerning you.

"Taste the rainbow,
always, always taste the rainbow
in every moment of this richly colored life."

SJK

TASTE THE RAINBOW

A friend sent me a photo of her son with his head gently dipped back, mouth open, and — as it appeared from the angle of the photo — one end of a double rainbow streaming into his mouth. She captioned the photo, "Taste the rainbow." That photo and caption stopped me in my tracks: taking something so lovely, yet seemingly untouchable and far away as a rainbow, and turning it into something so close, so tangible that we can put it in our mouth and taste it, make it a part of our self. That is what it means to fully experience a moment in life. Taste the rainbow — always, always taste the rainbow, in every moment of this richly colored life.

BRING IT TO LIFE!

Take five minutes to imagine and describe the experience of tasting a rainbow.
What flavors, textures, temperatures, and scents (smell is part of our taste experience)
show up in your mind?
How might you apply this "taste the rainbow" idea
to other experiences in your life?

"It's in those highest, lowest, and deepest moments of our existence
that we experience the place beyond words."

SJK

IN THE PLACE BEYOND WORDS

Words hold a hugely important place in our lives. They allow us to communicate our inner selves to others, connecting us to the external world beyond our thoughts as we speak and write our minds. As a writer, I find particular comfort and satisfaction in being able to put something into words, and feel great kinship to the colleague who collects interesting words on sticky-notes around her home. There's a limit, though, to words. They fail to be adequate for conveying those sunsets that drench our souls with exquisite joy, or the unspeakable grief as a loved one takes their last breath, or the all-consuming awe of a moment of deep worship. It's in those highest, lowest, and deepest moments of our existence that we experience the place beyond words — a state of being fully alive, fully conscious, and fully awake. We all need to spend time in that place beyond words, for it's here that we meet with what is divine and profound within us, and our tired, inadequate words germinate to surface later with increased depth, meaning, and beauty.

BRING IT TO LIFE!

Take a moment to remember a time you experienced a place beyond words.
What were you doing? How can you recreate that experience (for example, focused attention
to music, nature, silence, a photograph, gentle touch)? Reserve 10 minutes in your day
to discover your own place beyond words, and notice the impact.
Might this be a place you want to visit more regularly?

"Let's remember to thank the people who have influenced us, fueled our fires,
sparked our creative genius, and given us tools to live differently,
deeper, and with more daring."

SJK

HAVE YOU THANKED THEM?

When Steve Jobs died in 2011, I posted a thank you note to him on my business Facebook page. It got me thinking about everyone else who has been part of my journey and the incredible value each and every one of them has provided (and been) along the way.   As humans, we have the capacity to connect to other humans, learning and growing from each other in an infinite variety of ways. Let's remember to thank those incredible people in our lives who have influenced us, fueled our fires, sparked our own creative genius, and given us tools to live differently, deeper, and with more daring. In sincerely thanking others, we honor their presence and actions, and we remind ourselves of ways we can offer the same support to others in our lives.

BRING IT TO LIFE!

Create a written list of attributes that you consider important to supporting others in your life. Beside each one, place the name of a person who has shown that attribute in connection with you. Send a thank you to three of those people today (email, phone call, text, Facebook post, handwritten note card — whatever works best for you) to honor their place in your growth.
Thank them directly, from the heart, and include specifics.
Consider also thanking the rest of the people on your list over the next week.

APRIL

"We humans need growth in both directions:
grounded to the earth and soaring to the heavens."

SJK

IN BOTH DIRECTIONS

Most plants are programmed to grow their roots in the direction of gravity, and their stems away from gravity. The roots reach to the nutrients in the depths of soil, anchoring tight as a foundation for the stems as they follow the light and lengthen their reach. If all plant parts grew in one direction, it just wouldn't work: all stem, and the plants would topple over with no anchor, and if all root, they'd exist as subterranean creatures out of touch with the glories of light and open life. We humans also need growth in both directions: a grounding growth in the natural direction of our deepest inner strengths and a stretching growth in the direction of uncharted lightness of the unknown. Ground to the earth, soar to the heavens.

BRING IT TO LIFE!

What grounds you, helps you feel your strength and confidence?
What releases you, helps you feel your faith as you let go and stretch?
Choose one activity for grounding and one for release,
and carry them both out today.
Notice the impact of growth in both directions.

"The truest beauty is felt, not just seen."

SJK

WHEN YOUR HEART IS BLOCKED

The truest beauty is felt, not just seen — felt and integrated into our very cells as divine fuel for full living. Yet there are days when feeling seems to be inaccessible: days when I can look at the ocean and merely see waves, brush against a flower and not notice the velvety touch, or look into a loved one's eyes and not even see their color. Those are the days my heart is blocked — for any variety of reasons — and closed to the experience of sensation. Whether it's drowning in grief, shored up against hurt, or beating heavily within the lethargy of internal darkness, a blocked heart wraps tightly around itself in a cloak of protection. But isn't the feeling of awe when examining the aerodynamic structure of a dandelion seed worth a few minutes of heart-opening deep breaths? Isn't a full-hearted, loving tear on your cheek worth the risk of looking deeply into another's eyes with your heart cracked open? Isn't the potential flash of understanding your own beauty in this world worth the effort of keeping your foot gently wedged into your heart's door so it stays open ... always? I think so.

BRING IT TO LIFE!

Take a few moments to become aware of your heart. Close your eyes, and picture that spot in your chest as you feel the heartbeat. Breathe deeply into your heart, notice any resistance, and breathe anyway. Do this until you feel your heart become more open.

Approach today with that open heart, no matter how much courage it might take, and see how much beauty you can feel. At the end of the day, note your observations.

"Now serving love and gratitude for breakfast!
Would you like coffee with that?"

SJK

SACRED INGREDIENTS

Fresh rosemary sprigs sprawl in disarray across my cutting board, and each cut I make into their sturdy structure releases a waft of bold floral earthiness. ✑ I gently strip the fresh ginger root's bark and marvel at its pale yellow heart, a complex structure of juice and fiber with the aroma of sunlight. ✑ Nutmeg dares me to get lost in the memories evoked by its all-consuming scent, but I instead follow the allure of the silky cinnamon dust beside it. ✑ Maple syrup carries the life of its trees in sweet nectar to each rolled oat, while dark molasses adds its bittersweet reminder that life's most important experiences may have nothing to do with puppies and roses. ✑ Wrinkled, golden raisins clump together as they tell each other tales from their glory years on the old vines out west. ✑ Slivered almonds shiver without their skin in this embryo form, happy to finally be warmed with the rest of the crew in a gentle oven bake. ✑ To some it's just a homemade granola treat. To others, it's a collaboration of sacred ingredients and the chance to get up close and personal with the nourishing gifts of nature. ✑ Now serving love and gratitude for breakfast! Would you like coffee with that?

✑

BRING IT TO LIFE!

Eat a combination of two or more raw fruits (and nuts if you don't have allergies) today.
If feasible, add a sprig of fresh rosemary. Notice and appreciate
the natural flavors, textures, scents, colors of each. *How does this impact your mood?*

The periphery — that nebulous place that warehouses our greatest inspirations,
clearest inner wisdom, and most profound glimpses of the divine —
apparently works best when it's not under the spotlight."

SJK

THE POWER OF PERIPHERY

Something mystical happens when we focus wholly on something — say, for example, the insect-chewed pattern on a leaf, the repetition of a particular note in a song, or the undulating caress of a tender breeze across our skin. ✎ That laser-sharp focus on what's front and center seems to leave the subconscious (and self-conscious!) part of our soul unoccupied and brave enough to scootch from our periphery closer to our conscious awareness. The periphery — that nebulous place that warehouses our greatest inspirations, clearest inner wisdom, and most profound glimpses of the divine — apparently works best when it's not under the spotlight. ✎ It's in those super-focused times (examining nature, cooking, listening intently, loving deeply) that the periphery tilts its contents toward our awareness and words come flowing in to the writer; music appears to the composer; a flash of insight appears to the CEO, the homemaker, the coach, anyone. ✎ It's counterintuitive, I know, this idea that the more closely we focus on one thing, the more clearly we see something else, so I guess you'll just need to try it for yourself.

BRING IT TO LIFE!

Set aside five minutes, and describe something in front of you. Write down every detail
you see, feel, hear, taste, and smell. If you run out of observations before the time is up, focus
more closely and keep describing. At the end of five minutes, jot down thoughts that come
to mind, no matter how random. *What is new in those thoughts?*

"When life's meaning escapes us, perhaps that's what we can remember:
we're always a necessary part of someone's story."

SJK

PRESENT HISTORY

One day, soon after moving to historically-rich Philadelphia, I was sitting in the upper level of a corner coffee shop taking in my surroundings. As I looked at the time-worn, exposed brick wall, the modern trappings in my vision faded out, and I imagined the warm glow of a fireplace surrounded by men and women in colonial dress, coming in from a cold night after hitching up their horses outside. 〜 It only lasted for a minute until my awareness came back to my present-day experience, but something still lingered there, and still does each time I revisit that same coffee shop. I think it's the history that meets me there, strong enough that it takes over my vision and draws me away for a moment, back to the early days of that building and that town. 〜 This city is the continuation of the work of many people for many, many years. That brick wall was likely laid by the hands of a several-times great-grandfather, and that mortar stirred by some strapping young boys apprenticed to the construction business of the time, supported by the strength of women who held whole families together with their love and caring while their daughters snuck one last visit to the horse barn to feed carrots to Bessie. 〜 Our stories start well before us and carry on long after us. When life's meaning escapes us, perhaps that's what we can remember: we're always a necessary part of someone's story.

BRING IT TO LIFE!

What is the history of the town you live in? Whose stories began there before yours?
Who might be the continuation of your own story?

"You have 1,440 minutes today. Savor them."

SJK

ONE SAVORY MINUTE

We tend to put time in a chokehold of lack, using phrases like, "There's never enough time," or "I don't have time," or "So many _____, so little time." Yet, if we take a slightly different perspective, time magically expands: 1 day ... or 1,440 minutes? One minute is enough time to

Laugh,
Step outside and take three invigorating deep breaths,
Touch a flower and feel the velvety-soft or prickly texture,
Pick the spent blooms off a daylily,
Savor a cookie,
Call a friend and say, "I was just thinking about you,"
Start something over, better,
or say, "I'm sorry" and "Love you" and "Let's dance."

You have 1,440 minutes today. Savor them.

BRING IT TO LIFE!

Take five non-consecutive minutes in your day to intentionally savor something.
At the end of your day, write down each of those actions, and describe as much
as you can remember about each one.
How did each of those five savory minutes impact your day?

"Devour the fruits of the day with the hunger of a starving soul."

SJK

FAMISHED

Devour
the fruits of the day
with knife-sharp eyes
Let the juice of beauty
run in honeyed rivers
through your heart
as you pierce
each experience
with the hunger of a starving soul
famished
for a taste
of
God.

BRING IT TO LIFE!

Today, take in each experience with your full senses,
relishing each satisfying and fulfilling moment as completely as possible.
Notice how this full experience impacts your day.

"What if we said or gave just a little something extra
to our interactions?"

SJK

A LITTLE SOMETHING EXTRA

"Thank you so much ... have a good meeting," the young woman said as she accepted the laptop handed to her by another woman I assumed was her co-worker. As they each walked away in opposite directions from the outdoor café area, she turned and yelled back, "Oh! And I like your dress!" What if we said or gave just a little something extra like that to each of our interactions?

BRING IT TO LIFE!

Today, give a little something extra with every interaction.
Notice what little somethings were most impactful with the most ease.
Are they something you might want to do more regularly?

"When we identify the unknown parts of our living world,
we move one step closer to love."

SJK

ONE STEP CLOSER

I have bird books and butterfly books and garden plant books and tree books and even bug books, all to help me identify the names of these various specimens of nature. I constantly interrupt walks and drives asking, "Oooh, I wonder what kind of [bird, plant, tree, bug] that is?" ⤳ On one hand, we might say it doesn't really matter whether I can identify a certain living thing or not. A flower isn't less physically beautiful if I don't know its name, and a bug doesn't lose its magnetizing creepy factor if I don't know its name. ⤳ On the other hand, though, it matters to my heart. If I know that deep, shimmery-blue color belongs to an Eastern Swallowtail rather than a more generic "butterfly," I'm one step closer to knowing it, which easily expands into some sort of connection, which can turn into love. ⤳ When we identify the unknown parts of our living world, we move one step closer to love.

BRING IT TO LIFE!

Find a plant or bird you see often near your home, and identify it by looking online
or in a library for its key identifiers: colors, patterns, shapes, size, and location.
If this feels troublesome, assign a name to a certain plant or a bird you see today —
just as you might name a cat or a dog.
Notice the impact that naming has on your feelings about what you see.

"Joy is that pilot-light we have constantly burning deeply within,
quick to grow into an intense heat when fueled by meaningful experiences."

SJK

IN DEFENSE OF JOY

Unfortunately, "joy" seems to have become little more than a buzzword, often empty of meaning due to overuse and oversimplification. Devoid of depth, the term is easily equated to some Pollyanna ideal having something to do with a rose-colored life without any pain, sorrow, or hardship. ❧ Reluctant to use options from the buzzword pile, I stopped using the word "joy" for a while, but soon found there was no substitute for the richness of that word, and that a life without the concept of joy was one with a substantial hole in it. Joy is that pilot-light fire we have constantly burning deeply within, quick to grow into an intense heat when fueled by meaningful experiences — whether pleasing or difficult. ❧ Joy is the inexplicable feeling that burns high through the support of loving family members during a parents' death, and the appreciation of a friendship so deep that it brings tears to our eyes, and the awe of ongoing synchronistic experiences that light torches of guidance on our path. Joy is the feeling that burns bright into a celebration of gratitude for the meaningful experiences in our lives. Joy is, in my experience at least, what God feels like. Let's keep it a sacred and honored word.

BRING IT TO LIFE!

What does joy mean for you? Where do you feel it in your body?
What experiences have fueled joy in your life?

"In the midst of any variety of unspeakable duress,
we have a Hand to hold."

SJK

A HAND TO HOLD

It was about two years ago, at a time of ongoing change in several areas of my life. My inner foundation was crumbly, the highly imbalanced ratio of questions to answers in my everyday life had worn me down, and I just needed to rest in the arms of some source of strong comfort. ᐬ Writing only gave me more words of confusion and frustration. ᐬ Working pulled more from me than I had to give. ᐬ Waiting offered no peace. ᐬ So I found a ray of sunshine waiting for me on the soft carpet in my meditation room and lay down in *Shavasana* (corpse pose), flat on my back in deep surrender with the sunlight pouring over me. Within a few breaths, the tears came and I began to relax into meditation. ᐬ And then I felt it: an unmistakably gentle, yet firm touch of a solid hand, fingers intertwined with mine for the briefest of moments, and when the sensation left, so did my angst, leaving me with deep peace and an absolutely certain knowledge that we have support beyond what we ever imagine in this life. ᐬ In the midst of unspeakable duress, we have a Hand to hold.

BRING IT TO LIFE!

Take five minutes to close your eyes and imagine a gentle hand reaching into yours
and simply holding it with deep compassion and strength.
Carry that image with you today, and notice how it impacts your day.

"When I was young I used to be known as the crazy one
for talking to the animals.
I still do. I think animals do understand us."

TERERAI TRENT

ANIMAL COMMUNITY

Today after talking with a colleague about her meaningful multi-generational relationship with a bear family, I saw a picture of a beautiful African woman kneeling in tall grass, just inches away from a cow with some disturbingly sharp horns. I stared at that photo for a while because it seemed I could actually feel the connection between the woman and cow; they looked somehow as though they were interacting as dear, comfortable friends. I commented about how much I loved the photo, and the woman responded, "I used to graze the great-grandmother of that cow!" and went on to explain that when she was a child, people thought she was crazy for talking to the animals. "I still do," she adds. "I think animals do understand us." Two women in two different continents with two different animal families, on the same day sharing stories of their incredible connection to animals. I, for one, think there's something to it ... .

BRING IT TO LIFE!

Today, pay attention to the animals around you.
Is it possible there's more of a connection between you than you thought?

"Below the heights of success, our ground level reality
offers us a different way to walk in this world."

SJK

EVEN THE FALLEN

As the cherry, pear, and redbud trees begin to lose their blooms after a couple weeks of ecstatic display, I find myself wistfully wanting them to hang on. "Give me just a little longer to see you at your peak," I whisper into the bloom clumps, their ruffled layers of velvety softness held high above the ground like attendees at a rooftop soiree. ⪍ Then my eye follows a petal as it drops erratically to the ground, joining a thickening pink carpet of spent blooms, and I realize that even the fallen petals have an exquisite beauty, providing a tender layer of soothing color instead of the usual gray sidewalk brusqueness. ⪍ Even our fallen parts and people deserve attention and appreciation for what they and we bring. Below the heights of success, our ground level reality offers us a different way to walk in this world: blooming with compassion, empathy, and a grass-roots appreciation of the value of every phase of each person's life process.

BRING IT TO LIFE!

Today, look for things that you would normally consider to be past their prime
or their peak (nature, pets, people, buildings), and find the beauty and value in them.
How does this impact your opinion of and response to these things?
What if you integrated this perspective into your life every day?

"Morning is when the night gremlins have to be subdued and vanquished
with a counter-onslaught of coffee and exercise,
and the occasional sunrise."

STEVEN WIEBE-KING

MORNING ALLIANCE

Morning is an incredibly powerful time of day, magnifying whatever is topmost in mind as we emerge from sleep with our inner core vulnerable. Some fortunate souls naturally wake with the dawn, feeling joyfully alive, but for others, mornings are more about lingering night gremlins than welcoming a beautiful, new day. We can, however, shift our relationship with morning by building a simple alliance with her: we can take the time to notice, appreciate, and spend intentional time with her, let her help us build our day on beauty instead of fear and on expression instead of depression.

BRING IT TO LIFE!

If you don't already do this, experiment with taking an extra five to thirty minutes
early each morning to pay attention to the stillness.
It might be simply sitting with coffee, watching the sun rise, or taking a walk around the block
while listening to your favorite song or the sounds of the city or country.
Engage with the morning in a way that serves you and sets the tone you want for the day.
What are different ways you might collaborate with the morning?

"Catch that glorious glimpse of the fresh, unprotected shine of our soul's newest artwork that sparkles for just a moment before it dries."

SJK

BEFORE IT DRIES

Writing with pen and notebook in the clear morning sunlight, I noticed brief glints on the page — each one lasting for just a split second as I wrote each word. It was the sheen of the wet ink, gleaming before it dried, shining for that split second while it was most vulnerable to the smears and smudges that could render a word unrecognizable. The same goes for paint. And mascara. And Polaroid photos. And, perhaps, our own lives? That moment when we've added a fresh word of meaning and purpose to our identity, and we're still damp with the vulnerable newness of it. That moment when we're painting a new picture of our lives through a significant change in perspective or behavior, and old patterns threaten to run their careless footprints over our canvas. That moment of transition between who we were just a minute ago and who we are always becoming. Those are the moments to watch for, to catch that glorious glimpse of the fresh, unprotected shine of our soul's newest artwork that sparkles for just a moment before it dries.

BRING IT TO LIFE!

If feasible, find a gel pen for this exercise; ballpoint ink dries too quickly.
On a piece of paper, write, "Before it dries." See if you can catch the shine from the wet ink.
Tuck this image away, and bring it forward next time you experience change that makes you feel vulnerable. Those moments bring great beauty and an extra shine.

*"Different was delightful, and doughnuts in the break room
allowed us to get happily sidetracked with the shared excitement
of little deep-fried bundles of joy."*

SJK

DOUGHNUTS IN THE BREAK ROOM

Back in my corporate employee days, nothing — and I mean nothing — was as thrilling as the announcement that there were doughnuts in the break room.   Although I managed to be quite professional when necessary, all that went out the window on doughnuts-in-the-breakroom days. So much so that people started going out of their way to let me know about the presence of doughnuts ... so they could watch me run (literally) to that culinary treasure.   It wasn't so much the doughnuts themselves, I think, as it was the change from ordinary: an ordinary job on an ordinary day in an ordinary mood. Different was delightful, and doughnuts in the break room allowed us to get happily sidetracked with the shared excitement of little deep-fried bundles of joy.   I know, doughnuts are so not good for you, and I don't advocate eating many of them, ever. But we all need a good dose of some version of doughnuts-in-the-break-room excitement from time to time.   Treat yourself to delight.

BRING IT TO LIFE!

*What small treat (edible or not) feels as delightful as the unexpected announcement
of doughnuts in the break room during a long, tiring, way-too-ordinary day?*
Do that today.

"Today, I'm going to close my eyes in Virginia and put my face up to the sun
to soak it in before I get to the airport.
I'll be inside for hours and will wake up to the sun (hopefully shining) in France.
I'll do the same once I step outside there, and know it is shining the same for us,
no matter where we are."

REBECCA P. COHEN

THE SAME SUN

We all feel the same sun. Not all at the same time, or with the same intensity, but nonetheless, we all feel the same sun. Think about that for a moment. What a beautiful connection we all have, something we ALL share: the sun! Something we can see. And feel. And bask in when we can't be physically in the same space of each other's warm, healing energy. And just like the sun, even when we can't feel — and we lose faith in that connection — it is merely hidden, not gone. We all feel the same sun.

BRING IT TO LIFE!

Take five minutes at three different times today to stop and be aware of the sun
(even if it's hidden by clouds), thinking of someone you want to feel connected to.
Allow yourself to bask in the knowledge that you share the same sun.
Consider letting that person know that you thought of them
through your shared view of the sun.

"All genuine expression is creative, as it gives visibility
to the non-visible within us."

SJK

THE DIVINE ARTIST

No matter what you call it — God, creativity, inner wisdom, universal energy, higher power, spirit, the divine, your truest self, or something else — there's a beautiful presence that shows up through creative awareness and expression. Never mind if you don't consider yourself creative, because really, isn't all genuine expression creative, as it gives visibility to the non-visible within us? Expression of any form — whether it be singing, laughing, crying, loving, talking, painting, writing, etc. — allows us to engage with that mystical presence within and around us. It's like walking through the open door of the divine and realizing that his/her/its living room is, indeed, your own heart.

BRING IT TO LIFE!

Set aside 15 minutes, and engage in one of your favorite forms of expression today,
allowing yourself to step through the door of the divine.
What do you find there?
Is this a place you'd like to visit more often?

"Each day, in all situations, we have this choice
between fear and faith."

SJK

SIGN OF PROTECTION

On our city street, overnight, five cars in a row were damaged: some with flat tires, others with fenders and hubcaps littered around the street beside their wrinkled vehicles. Expecting to see similar issues with our car, we were thrilled to realize that all the damage stopped just before our vehicle — not a scratch, bump, or dent there. I could choose to go through my day after that consumed by anxiety about the very real dangers of city living, or I could choose to wrap myself in the equally real signs of Protection. Each day I choose protection — the choice that allows my heart to stay open. Each day, in all situations, we have a choice between faith and fear. What will it be for you today?

BRING IT TO LIFE!

Write "Faith or fear?" on a sticky-note and take it with you today.
Pay attention to your responses today, and at each one ask yourself, "Faith or fear?"
What do you choose most often?
Is it the choice that best serves you and those around you?

"They say no man is an island;
what if the same is true for religion?"

SJK

BLENDED WORSHIP

I wish our world was better at encouraging blended worship — time spent in deep gratitude in a way that combines self-selected practices from any organized religious, spiritual, natural, or other groups. Not that the more standard purity of sticking fully to one core set of practices and beliefs isn't valuable; just that perhaps we also need to consider the possible value in blurring those lines. ᛉ This morning, I sat on my meditation mat in half-lotus yoga posture, eyes closed, listening to Christian hymns with a cat curled into my lap. I soon raised my hands, palms up, in a natural expression of allowing and receiving — with thumbs and forefingers in the circle of *chin mudra,* an Eastern energy and consciousness technique. Then, bringing my creative soul into the mix, I added my notebook and pen and wrote from that physical, spiritual, and energetic space. In that experience, I felt the depth of inspiration multiplied exponentially through the blend of various components that felt like worship to me: Eastern, Western, nature-focused, creative, traditional, and non-traditional all together. ᛉ They say no man is an island; what if the same is true for religion?

BRING IT TO LIFE!

What are your favorite ways to experience the parts of life that touch you deeply?
How might you combine more of those to create an even deeper experience
of inspiration or worship?

"Our actions are inner wisdom turned inside out."

SJK

INSIDE OUT

In an awake life, we often see clues to our inner workings by looking at our outer actions — like the way I selected seashells on day three of a highly introspective writing retreat. I had spent quite a bit of time reading, writing, and ruminating on recurring questions regarding my relationship with myself, plus inner work on honoring my imperfections as an equally sacred part of myself. I was still tossing those ideas and feelings around as I went for a walk on the beach, and was soon drawn to an expanse of shells littered across the sand. I began, as usual, to look for the most perfect shells, fine specimens of nature to offer my wife back home, but my attention quickly went to the shells with chips out of their rounded edges, cracks toward the center, and holes interrupting the smooth flow of their colored bands. I realized I was seeing more beauty in the imperfect shells than the perfect, feeling a deep compassion for their cuts, cracks, holes, and chips. I was seeing and collecting me. Our actions are inner wisdom turned inside out.

BRING IT TO LIFE!

Pay attention to your actions today, and notice any particularly strong reactions
or feelings about any of those actions.
If those actions are your inner state turned inside out, what might they be telling you?
How do you want to respond?

"Spring opened its mouth today
and I fed it my love."

SJK

THE MOUTH OF SPRING

Spring opened its mouth today
licking gently at my heart
asking if it was time to play yet. Or now. How about now?
Now?
Finally I said an internal yes
and my emotional shadows merged into
sunlight
blooms
and the courage to see beauty sharp enough
that it could cut my undefined fear.
Spring opened its mouth today
and I fed it my love.

BRING IT TO LIFE!

Find signs of spring or nature in your world today,
and see what questions and answers come to mind for you.

"How often do we miss the incredible capabilities
of a human being simply because we forgot to put the 'un' in front of 'limited'?"

SJK

UNLIMITED

Derek Paravicini was born over three months prematurely, too early to sustain sight and full brain functioning. Yet, now in his thirties, there he sits at the piano keyboard improvising songs so intricately that it sounds like several pianists on several pianos at once. Never mind that he can't see; never mind that he has severe autism; this man is apparently unlimited in his musical capacity and subsequently in his ability to amaze and inspire others. ⤳ How often do we look at and look for the limited rather than the unlimited — in others, and in ourselves? ⤳ How often do we miss the incredible talents and capabilities of a human being simply because we forgot to put the "un" in front of "limited"?

BRING IT TO LIFE!

Today, put the "un" in front of all the limits you encounter — in yourself and others.
What becomes possible?

"Although we still shine on our own, when connected to other like-minded or like-souled folks, we gain strength for a stunning impact of exponential beauty."

SJK

SEQUINS

Waiting at the airport in Charlotte, North Carolina, I noticed a small, blue sequin on the empty seat beside me. Have you ever examined a sequin? They're quite amazing: this one was a shimmery, metallic circle surrounding a six-sided, shiny blue geometric figure with a hole in the middle and one side curved in — all features designed to catch and reflect light. On its own, this individual sequin's light gets lost in the vastness of its environment, but put it with a community of other sequins on a shirt collar or dress, and the combined sparkle catches the eye of everyone nearby. Like this sequin, we each have a sparkle that comes from our multi-faceted selves and the interesting shapes of our personalities. Although we still shine on our own, when connected to other like-minded or like-souled folks, we gain strength for a stunning impact of exponential beauty. When your individual light dims or your solo sparkle longs for a broader impact, reach out for your community, and nestle in with the shared wattage.

BRING IT TO LIFE!

What area of your life is wishing for community to enhance your sparkle, your impact, your connection to the world around you? What are three ways you can connect to others who might be looking for similar connection? Do one of those things today.

*"Let's bring it back, the reading aloud of connecting stories
given life through our own voices."*

SJK

READ TO ME

During the first evening of an informal writing retreat, two women read their stories out loud to me. I was immediately soothed by the cadence of their sentences and the easy flow of words effortlessly carrying me into their stories. ⌇ We read stories out loud to the little ones in our lives, using the words to wrap them in our love and comfort as they sleep, but at a certain age, most of us just stop. Reading out loud to each other falls by the wayside along with tattered dolls, toys, and teddy bears. ⌇ Let's bring it back, the reading aloud of connecting stories given life through our own voices. Bring back the dusty, warm memories of sleepy childhood bedtimes bathed in warm lamplight, or make memories you never got. Bring back the total absorption in a world of possibility and adventure and experience made real through our imagination. ⌇ Let's remember, in this digitized, electronic world, that it doesn't take technical skill to turn print words into practically-alive 3D; it merely takes a voice and willingness to read aloud. ⌇ Gift someone with words today, wrapped in the gorgeous timbre of your voice.

BRING IT TO LIFE!

At some point today, take the time to either read something out loud to someone,
or to ask someone to read to you. If you're feeling quite shy, it can be a quick paragraph.
Feel the connection of stories read out loud, and consider making this
a regular part of your routine.

"Start wondering about everything, everywhere, all the time."

SJK

THE WONDER OF WONDER

As the majestic, newly retired space shuttle rode on a 747 jet's back through the east coast airspace, people stopped their cars on the highway and interrupted work at their desks to watch this incredible sight. Facebook and Twitter buzzed with commentary on this fascinating event. ✍ What was it that transfixed and transformed all of us in those moments of awe? What was it that had me race to my TV and literally cheer out loud when the shuttle-loaded jet gently landed at Dulles Airport? ✍ It was the surrender to WONDER: energy that comes from seeing proof that things well beyond our imagination can actually become reality, that the seemingly impossible is actually possible. ✍ It was the transporting experience of soaking in the "How in the world … ?" questions and feeling the answers as pure inspirational energy. ✍ You want to be inspired? Insightful, energized, creative, and innovative? Cutting edge? And happy? ✍ Start wondering — openly, curiously, and non-judgmentally — about everything, everywhere, all the time.

BRING IT TO LIFE!

In conversation today, start three sentences with the phrase "I wonder."
Notice how that impacts the conversation.
What might happen if you shift your life filters to WONDER?

"Apprentice yourself to the practice of seeing."

SJK

THE PRACTICE OF SEEING

Apprentice yourself to the practice of seeing.   Start in the gift shop of nature, getting used to this business by sorting through the mass-produced beauties of wildflowers, flocking birds, and inter-living aspen groves. Move next to the workshop where you hone your seeing through practice, to notice the diamond in the coal, the blackberry in the brambles, the miraculous speed in a snail carrying its whole life on its back. Before you know it, you'll be working side by side with the Master, polishing the mirror of yourself as you see the promise of your soul playing in your newly minted smile.

BRING IT TO LIFE!

Spend time in your practice of seeing: pay close attention to everything you see around you.
Notice, initially, the things you easily see at first glance, then look more closely to see more
and different things, appreciating each new detail.
After this day of "seeing practice," look in the mirror and see yourself
as deeply and appreciatively as you are able.
Engage in your seeing practice regularly, and notice how your external
and internal seeing capacity expands and deepens over time.
If your vision is limited or non-existent, use the sense of touch instead of sight.

"Our lives have more than one speed; which will you choose?"

SJK

THE SPEED OF LIFE

It had been a packed work and social week, and my mind was tired even though it was only Wednesday. Although I still had significant items on my To-Do list, I let the early afternoon sunshine lure me outside.   Following the sunshine, I ended up at a local plaza with a small urban garden, so I sat on the low cement wall near the plants and drank in big gulps of nourishing sunlight while my mind soldiered on, working on a tagline for a client's business. ⮷   Then a small bubble floated past ... and another ... followed by a third. My mind lurched, and my thoughts immediately melted into a mental calm that followed the lazy floating of each bubble. ⮷   In the midst of my fast-paced internal and external life, that slow, meandering visual took the reins and pulled back — gently, but oh so insistently — and shifted my speed of life. ⮷   Our lives have more than one speed; which will you choose?

⮷

BRING IT TO LIFE!

Take a moment to notice your current "speed of life."
Is it a speed you're truly comfortable with?
If not, which direction do you want to take that speed?
Find three things in your day today that model the speed you want your life to take,
even if only for a few moments. At day's end, note what those three things were
and how your day was impacted.

"In the arms of nature, we were given life
when death threatened to take over."

SJK

IN THE ARMS OF NATURE

My sister died on April 29, just months before she would have turned 40.   When I think of that day, I remember first being at my sister's bedside after watching her last breath, then turning away to be wrapped in my brother's waiting arms — a place unknown to me before that moment. I remember his heartbeat on my cheek, and thinking how appropriate it was to be held by the man with a chest full of scars (from childhood accidents).   And then I remember being in the arms of nature. How all eight siblings sat on the ground outside the hospital in the dappled sunshine, sheltered by a grove of blooming, weeping cherry trees. Sitting there in the arms of nature, alternately laughing and crying as we talked about our sister and her richly-storied life of mental illness, we began to heal together. In the arms of nature, we were given life when death threatened to take over.   We always, all of us, have a place to rest our hearts in the arms of nature.

BRING IT TO LIFE!

Take 15 minutes today to spend time with nature — surrounded by it if possible:
sit under a tree, lie down in the grass, bury your face in a bouquet of fresh flowers,
or slowly look through a nature photography book or website.
Pay close attention to your heart as you near the 15-minute mark of your time with nature.
Can you feel the healing potential?

*"Our willingness to see more in the world around us
is one of the most powerful life jackets we can wear."*

SJK

EVERYDAY ABUNDANCE

It's so easy to get swept along by the tidal wave messages of lack in our world: we need more money; we don't have enough time; we need to do more and better; we're less than we should be; and on and on. ➤ How can we possibly stay out of that undercurrent? ➤ We can anchor ourselves to a perspective of abundance in our everyday experiences. We have a choice. ➤ We can see only one plant, or a full complement of 43 leaves. We can see not enough sun, or the plentiful comfort of a cloudy sky. We can see lack of happiness in tears, or the wealth in being able to feel. We can see a sidewalk missing nature, or the myriad of calming geometric patterns in the cement and stone. ➤ Our willingness to see more in the world around us is one of the most powerful life jackets we can wear. Let's hone that skill through the lens of everyday abundance.

BRING IT TO LIFE!

Today, challenge yourself to see abundance in everything.
How does this impact your day?

MAY

"Put a prayer on my lips, Beloved."

SJK

PERPETUAL PRAYER

Prayer can be a loaded word. For me, it conjures up contrasting images of long, tedious convocations and benedictions, and childhood moments of great comfort when writing out my thoughts and requests to God.   Those concepts of prayer have morphed for me over the years to a broader idea that prayer is simply what we express in response to deep feeling. Like the following poem that came to my page as soon as I started writing:

Perpetual Prayer
Put a prayer on my lips, Beloved.
Let me whisper that sweet kiss of words
barely breathed
As each beat from my soul
speaks
You.

BRING IT TO LIFE!

What are your thoughts and feelings about prayer? Take five minutes to write them down.
Then take five more minutes to describe different ways you respond to different deep feelings.
Are there similarities in your lists? What does your answer tell you?

"It turns out some weeds smell like lavender,
others like garlic from the wrong side of the tracks, and still others
like sunshine mixed with gently crushed grains."

SJK

THE SCENT OF LIFE

The other morning I had an unusually intense need to get outside. At first, I thought it was just the beautiful weather that lured me away from my work with its sexy breeze and scantily clad sky, but within seconds of stepping out, I noticed something else. All I cared about was getting the scent of plants. ✎   My eyes typically run my outdoor experience, but on that day it was all about scent. I just wanted (needed!) to smell fresh greenery, the earth-cologne clinging to each leaf from the inside out, the very perfume of pure health, hope, and love. ✎   So I found the closest greenery — an overgrown clump of weeds — knelt down, and opened my nose and lungs wide. It turns out some weeds smell like lavender, others like garlic from the wrong side of the tracks, and still others like sunshine mixed with gently crushed grains. ✎   They say we usually don't breathe deeply enough, that we shortchange our cells with our usual, tight-chested sips of air in too-full lives, too-stressed jobs, too-busy days. Well, after a morning of drinking in plant-drenched air, I add that we also shortchange our hearts and souls. ✎   There's a reason they tell us to stop and smell the roses. Go discover it!

BRING IT TO LIFE!

Take five minutes today to find some plants and deeply breathe in their scents.
Describe them in your head as though you were tasting a highly nuanced glass of wine
or smelling an exquisite perfume. Notice the impact on the rest of your day.

*"We don't need to compromise the fullness of life
to find emotional balance; we just need to know our center."*

SJK

ON BALANCE

I used to think that a balanced life was a steady experience of even emotion: no upheavals, no turbulence, and no stomach-dropping roller-coasters, just smooth sailing. It makes sense that in my depression years, that definition of balance sounded like heaven — anything that might keep my emotions above sea level was worth striving for. I've since discovered, however, a very different definition of balance. This one includes the richness of significant drops and climbs, deep dives and pinnacle experiences. What's changed is not so much my life experiences, but the fulcrum on which that seesaw rests and the force of my push back to center. Self-learning, self-compassion, self-care, and a habit of looking for the divine in every aspect of life are the tactics that keep our centers strong and give us the strength to tip the seesaw back to balance time and time again. We don't need to compromise the fullness of life to find emotional balance; we just need to know our center.

BRING IT TO LIFE!

Make a list of all the things (activities, practices, relationships, etc.) you can think of that help provide "balance" in you. Today, engage in one of the activities you listed, and notice the effect it has on your sense of internal balance.

How might you regularly strengthen your center?

"What a gift it is when we are allowed to connect with the metaphorical underbellies of our loved ones."

SJK

THE SOFT UNDERBELLY

Every morning as my wife and I gently start our day with a cup of coffee in bed, our rambunctious feline, Jazzy, joins us for some family time. This cat's presence always boosts my energy, but what melts my heart is the way she drapes herself over my leg each morning, settling across my shin with her paws outstretched and crossed in front of her. Maybe it's her lack of belly bones or the warmth of that little body draped over mine, but I suspect it's the inherent vulnerability of the underbelly that really tugs at my heart as I feel the tender, feline softness across my leg. What a gift it is when we are allowed to connect with the metaphorical underbellies of our loved ones. We tend to protect our vulnerable underbellies at all costs, yet, in doing so, are we denying those around us the heart-expanding comfort of our own softness? Perhaps we can find the courage to more often offer that tender gift to others and see what profound experiences await in that place where our underbellies touch.

BRING IT TO LIFE!

As you go through your day today, notice when you are protecting your underbelly, and see if it might be safe to risk showing a bit of that vulnerability. Notice how this approach impacts your day.

"What makes you cry is what makes you live."

SJK

WHAT MAKES YOU CRY

It was a cloudy day, rain threatening to chase me home at any moment as I walked past the small corner bakery, inhaling the sweet smell of fresh-baked goods. For the thousandth time, I looked at the mural painted on a nearby wall, smiling a bit at the whimsy of random parts (bees, a birdhouse) expanded into 3D. Then I drew my gaze back to include the unruly flower garden patch fronting the wall, and the abundance of nature, color, art, and community brought tears to my eyes from an overflowing heart. ✎ These things that make us cry, these are the profound morsels of our lives. ✎ The tears that flow with the harmony of song dancing in our veins. The tears at a funeral that flood us in an attempt to soothe our shattered hearts. The tears that sit behind the words of a poem, waiting for us to read our own souls on the page. The tears that splash like confetti on our cheeks during a joyous celebration. The tears that flush out our burns and scrapes when things just plain hurt. The tears of joy that flow into little puddles for our inner toddler to splash around our hearts in. ✎ What makes you cry is what makes you live.

BRING IT TO LIFE!

Take 10 minutes (set a timer) to write a quick list of what makes you cry tears of any sort.
Don't ponder or think much about it, just quickly write what comes to mind.
At the end of the 10 minutes, read over your list and offer a quick whisper
of gratitude for the richness of life as evidenced by the tears.

"If only the weeds weren't there,
covering the glory of that colorful, spring display."

SJK

AMONG THE WEEDS

One of the greatest joys of living in a city is walking through the neighborhood on a warm spring afternoon to take in the variety of container plantings just off the sidewalk. As expected, one of my favorite houses was showcasing a stunning display of bold purple hyacinths and gentle yellow daffodils. The container was an old, wooden barrel half, and the contrast of that deep, textured brown against the bright flower colors and rich, black potting soil stopped me in my tracks. "Oh!" I reverently whispered as I bent down to breathe in the beauty. My heart saturated, I moved on to the next house and was disappointed to see a similar barrel, but this one full of weeds. I was almost past it when I realized that barrel also had flowers: hyacinths and daffodils combined to make a potentially breathtaking display — if only the weeds weren't there, covering the glory of that colorful spring display. We have a choice in our lives. Do we want to ignore the things that are dimming our souls and confining our talents, or do we want to take the time and effort to remove the pieces that hide our most impactful areas of beauty?

BRING IT TO LIFE!

What are your hyacinths and daffodils — those areas of brightness you hold?
What are your weeds — those things that confine and cover your natural light?
Create a simple plan for taking the first steps in weeding your internal flower garden,
and take one step forward today.

"It's my husband's birthday party on Saturday,
and I'm going to dance my face off!"
EILEEN KENNEDY

DANCE YOUR FACE OFF

I was talking with a colleague the other day, looking with her at all the things that were occupying her time and keeping her "really having fun" times at an arm's distance. After going through a daunting list of significant life change events intertwined with the necessary busy-ness of getting to that next stage, she added, "Oh, and did I mention I'm throwing this huge party for my husband's birthday next weekend?" ❧ As I was about to groan on her behalf, she added, "and I'm going to dance my face off!" Oh, how I laughed! ❧ I keep hearing that phrase in my mind, each time chuckling to myself at the glee, anticipation, and utter determination to squeeze every last drop of goodness out of that evening. ❧ I suspect most of us could benefit from an all-out "dance your face off" evening, bringing our bodies into connection with our heart, soul, and mind for an integrated full-self expression.

BRING IT TO LIFE!

What is your reaction to the idea of having an evening to "dance your face off?"
If you're even slightly intrigued, set aside an evening to do just that — dance your face off in
any way that works for you (with or without others or music, publicly or privately).
If dancing feels like too much of a stress or push for you, what might you substitute for dance?
Do that thing: _____ your face off!

"May we all have some moments to shoulder only the sun."

SJK

SHOULDER THE SUN

Needing to fill my energetic well, I grabbed my camera one morning and headed for Philadelphia's Fairmount Park. As I walked along the Schuylkill River, I noticed that the rising sun looked as though it was resting on the shoulder of a statue. That image stuck with me for hours.

Shoulder the Sun
You knelt in the grass, head bowed
in another early morning ache
knees damp with dewy tears
and shoulders cracking
under all that weight
Yet you stayed there
folded inside out as dawn turned to day
and the sun gently rose just enough
to rub the tender nape of your neck
and give you a few moments to shoulder only the sun.

May we all have some moments to shoulder only the sun.

BRING IT TO LIFE!

If the sun is out today, take a moment to bow your head and feel the warmth on the back of your neck and shoulders. If the sun's not out, bow your head anyway, and imagine the warmth.

"Step 1: Notice. Step 2: Share. Step 3: Connect. Repeat."

SJK

BIRD ON A WIRE

Walking home from a meandering, city photo-walk, I passed a young child wearing pink and yellow rain boots (in bright sunshine, not a cloud in sight), walking a dog almost as big as she was. I grinned as I passed, and was surprised to hear her speak. "There's a bird over there," her small, strong voice said as she pointed with the hand holding the dog leash. I followed her gesture to the bird balancing easily on a wire stretched over a garden of weeds and tulips. ⤳ "Sure enough!" I responded, "He must've come over to say hi." The girl just shrugged her shoulders and wandered off nonchalantly. No big deal to her, apparently, but the random connection of that interaction stayed with me for days. ⤳ A bird, a dog, a little girl in rain boots, and me, all connected in one delicious moment, simply because there was "a bird over there."

Step 1: Notice
Step 2: Share
Step 3: Connect
Repeat.

BRING IT TO LIFE!

Today, pay attention to little things around you, and point three of them out to someone else.
How does this impact your view of the day?
What responses did you get from the people you pointed things out to?

"In-person time allows us to expand the interaction experience to include movement, scent, hugs, and hearing laughter bounce off the energy of our shared physical space."

SJK

IN REAL LIFE

I recently hopped on a plane to meet Facebook friends IRL (In Real Life) for the first time, and as synchronicity would have it, I also got to spend time over breakfast there with a new client. Although I'm a huge fan of online communication, those few days also reminded me of the deep value of real-life interaction. ⤳ I noticed how the in-person time allowed me to take a break from the laser focus of online communications that overwork my eyes and hands, expanding the interaction experience to movement, scent, hugs, and hearing laughter bounce off the energy of our shared physical space. IRL gave me the featherlight touch of a hand on my arm during conversation, the sparkle in the eye that written words might dilute or confine, the perfume that hints at flowers and earth intermingling happily, and the communion of a shared meal over meaningful conversation. ⤳ Although virtual interaction has incredible power in our lives, let's not forget to keep a healthy dose of IRL.

BRING IT TO LIFE!

Schedule a time to meet a friend or colleague at a coffee shop, park, living room, or anywhere else that allows for meaningful interaction.
Soak in the treat of spending In Real Life time with that person, noticing everything about them: their eye color, expressions, perfume/cologne/neither. Touch them in greeting with a hug or quick shoulder squeeze, feel their energy, and hear how their voice dances around you.
How did meeting in person instead of virtually impact the interaction?

"A simple, open, internal allowing, plus a few moments focused
on a particular person, and a prayer is sent."

SJK

PRAY IT FORWARD

We can hold our gratitude for ourselves, or we can pray it forward. ✍ We can hoard our friends' energizing support, or we can pray it forward. ✍ We can cling tight to our resources, gifts, observations, wisdoms, intuitions, and works of art, or we can pray it forward. ✍ A simple, open, internal allowing, plus a few moments focused on a particular person, and a prayer is sent. ✍ Why keep all our blessings to ourselves? Pray it forward.

BRING IT TO LIFE!

Write five things you are grateful for right now.
Then think of five people in your life who might each need one of those five things.
Visualize your heart opening (in whatever way works for you),
then spend one minute "sending" your first gratitude item to the corresponding recipient.
Repeat for all five gratitudes and people.
Notice how you feel after praying it forward.
Is this something you might want to do more often?

"Work hard, play hard, and rest just as hard.
Then ask for a belly rub."

SJK

LESSONS FROM THE HOUNDS

I am in awe of greyhounds. With friends who have rescued greyhounds as pets, I have gotten to watch those gorgeous animals run like the wind, chasing each other around the yard at spectacular speeds. But even more impressive to me than the speed is the sheer delight you can feel coming from those dogs as they feel their freedom, flying around our friends' back yard in a blur.  Five minutes later, those whirling dervishes crash out on the lawn, soaking in every ounce of rest and relaxation they can. One minute they're pure energy; the next minute they're lying languidly in the grass asking for belly rubs. ➤ I tend to gravitate to a more even flow of energy for myself, but it occurs to me there could be great value in following the ways of these hounds: work hard, play hard, and rest just as hard. Then ask for a belly rub.

BRING IT TO LIFE!

At the end of your workday today, find a way to play hard, really hard.
Play tag with your children, or go bowling on a school night with your partner,
or head by yourself to the nearest swing set and give it a run for its money.
Then come home and relax so hard you're not sure where you end and the ground,
floor, couch, or chair begins.

"When we create, we have a chance to see our soul."

SJK

THE VISIBLE SOUL

What is it that brings the painter to the canvas time and time again, the writer to the page day in and day out, the actor to the stage, the musician to the instrument, the sculptor to the clay, the chef to the kitchen, and any one of us to the similar activities that transport us to a different realm? Perhaps it's what author Oriah Mountain Dreamer posits: that creative expression is the way we make our souls visible. When we create — in any form, any medium, at any skill level — we have a chance to see our soul, that incredibly precious central force of who we are and why we're here.

BRING IT TO LIFE!

Set aside 15 minutes. Pick a creative activity (anything that makes something different out of what is already there), and for 15 minutes focus completely on that activity. When the time is up, take a few deep breaths and think about what part of the past 15 minutes might have been your glimpse of your soul. Experiment with this on different days with different activities.

"Those briefest moments, smallest ideas, and most unique spaces
for capturing our fleeting expressions are the sparks that light the forest fires of our soul."

SJK

WHAT ARE YOU LOOKING FOR?

Stumbling to the gym just before sunrise, I was nudged out of my stupor by graffiti letters scrawled boldly across the street's white crosswalk paint. It wasn't the graffiti that surprised me, it was the placement of it on a crosswalk canvas I hadn't seen before. ✎ We can learn from graffiti writers: they see opportunity for expression in every blank space around them. The small edge of a brick in an alleyway entrance has space for a signature in thin marker, an open expanse of wall allows for spray-paint grandiosity, and utility posts are a chance to turn the writing vertical. ✎ Like the graffiti writers, we need to look for those brief moments of inspiration and use them, playing with them like fireflies on a warm summer night: chasing them, holding them in our hands for a moment as their little lights flash, then releasing them. ✎ Finding the time for creative work-play is less about time and more about what you're looking for. Yes, we still need to carve out time to get fully immersed in our deepest creative work, but those briefest moments, smallest ideas, and most unique spaces for capturing our fleeting expressions are the sparks that light the forest fires of our soul.

BRING IT TO LIFE!

What are you looking for? Carry a small notebook and pen with you today, or leave one open
near your workspace, in your kitchen, or wherever you will spend time today.
Jot down any sparks of inspiration you notice in your day. At the end of the day, notice
all the inspirations you found, and consider repeating this exercise regularly.

"Give energy to that which you want to grow."

LORIN BELLER

MANUAL FOCUS

After years of acquiescing to automatic focus, I finally figured out how to use the manual focus feature on my fancy-schmancy Nikon digital camera. It wasn't difficult to learn, but it changed everything. Instead of endless minute camera shifts to try to trick the autofocus into a near or far focus, I was able to set up the scene composition in my camera viewfinder, taking full control by manually adjusting the focus to create exactly the visual impression I wanted. We have that same control in our lives, if we choose to shift the setting to manual instead of auto focus. If you want your day's view to be full of beauty, focus there. If you long for assurance of a benevolent universe, focus on the evidence that is here with you today. Control your focus, and your experience will follow.

BRING IT TO LIFE!

Choose a focus for your day, such as ease, joy, beauty, possibility, abundance,
or whatever else you truly want to experience.
Write the word in small letters on your hand or wrist
where you will see it throughout the day.
How does this intentional focus impact your experience today?

"We each need to find our own answer
for what gets the front and center space on our life windowsills."

SJK

FRONT AND CENTER

The first improvement we made to our new urban home was to add a security system, complete with door alarms and motion sensors. After installation, we put a "Secured by ADT" sticker in each street level window, front and center. Shortly afterwards, we started adding plants to the large, sunlit window ledges, front and center. Which means that from the outside, each plant is partially hidden behind a "Secured by ADT" sticker. Yes, I want to discourage people intent on vandalizing or stealing, but don't I want even more to offer love and beauty and the promise of life that nature gives us? It's a tough one, the quandary between vulnerability and (perceived) protection, and as much as I'd love to offer an easy solution, we each need to find our own answer for what gets the front and center space on our life windowsills.

BRING IT TO LIFE!

What currently gets front and center placement on your actual windowsills?
How does (or doesn't) that reflect what you want to offer those
who pass by or stop in to visit your home?
If it's not the message you want to send, change it — today.

"Perhaps our strongest lives are lived not in the solid structures
of constant protection, but in the grace
of what travels through the cracks."

SJK

THROUGH THE CRACKS

City sidewalks display determined weeds and wildflowers through cracks in the solid façade. Building foundations refuse to let anything root until the weather-worn mortar crumbles just enough for plant life to push through. Reflective puddles of water gather only in the holes and depressions of the asphalt that give in to the pressure of day-to-day traffic. We build stunning, powerful, and strong man-made structures to stand firm and unyielding through the pressures of existence, and in doing so, we often shut out the natural vibrant growth of the plant world. ✎ Perhaps it's the same with our emotional structures that we build to unbendingly weather every internal storm without breaking. Perhaps it's through the cracks that our natural inner growth reaches hungrily for the sun, the richness of our inner beauty sprouts, and the interchange of life hums freely. ✎ Perhaps our strongest lives are lived not in the solid structures of constant protection, but in the grace of what travels through the cracks.

✎

BRING IT TO LIFE!

Notice the actual cracks and crumbles in your environment today,
and see what each "weak" spot allowed to grow or shift.
How might you allow for more gentle cracks in your own emotional life,
or to more intentionally honor the ones already there?

"We track the quiet mind like a gazelle in the jungle."

SJK

HUNTING THE GAZELLE

We track the quiet mind
like a gazelle in the jungle
Tiptoeing thru the dry grass of thought
freezing motion at each crunch
as our untrained feet stumble
on memories & plans
and the gazelle bounds away
eluding capture time and time and time again.
So finally we sit
weary of hunting the silence within,
and folding our legs like a prayer,
behind our closed eyes we rest.
Thought becomes breath
Breath becomes body
Body becomes heart and all is still
as the gazelle climbs into our lap and sleeps.

BRING IT TO LIFE!

Simply take three long, deep breaths in and out. Let the gazelle go.

"Follow those urges to bring certain experiences closer to you
for gentle examination through a clear focus. "

SJK

BRING IT CLOSER

Five-year-old Siena and I were sitting on a stone wall around the lake, watching a Mallard duck in the distance and wishing it would come closer so we could talk with it. "I'm going to look at it through my binoculars," she said, shaping her thumb and index finger on each hand into a circle and holding them up to her eyes. "Oh, there, now I can see him better!" she exclaimed happily. Following her lead, I curled both hands into cylinders, and stacking one behind the other, looked through my "telescope." ⤳ The odd thing was, the duck really did seem closer, simply because I had given my eyes a clearly defined focal point. ⤳ Even pretending, Siena and I were able to bring that duck closer in our minds' eyes, and through our "binoculars" and "telescope," we held a one-sided conversation with our new little duck friend, watching the sunlight glinting off his head in metallic hues of blue, green, gold, and black. ⤳ Follow those urges to bring certain experiences closer to you for gentle examination through a clear focus. You do, after all, have a built-in telescope.

BRING IT TO LIFE!

Create a "telescope" or "binoculars" with your hands, and focus on an object in the distance.
Notice how it seems more clear, and even a bit closer, from this focused perspective.
What in your life could benefit from a closer, focused look?
Spend time with that today.

"It was just two pillows, but they showed an entire night's truth
of unconscious tenderness."

SJK

THE SLEEPING TRUTH

When my wife and I made our bed the other morning, I noticed with a soft grin that our pillows were overlapping, still snuggled together in the middle of the bed, showing us how closely we had slept. It was just two pillows, but they showed an entire night's truth of unconscious tenderness.   Our visible lives are just the tip of the iceberg, an indication of the deeper happenings in our subconscious. We get to find those visible clues, decide what they tell us about our inner state, then cultivate even more of what we want to have seep into our consciousness and our actions. What is your sleeping truth — anywhere in your life?

BRING IT TO LIFE!

Notice today the visible clues to your inner state.
Which clues make you grin?
Do any of them surprise you?
Are there any changes you'd like to make?

"When was the last time someone said
it was good to see you again, letting you know that you matter
by simply being present at that moment?

SJK

GOOD TO SEE YOU AGAIN

It was only my second time at this coffee shop (The Sweet Spot — what a fabulous name!), but as I was spooning rough grains of raw sugar into my steaming coffee, I heard someone cheerfully say, "It's good to see you again!" I looked up, and to my surprise, the comment was directed to me, accompanied by a broad smile from the shop manager (or owner?). The sparkle in his eyes easily lit an answering one in mine, and it got me thinking. When was the last time someone said it was good to see you again, letting you know that you matter by simply being present at that moment? Maybe it's time for us to be that person to someone else today.

BRING IT TO LIFE!

Today, make it a point to say, "It's good to see you again,"
or "It's good to hear your voice again," in full sincerity and appreciation
for that other person's presence. Do this for three people today.
Notice how this exercise impacts your day.

"It is not enough to have thought great things before doing the work.
The brush stroke at the moment of contact carries inevitably the exact
state of being of the artist at the exact moment into the work … "

ROBERT HENRI

EXUDE YOUR MESSAGE

Technique can be taught and, to a certain extent, learned by anyone, and skills can be mastered with enough dedication and practice. But what makes the difference between work that shows just skill and work that moves people? It's what we bring to our work. ⟋ If, as Robert Henri says, our art [work] is imbued with our "state of being," we would do well to place high importance on the preparation phase of our work. We increase our potential to impact the people around us if we work from the state of being that exudes our intended message. ⟋ For example, if I write about the healing power of compassion while I'm angry, resentful, or bored, the words will come from my head, not my heart, and come across as flat commandments or directives. If instead, I write from a space of compassion, the words come from the fullness of that state of being, having a much greater chance of providing a message that reads as an offering, a salve, and a heart-wrapped gift of healing.

BRING IT TO LIFE!

Take five minutes right now to write a list of ways you can get into your intended internal work space. For example, take a stroll outside, read a book that inspires you, write down how you want to positively impact those around you, remind yourself of things you love.
Try two of those preparation activities today, and experiment with them over the next couple weeks with different activities. Keep the ones that work for you, and forget the ones that don't!

"Sunlight through ears makes me weepy."

CHERYL PEACHEY STONER

LOOK FOR THE LIGHT

It's easy to take light for granted, knowing each day at sunset that the sun will rise again in just a few hours. Sure, we think about light when our electricity goes out and it takes more than a flick of a switch to illuminate our surroundings, or when we're met with a cloudy day at the beach, but for the most part light is simply an afterthought. ⮠ Oh, how we're missing out if we don't look for the light, for it's in the light that we see the most magical parts of our lives and environment. To remind myself of this, I regularly take a walk at sunrise or near sunset for the sole purpose of looking for the light. ⮠ Light transforms everything it touches: a backlit, red-orange daylily becomes a gentle flame; top-lit trees become shadows dipped in gold; any solid form blocking the light becomes a mirrored whisper of itself as a shadow. And sunlight shining behind a young boy's ear softens it to the point that his mother writes, "Sunlight through ears makes me weepy." ⮠ We so easily notice the darkness, so why not notice the light?

BRING IT TO LIFE!

Write yourself a note to "Notice the Light," and carry it with you today.
Everywhere you look, notice the light and the way it interacts with everything around it,
transforming it in some way.
At the end of the day, ask yourself what was different about this day.
What changes when you are focused on looking for the light?

"Enthusiasm can be a passing feeling, or it can be a way of life.
You choose."

SJK

ENTHUSIASM

Enthusiasm. I've often thought of it as a high-strung, high-energy approach to life, exhausting for sure.   Until, that is, I read in Gurumayi Chidvilasananda's book, *Enthusiasm*, that the origins of the word enthusiasm are from the Greek *enthusiasmos*, which means "carrying God within." In other words, enthusiasm is life-giving, energizing, and divine. Gurumayi encourages us to live in the "divine experience of enthusiasm," whether in joy or sorrow or any other experience in the spectrum of life. We do this through expressions of love, times of worship (in whatever way we personally touch the divine), interactions with the heart of nature, and an ongoing search to see the beauty in every aspect of life and every person we meet. Enthusiasm can be a passing feeling, or it can be a way of life. Which do you choose?

BRING IT TO LIFE!

Take five minutes to write down your feelings about the unfolding day.
Then take five more minutes to write down how you could switch each of those feelings
and expectations into enthusiasm — if they're not already there.
Go live your day through the energy of enthusiasm.
Is enthusiasm something you might want to make a habit?

"Change is a process, not an event."

SJK

THE SPEED OF CHANGE

In our fast-paced lives, we often expect change to also happen in the blink of an eye. True, sometimes it does, but often in those cases, traumatically so — because change most naturally happens slowly. I love the example of nature as a guide for the pace of change: flowers grow, strengthen, expand into full bloom, provide fruit, fade (though often first increasing color depth or spectrum in the process) die back, rest quietly — invisibly gathering strength while protected under soil or in seed - then begin the cycle again. ✑ Many plants have a yearly cycle, while 17-year cicadas take, well, 17 years underground as nymphs until they emerge and spend a few crazy pre-death weeks as adults mating and laying eggs to keep the cycle going for another 17-year span. ✑ Change is a process, not an event. Let's take nature's example, and allow ourselves the space for steady, non-rushed growth.

✑

BRING IT TO LIFE!

Are you currently trying to push through a change in your life?
If so, what is truly the hurry?
Is there a way you can allow yourself time for the change process
to unfold more naturally?
If so, take a step in that natural direction today.

"'Your color choices are genius!' I exclaimed to God
in her gallery of fresh fruit chunks."

SJK

DARSHAN*

I spoke with God today
directly
several times:
I love your dress!
I told her, the fully-bloomed cherry tree in the park
Your color choices are genius!
I exclaimed to her in a gallery of fresh fruit chunks
How did you ever think of that?
I asked in creeped-out wonder, jumping away from the crusty black beetle
But most of all, Oh … oh how I love what you've done with this place
I whispered in awe as I caught a glimpse of my heart's layout on the page.

Darshan is a Sanskrit term meaning sight, and often refers to an
energetic interaction between human and divine.

BRING IT TO LIFE!

Today, initiate specific interactions with whatever you consider to be God (creativity, inner
wisdom, universal energy, higher power, the divine, your truest self, or something else).
What showed up for you? Were you surprised by any of the interactions?

"Whether our goal is to walk with healing in this world,
or to just make it through this life relatively unscathed,
working to increase the depth of our smile is a divine gift to all involved."

SJK

THE DEPTH OF YOUR SMILE

I've noticed a consistent pattern recently: life seems to respond to the depth of my smile. On days I've experienced deep meditation, or had extra healing time with nature, or when I give myself intuitive freedom in my writing, my smile begins in the depth of my soul, carrying with it a natural offering of my heart. ⟋ On those days, strangers who pass me in the neighborhood greet me with a warm "Good morning," the receipt-checker at Lowe's beams as she bursts out with "OH, you are SO CUTE!" and the toddler in the coffee shop reaches her arms out to me as if to say, "Oh yes, I feel it too." And on those days, the only thing I know is different? The depth of my smile. ⟋ Whether our goal is to walk with healing in this world, or to just make it through this life relatively unscathed, working to increase the depth of our smile is a divine gift to all involved — starting with ourselves.

BRING IT TO LIFE!

Think of a time when you were aware of an extra depth in your smile.
What were you doing? What had you done earlier in the day that may have impacted the
depth of your smile? How did a deeper smile affect you and those around you?
Make a list of ways you might be able to deepen your smile,
bringing to it more of your heart and soul. Do one of those things today.

MAY 28

"If our impatience can be triggered so strongly,
is it possible that our patience can likewise be triggered?"

SJK

IN SEARCH OF PATIENCE

I feel it bubbling up, the froth of impatience churning my insides as I repeat an email request for the umpteenth time, or wait for a late delivery or medical test result, or my sense of time clashes with that of someone I'm meeting with and we continue conversation way beyond my attention threshold. ⟿ I'm usually quite patient, but when I'm not, I'm really not. ⟿ If my impatience can be triggered so strongly, I wondered today, is it possible that my patience can likewise be triggered? ⟿ So I went in search of "patience triggers." Sure enough, I found my cat sitting patiently waiting on the desk for my attention, my journal waiting patiently as always to carry the weight of my words, my calendar for next month waiting patiently for this month's days to pass, and my water bottle waiting patiently on the coffee table to offer me a cool, liquid respite. ⟿ It didn't happen immediately, but before long, the patience triggers took hold, and impatience left the building.

BRING IT TO LIFE!

Next time you feel your own impatience bubble up,
look immediately for "patience triggers." As you continue through your day,
make a running list of things that could act as patience triggers for you in the future.
How does this exercise impact your day?

MAY 29

"It turns out we can find bliss
by breathing in the confluence of the divine, nature, and human
that come together in the space of spring blossom fragrance."

SJK

THE BUDDHA IN THE BLOOMS

I've discovered that the heady scent of blossoms and blooms in springtime brings tears to my eyes. In part, I'm responding with great relief to a break from the human-made scents of a long, cold, urban winter, but for the most part, the tears are a natural overflow from deliciously abundant sensory saturation. ⤚ In our spiritual lives, we long and pine for the brief experiences of inspiration, bliss, or enlightenment. It turns out we can get exactly that by breathing in the confluence of the divine, nature, and human that come together in the space of spring blossom fragrance. ⤚ Let's not miss the Buddha on the corner, greeting us in the blooms.

BRING IT TO LIFE!

Look for inspiration in the blooms
(in real life if possible, or in photos if necessary)
around you today.

"Letter writing is a process like no other;
it reveals the essence of the relationship."

NANCY J. DUNCAN

WHEN YOU WRITE A LETTER

In my constant quest for spiritual growth, I've gone through several iterations in my understanding of God, deities, the universe, the divine, gurus, spiritual teachers, and the existence of spirit in my everyday life. The rickety bridge between each phase of understanding seems to be questions deep enough that they're hard to clarify, and a sense of distance from that divine energy I so long to experience. ✑ In the midst of a recent "bridge time," I turned to my pen and notebook and started writing a letter to the guru I was confused about. Even though I had no intention of sending that letter, I poured my heart out with question after question, requests, concerns, gratitude, frustrations, appreciations, and more questions. And when I finished writing, I had peace. I didn't have answers to many of the questions, or clarity on all the confusion, but I had an explicit sense of connection with that guru and the love and wisdom there. ✑ When you write a letter — to a guru, God, friend, or to yourself — you open a one-to-one energetic connection between you and the recipient (even if you never send the letter) that allows you to show and hear yourself in context of that relationship. ✑ Keep a pen handy — it's one of the most important relationship tools you'll ever use.

BRING IT TO LIFE!

Who did you think of during today's reading? Write a letter to that person (whether or not you intend to send it), and see what you need and want to express. *How does the letter-writing process impact your perspective of that person/concept? Of yourself? Of the relationship?*

"Let's not miss the best parts, okay?"

SJK

THE BEST PARTS

One winter morning after our sleepy, shivery, 10-block stumble to the gym, the sun was rising just as we arrived for our morning torture … err … exercise. The sunrise was so magnificent that it stopped us in our tracks, waking us instantly as both of us breathed a wide-eyed "WHOAaaa!" ⟿ When we entered the gym, the owner grinned at us, pointed to the sunrise, and disappeared. I found him on the other side of the glass-enclosed gym sipping his coffee, quietly watching the reds and oranges grow deeper, richer, and more stunning across the entire 180° view. ⟿ "I've interrupted training sessions for this," he said, talking to me but still focused on the sunrise. "I used to just glance, then hurry back to work. But now I stop sessions and tell my clients, 'Wait. Look at this. I don't care if you have a problem with stopping your workout, come look at this,' because I know the best part only lasts for a few minutes." ⟿ Let's not miss the best parts, okay?

BRING IT TO LIFE!

Today, make a pact with yourself to be fully present to all the best parts of the day.

The first sip of coffee, tea, water, or juice in the morning.

The moment you finish a task.

The word "love" (or "I" or "you") in the sentence "I love you."

The seconds just before the sun sets.

The three notes in your favorite song that melt you every time.

The way your cheek dimples when you grin.

How does this approach impact your day?

JUNE

JUNE 1

"It was a mess, eating those delectable packages of sunshine,
but as kids we didn't care."

SJK

HOW TO EAT A MANGO

I knew this mango was going to be a good one when juice squirted out from the first scrape of the peeler. I managed to get the whole luscious fruit disrobed without its slippery, orange-gold body skittering across the counter, and as I took my first big bite, I was transported to the mango-eating sessions of my childhood Florida visits. It was a mess, eating those delectable packages of sunshine, but as kids we didn't care. With both hands, we'd dig fingerholds into the escape-prone fruit, sinking our little faces deep into the rich, juicy sweetness to more fully experience the delight, finally coming up for air with cheeks smeared in orange, juice trailing to our elbows, and teeth threaded full of the fibers we'd scraped from the seed. So today I put down my knife, dug instead my fingers into the easily-yielding mango flesh, and dove in headfirst, completely, into the healing memories of childhood and present sensory experience of today.

BRING IT TO LIFE!

Select a natural treat today that you remember enjoying from childhood
(the juicier/messier, the better), and eat it with the fervent all-out attention
you gave that treat as a child.
What do you notice about the experience?

"I wanted to honor not the graffiti
but the potentially wounded heart of the person who did it."

SJK

AT THE HEART OF IT

The pristine surface of our new urban alley door survived for about six months before becoming a canvas for graffiti scrawled across it. My first reaction was a twinge of fear followed by a brief feeling of being somehow violated. As I tried to read the letters scrawled down the door, however, the fear turned to curiosity, then to empathy. ✎ We've hired a contractor to remove the letters and stain the door, effectively erasing the (gang-related?) message that's there now, and I just keep thinking, "What were they trying to express? What did they say with those letters? What drives someone to use other people's property to make their mark?" ✎ I was tempted to paint a frame around those quickly-scrawled letters, turning them from a declaration and violation to an offering. I wanted to acknowledge the voice that was unheard enough that it felt a need to shout. I wanted to honor not the graffiti but the potentially wounded heart of the person who did it. ✎ Uncertainty won out this time, as the graffiti gets removed, but one day, I'll find the courage to look only at the heart of the action, not at the action itself. ✎ May we all do the same.

BRING IT TO LIFE!

What in your life has offended, angered, or disturbed you in some way?
Take a moment to think about the person behind the action and what pain
might have been at the heart of it for them.
What changes when you see the heart first?

"Word play — like a shoehorn for your heart."

SJK

WORD PLAY

During her chemo treatment, my friend Laurie Foley posted this "chemoku" on Facebook:

My hard-working friend
Is a tiny pouch of pink
scrubbing cells away.

In three brief lines, she brought me into her experience and opened an easy compassion for her time in chemo and for the tireless heart-wrenching work of the chemo itself. It can't be easy for those cell-scrubbers fighting the bad guys, especially knowing that they're also hurting the human they're serving. ✎ Others quickly followed my friend's original prompt, posting their own chemoku verses, and now I've spent the afternoon energetically sitting in a chemo room buoyed by a circle of poet-minded folks surrounding that tiny pouch of pink with our words. ✎ All this because a creative brain created a word "chemoku" that engaged my curiosity, that evoked my imagination, that teased open my heart. ✎ Word play — like a shoehorn for your heart.

BRING IT TO LIFE!

In the course of your regular day, make up three words
or use words playfully (i.e., incorrectly on purpose).
Notice how this impacts your interactions today.

"I saw the angel in the marble and carved until I set him free."

MICHELANGELO

GORGEOUS INSIDE

Michelangelo's approach could be the secret to enlightenment ... or at least the secret to creating our work and our lives. Instead of our default approach of adding to, we could consider that perhaps we already are and have all that we need, and our work is to take away the parts covering our answers and ourselves. There is an artist in each of us, sitting expectantly with exquisite carving tools, waiting for permission to work. There is a part of us that intuitively knows what needs to be carved away in any situation to set free our project, our art, our work of creation small or large. Each document we write is a carving away of all the words we don't need. Each painting we create is a carving away of the white space that sacrifices itself to color. Each presentation we develop is a carving away of all the possible facts, anecdotes, and tomes of wisdom that aren't relevant. Each mindful breath we take is a carving away of the inauthenticities we carry so tightly within us. It's in the carving away that we find the angel, the work of art, the divinity within.

BRING IT TO LIFE!

*What is your block of marble today: that thing that is encasing something in you
that's ready to be freed? What are your carving tools?*
Take five minutes today to do whatever you decide is a beginning
toward carving away what covers your inner light.

"Living prayer is action, thought, or state of being
that allows you to bring in strength as you exude compassion."

SJK

LIVING PRAYER

How
do we speak to the prayer in our hearts
find the words
to bend the bars of our cage and
open
all doors and gates and windows
to release
Love
our living prayer?

BRING IT TO LIFE!

What is your form of living prayer — that action, thought, or state of being
that allows you to bring in strength as you exude compassion?
Make a list of possible "living prayers," then choose three of those things
and engage in them today.
Notice how intentional "living prayer" impacts your day and those around you.

"The space between is a profound, yet seldom-noticed, thing."

SJK

THE SPACE BETWEEN

The space between is a profound, yet seldom-noticed, thing.
In meditation, it's the space between the in-breath and the out-breath
and the space between our cells.
In consciousness, it's the space between sleeping and waking.
In time, it's the space between the past and the future.
In art, it's the space between lines and shapes and colors.
In music, it's the space between notes.
In nature, it's the space between raindrops and wind gusts and sunset and sunrise.
In transition, it's the space between leaving and arrival, beginning and ending.
In love, it's the space between heartbeats.
And, in life, it's the present powerful moment:
the space between just existing and deeply, fully living.

BRING IT TO LIFE!

Today, notice as many experiences of space between as you can.
At the end of your day, write down what you noticed about those spaces between.
What new perspectives showed up?
What might happen if you expand your attention
to include more space between on an ongoing basis?

"What do you carry with you each day?"

SJK

A FULL TANK

The other day I passed three Starbucks employees on a street corner — each with a tank of coffee on their backs, complete with a hose for serving samples of the latest coffee roast. What is in your tank? What do you carry with you each day, and how is it serving you and those around you?

BRING IT TO LIFE!

Take a careful inventory of that tank on your back.
How big is it? How much does it weigh? What is it filled with?
What are the decorations (if any) on the outside?
If any parts of it are not what you want or need, write two lists:
"I will let go of ..."
and
"I will add ... "
Make these "living" lists by updating them regularly.

"The next time you feel a twinge of fear,
turn your thoughts to the warmth and light of sunshine."

SJK

AN ANTIDOTE TO FEAR

Sun
warms the fear under my skin
spreading it out to
dissolve
harmlessly in the space between cells
leaving only room for
Love.

BRING IT TO LIFE!

The next time you feel a twinge of fear, turn your thoughts to the warmth and light
of sunshine. If feasible, actually step into the sunshine for a moment and feel the warmth
on your skin and raise your face to the sky, seeing the light behind closed eyes.
What effect does the actual or envisioned sunshine have on your fear?

"Hear today, touch today, smell today, and taste today
as though it is our last chance to experience that sensation."

SJK

AS THOUGH YOU NEVER WOULD AGAIN

For some reason the phrase, "Live like you were dying," never sparked much motivation for me. I realize the phrase is meant to encourage us to live fully and squeeze the most out of every minute of life, but I just picture someone on their death bed unable to move, communicate, or barely even breathe. Helen Keller, however, found a way to express that same "live fully" idea in a way that completely grabbed my attention. She asks, as a blind person, that those of us who have sight use it as though we might never see again after today, and to honor the gift of each of our senses in the same way. She asks that we hear today, touch today, smell today, and taste today as though today is our last chance to experience that sensation. Give each moment your full attention today, _____ing as though you never would again.

BRING IT TO LIFE!

Today, set a timer (your phone, watch, or other time-keeping device)
to alert you at hourly intervals. For each hour, select one of your senses and use it.
Pay attention to it as though you never would experience that sense again.
At the end of the day, take a few quiet minutes to reflect on your day's experience.

"Share your good in the mornings."

SJK

GOOD MORNING

I don't know his name. I don't know where he lives or works or shops for groceries. In fact, I know nothing about him except that he walks down George Street every morning around 6:50. ✎ I don't know him, but in some small way I love him — because every morning on my way back from the gym, we smile openly in recognition of each other and quietly say, "Good morning." ✎ Two words, two smiles, and a world of difference. Share your good in the mornings.

BRING IT TO LIFE!

This week, say good morning to people you pass and mean it.
Notice their responses, and yours!

"Silence amplifies the sound of your heart's desires."

SJK

ARE YOU LISTENING?

Nature whispers divine secrets at dusk.

Silence amplifies the sound of your heart's desires.

Words unspoken tell of your wounds as the sighs of your breath point to your salve.

Are you listening?

In the depths of your soul, are you listening?

BRING IT TO LIFE!

Today, listen to your life.

Listen for the message in sounds around you and feelings

and longings within you.

At the end of the day, write down what you heard,

and consider the messages therein.

"These signs could mean nothing, but I choose to fill them
with meaning that re-sparks my work in this world."

SJK

MAKE MEANING

I was in an uncomfortably long stint of not writing — a daunting (okay, terrifying) place for someone whose livelihood and daily strength comes in large part from the act of writing. ☜ As I left the house to prime my inspiration pump at a different coffee shop this morning, I whispered a quick request to the universe for an encouraging sign of support to help me rediscover belief in my work. I looked up and saw the workmen at the house down the street waving as they both beamed a cheerful "Good morning!" to me. ☜ I stopped for a moment down the block to breathe in the heady scent of Butterfly Bush blooms and was surprised to see a butter-yellow Swallowtail alight on a bloom near me — the first full-sized, fully-patterned butterfly I've seen this summer in the city. ☜ Then, as I walked across the parking lot, my phone buzzed with an email notifying me someone had just purchased my writing eCourse. ☜ And when I got to the coffee shop, the owner grinned and welcomed me with a cheery "Good to see you again!" ☜ Then I wrote 10 draft pages in 30 minutes. ☜ And, on the way home, the butterfly crossed my path again. ☜ These signs could mean nothing, but I choose to fill them with meaning that re-sparks my work in this world. Why not, right??

BRING IT TO LIFE!

Today, challenge yourself to find meaning — specific meaning that you might need right now — in as many things and experiences as possible.

"All good ideas start with mini good ideas."

SANDRA A. MANNE

THE LITTLE THINGS

I recently bought a tiny plant for a little geometric wall planter in our home, and it made me incredibly happy. The four itsy-bitsy leaves on teeny stems are so cute that I smile deeply every time I see that mini specimen of beauty. ⤶ It's the little things that matter, they say, and many of us nod in absolute agreement — yet, when it comes to the very important task of living, those little things so often get overlooked, overrun, and trampled ruthlessly in our mad rush to find and achieve bigger, better, more, and higher. ⤶ Consider this: what if that tiny little plant hanging in its little planter is what will keep my heart open enough to offer love in my smile as I pass a sorrowful-looking stranger on the sidewalk tomorrow ... and he takes that smile home to his family instead of his all-too-familiar anger? It is possible. ⤶ Little things can lead to big things. Books start with one letter; relationships start with a look, or a word, or a smile; an observation grows to a thought to a question to a pondering to a theory to a belief to an entire belief system; a person grows to a family to a tribe to a generation to a culture to a civilization. ⤶ Big things grow from little things, so let's honor those little things.

BRING IT TO LIFE!

What is a big impact you want to make in this world?
What is one little thing you can do today to get that impact started?
Do that.

JUNE 14

"Sitting in our own quiet meditation space,
we have a chance to hear the pause in our ongoing self-talk."

SJK

UNCONDITIONAL FRIENDLINESS

I love the way Buddhist Pema Chodron describes meditation as "a method of cultivating unconditional friendliness toward ourselves." Sitting in our own quiet meditation space, we have a chance to hear the pause in our ongoing self-talk, and in that pause, self-compassion (unconditional friendliness) has a chance to seep into our awareness. Consider how wonderful it feels when we find someone who can offer us truly unconditional friendliness; imagine the gift when we can offer that to ourselves.

BRING IT TO LIFE!

Schedule 10 minutes of interrupted time in a quiet space.
Set a timer for five minutes, and imagine you are sitting silently with a dear friend,
listening for their heartbeat and feeling their presence.
At the end of five minutes, write a description of your experience
and how you feel about that friend.
That friend is you.
Consider sitting with yourself in silence daily
to build unconditional friendliness toward yourself.

"Soothe my sandpaper soul."

SJK

THE ALCHEMY OF GRACE

During a recent conversation with a friend, she said she felt as though she was wrapped in sandpaper, rough against everything she was experiencing in her day. I remembered that today as I was sitting on a rough stone outside, feeling a delicate breeze wrap around me in a way that opened my heart wide. This is the result:

The Alchemy of Grace

Soothe my sandpaper soul
with Your warm breeze, Beloved
gently oh so gently buffing
the rough into divine silk
a golden tribute to the alchemy
of Grace.

BRING IT TO LIFE!

Is there a sandpaper-wrapped part of you or part of your life?
If so, what might be that warm breeze that could help smooth the roughness?
Forgiveness, self-compassion, laughter, all-out play, prayer, or what else?
Any of those things can alchemize to peace through grace ...
so practice one of them (or more) today, and notice the impact.

"Not everyone is wired for fully public expression;
some live even more beautifully as a quiet silhouette."

SJK

SILHOUETTE SHINE

It was one of those dream-like scenes the other morning in our bathroom (of all places!): early morning sunlight tapping at the far window for us to open the venetian blinds, back-lighting the small tropical plant behind the closed slats to create a stunning silhouette. Tiny shadow-flowers waved at the ends of delicate stalks, the light and shadow contrast so strong they somehow looked almost more than three dimensions. In all the times I've seen that beautiful plant preening itself in the sun's spotlight on our windowsill, it's never been as breathtaking as when it was displayed in full silhouette. We tend to favor and lend more attention to those who shine loudly and show their full bright colors as they interact with life. Not everyone, however, is wired for fully public expression; some live even more beautifully as a quiet silhouette. Be whoever you are, and give the same freedom to those around you.

BRING IT TO LIFE!

Look for silhouettes in your world today — any back-lit object that can't be seen in full detail because of the light and shadow effect. Notice the quiet beauty in each silhouette.
Also notice the people today — including yourself — who seem to be more like silhouettes in their interactions.
Appreciate their beauty and their similarity to or difference from you.

"How far do you go to taste someone else's flavor of life?"

SJK

HOW FAR DO YOU GO?

I watched a commercial this morning that turned my heart to mush.  A group of guys are playing an intense wheelchair basketball game, clanging into each other, crashing onto their sides (with wheelchairs strapped to them) in all-out lunges for the ball and clearly pouring their souls and bodies fully into that competition. The game ends, and after they congratulate each other on a game well-played, all but one of the players unstraps himself from his wheelchair and walks out of the gym. How far do you go to taste someone else's flavor of life, considering yourself an honored guest at their table instead of just inviting them to your banquet?

BRING IT TO LIFE!

Today, think about what it really means to step into someone else's shoes.
*How might you do this in a way that assumes no judgment of better or worse
in anyone's life situation?*
Look for ways today to taste someone else's flavor of life, and acknowledge it
as the incredibly generous gift it is.
How does this perspective impact your interactions today?

"Just because our outsides don't match
doesn't mean our insides can't understand each other."

SJK

NOT THAT DIFFERENT

She was wearing a black burqa, and from a distance, the only thing visible other than her clothing was her hands. I immediately thought of how different her life must be from mine, but just as I was stepping into my imagination to explore her home life, I was stopped short. She had just jumped onto a swing in the playground across from my office, and immediately a small girl wearing hot pink shoes jumped onto her lap. ⬧ For the next few minutes, they played on the swing together — face-to-face, with arms wrapped around each other — those little hot pink tennis shoes standing out like neon against the woman's dark coverings as they both kicked their feet up to go higher, higher, and higher together. ⬧ Just because our outsides don't match doesn't mean our insides can't understand each other. Just because outside says "different" doesn't keep inside from saying, "I recognize you." ⬧ We're all human, and in that realm, we're really, truly, not that different.

BRING IT TO LIFE!

Today, notice when you consider someone to be different than you.
What do you assume is the difference?
Is it possible that there's more similarity between you than you first realize?
Look for evidence of similarity.
How does this perspective impact your day and your interactions?

"Always doing our best doesn't mean doing the best we've ever done,
every single day. It means assessing our best for each day
and holding ourselves to that standard on that day."

SJK

THE FLUCTUATING NATURE OF CAPACITY

One of the agreements in Don Miguel Ruiz's book, *The Four Agreements*, is "Always do your best." ⤐ I cringed when I first read it. Aren't we already over-achieving and under-resting? Don't we need permission to stop striving, stop reaching, stop pushing ourselves to the edge of our capacities day after day? ⤐ There's an essential point Ruiz makes: on any given day, our best will be different. Like today, when I'm on hormone therapy meds and feeling cranky and irritable, so my best is several levels down. Other days, I've operated effortlessly on all cylinders, feeling my mind, heart, and spirit collaborating so easily that it felt quite close to divine. ⤐ So, always doing our best doesn't mean doing the best we've ever done, every single day. It means taking each day separately, honestly and compassionately assessing our best for that day and holding ourselves to that standard on that day.

BRING IT TO LIFE!

Write this question down: "What is my best IN THIS MOMENT?" Each time you see it, pause to take an honest inventory of your capacity. *Are you pushing beyond your best into burn-out, fatigue, or illness?* Regroup. Get back to it at a different level. *Are you letting your energy drain by tolerating boredom, inaction, or behaviors that go against your nature?* Regroup. Get back to it at a different level. *Are you at a level that beautifully matches your capacity?* Stay right there and enjoy the hum.

*"In talking with the trees, we are honoring the magical interconnections
of life, nature, wonder, and possibility."*

SJK

TALKING WITH THE TREES

Although I often whisper little greetings to birds, bugs, and blooms, it's rare that I'm with some-one else who does the same. You can imagine my thrill when I was recently exploring an unknown neighborhood with a friend, and upon seeing a tree variety neither of us recognized, my friend touched the tree gently and greeted it: "Well, hi! Who are you??" In that moment, I flashed back to over 30 years ago when we were inseparable childhood friends frolicking happily in the woods, pausing to examine tiny moss spores and fungi and anything that crawled. We're (somewhat) grown up now, but in talking with the trees, we are still honoring those magical interconnections of life, nature, wonder, and possibility.

BRING IT TO LIFE!

Talk to the trees today. If it feels too uncomfortable for you to do out loud,
simply say something in your head.
Ask how they're feeling today. Thank them for providing oxygen.
Acknowledge the beauty of their leaves and the careful growth of their bark.
Ask or share anything that comes to mind!
Notice how it feels to have a brief personal connection with nature.

"Let's hear each other, see each other, and care about each other."

SJK

HOW ARE YOU?

"How are you?" we ask in passing, seldom waiting around long enough to hear even an automatic "Finethanks" response. Insincere formality tires me, so, for the most part, I've stopped answering that question ... and, sadly, it seems the asker seldom even notices. Living an awake life means paying attention as much as possible to every moment and aspect of our lives — including paying attention to others around us. 🙢 Let's hear each other, see each other, and care about each other. Let's ask, "How are you?" as we look each other in the eyes and stop to hear each other's responses.

🙢

BRING IT TO LIFE!

Today, sincerely ask three people, "How are you?" and focus on hearing their response.
When someone asks, "How are you?" answer them with a rich smile,
responding honestly and intentionally.
How does this exercise impact your day?

"I believe the most powerful person in the room is the one
who can see all perspectives as possibilities rather than threats —
the person who acts first to be kind rather than to be right."

LORIN BELLER

KINDNESS

We hear a lot about the merits of kindness in our non-business interactions, but "kind" doesn't usually get the same caliber invitation to the business world. Being kind can be seen in business as being weak or ineffective — so being RIGHT is what gets applauded instead. Kindness deserves a higher valuation. It allows us to hear instead of insistently speaking, and to connect rather than shutting others out, all the while creating a space for collaboration and curiosity. Aren't these things that are absolutely essential to client relationships, co-worker relationships, and our relationship with ourselves at work, at home, and everywhere? Give kindness an open invitation to everything and everyone, everywhere.

BRING IT TO LIFE!

Write "Kindness" on a small sticky-note, and place it where you will see it
at least several times today (on your desk, in your kitchen, in your car). Each time you see that
kindness note, pause and notice what you're thinking or what you're doing.
Is it kind?
If not, take a deep breath and change the thought or action to a kind one.
What changes do you notice by the end of the day?

"Perhaps we're all here on this earth from century to century,
lifetime to lifetime, in one beautiful continuation of growth
through all generations before and to come."

SJK

CARRY ON

With the death of both parents in three month's time, my siblings and I quickly went from being sons and daughters to being a living legacy. ✏ The parts of my siblings I had long thought of as unique to them suddenly became instead glimpses of what my parents had passed on, parts of themselves that had become parts of us, always to carry on the spirit of our parents. ✏ I wonder, too, if part of our role in this living legacy is to not just carry on, but to carry on further. To expand upon the gifts our parents imbued in us and carry their spirit beyond what they were even able to think or dream of in their generation. To break the limits they didn't know how to escape in their own time. ✏ Perhaps we're all here on this earth from century to century, lifetime to lifetime, in one beautiful continuation of growth through all generations before and to come. ✏ What living legacy are you carrying on today?

BRING IT TO LIFE!

Think today about what your limits may have been or may be operating within.
Is there a stirring in your heart to take yourself beyond those limits?
If so, take one step toward that expansion today, and increase your living legacy.

"Change your words, change your world."

SJK

A DIFFERENT WAY WITH WORDS

I saw a movie clip a while back of a blind man begging on the streets with a sign that says, "I'm Blind. Please Help." Most people simply pass him by, until one person stops and writes something on his sign. Suddenly, person after person place coins in front of the blind man. The sign changer returns, and the blind man asks incredulously, "What did you do to my sign?" We see then the revised sign that now says, "It's a beautiful day and I can't see it." The sign changer replies, "I wrote the same, but with different words." That is the power of words. They impact and spark actions and reactions, and when you use different words, the impact, actions, and reactions change. My company tagline is "a different way with words," serving as a reminder and a challenge to myself and others that we can use different words to create a different way, and vice versa. Let's intentionally select what we say and how we say it, and use our words for healing (not destruction), for truth (not lies), and for love, (not hate). One word, one phrase, one intention can make all the difference.

BRING IT TO LIFE!

Today, pay close attention to the words you use and the impact they have.
Which word choices had positive impact? Which didn't?
How might you more consistently choose words that encourage, support, and show love?

"My body knows — even when the rest of me forgets — that I need this."

SJK

BODY WISDOM

Almost daily, I sit creakily down onto my meditation mat on the floor, easing into the pretzel-fold of crossed legs as I wonder if this is really necessary. Why not just toss myself right into the day and get going, get moving? Fortunately, on most days, discipline keeps me at the mat, so I close my eyes, take a deep breath into my spine, and feel my body settle into position with a sigh of relief so intense it brings tears to my eyes. After enough time spent in the quiet safety of this meditation posture, my body knows what's coming and now gets "there" (to some mysterious place of complete inner peace) before the rest of me does. My body knows — even when the rest of me forgets — that I need this. So often we drag our bodies along as an after-thought in our lives, yet they carry such incredible and personal wisdom for us. They remember. They anticipate. They are ready to sit us down in a quiet space to spend time in the place beyond words. Perhaps it's time to follow their lead.

BRING IT TO LIFE!

Take five minutes to sit quietly, close your eyes, and pay attention to your body
– the tightness, tingles, aches, comfortable spots, and imbalances.
What message might your body be giving you right now?

JUNE 26

"Trust there is meaning there for you."

SJK

THE SECRET OF LIFE

If you want to discover the secret of life, closely watch a bumblebee in a flower garden.

BRING IT TO LIFE!

Schedule 10 minutes in your day to watch a bumblebee interact with flowers.
If you don't have a place nearby to do this in person, find a video on the Internet to watch.
Look for messages or associations that come to mind as you watch.
Write down any hint of understanding, and trust that there is meaning there for you.

"In every moment, our hands are offering something."

SJK

IN OUR HANDS

In many religions, it is considered a great honor and divine experience to be in the presence of a master spiritual teacher. Curious about this idea myself, I recently sat in the virtual presence of a guru, watching a video of her meditating under a weeping cherry tree in full spring bloom. It was a gorgeous scene, but I didn't feel the divine part of it ... until, that is, I saw the close-up of her hands gently, reverently moving from bead to bead of her *japa mala* (prayer bracelet of sorts), and my heart melted instantly into unexpected, warm tears. As if in response, as I write this page, my own hands are tingling with a vibrant warmth of connection — to you reading this, to the guru, and to the divine. There's something so intimate, personal, and powerful about our hands. Our hands hold the capacity to heal or hurt, to grasp or release, to give or take away, to caress or bruise. In every moment, our hands are offering something. May we use them consciously to offer compassion, not rage; healing, not hurting; reverence, not dominance. May we use our hands to offer love.

BRING IT TO LIFE!

Sit comfortably with your hands on your lap, palms up, and focus your attention on them.
What do you feel? What do you see?
Close your eyes, and imagine touching someone's arm in a gesture of gentle compassion.
What do you feel in your hands? In your heart? Then gently cup your hand on your own cheek, palm to your lips. *What do you feel in your hand? In your heart?*
Today, pay special attention to the actions and feelings of your hands.

*"Our bodies carry such profound information;
let's pay closer attention to the guidance of feelings
in our resonant, internal cathedral naves."*

SJK

RESONANCE

A choir singing in a cathedral is one of my favorite sounds. Actually, it's one of my favorite feelings, as the acoustics of a cathedral nave deepen and lengthen the resonance of each note until the sound becomes an internal sensation. The deep vibrations of the bass voices seem to settle in and among each cell, nudging them to each tingle in the same frequency. ⤢ It's the same feeling when we hum a few rich notes, chant a heart-opening mantra, or nestle in with a cat purring loudly or baby sleeping softly on our chest. ⤢ That resonance is also one of our greatest, wisdom-indicating tools. You know how we talk about whether something resonates with us or not? That deep feeling of energetic alignment is one way our intuition tells us YES. That feeling of a choir singing in a cathedral? That's the feeling of your next right step. ⤢ Our bodies carry such profound information; let's pay closer attention to the guidance of feelings in our resonant, internal cathedral naves.

BRING IT TO LIFE!

Listen to a choir singing in a cathedral (search the Internet for "choir singing in a cathedral").
Use headphones or earbuds, if possible, to put the music close to your body.
Notice the notes and any matching resonance you feel in your body.
What does resonance feel like?
Do this exercise regularly so you can recognize resonance and use it to guide you.

"Begin in a way you want to have continue."

SJK

AS WE BEGIN

There's an old saying that suggests, "As we begin, so shall we continue."   What is your first thought when you wake up in the morning?   What do you first pay attention to in your day?   How do you first address yourself internally each day?   Take the time to begin in a way you want to have continue.

BRING IT TO LIFE!

Answer the questions posed above.
Are your answers what you want them to be?
If so, acknowledge your intentional approach to "beginning."
If not, what changes would you like to see?
Make one of those changes today.

"A heart beats with the strength of God, looking for a sky
to play its rhythms through the colors of a sunrise."

SJK

GIVE LOVE

I have days of general emotional discomfort: my breathing is tight, a small knot in my core seems to tie my inspiration and enthusiasm into a restricted ball, my focus is murky, and it feels like there's a haze between me and the beauty pouring out all around me — I see it, I recognize it, yet I don't feel it beyond an intellectual noticing. I used to think that feeling was a sign of emptiness, of a need to drink in fortifying sensory experiences and read words that might act as emotional elixir to refill my dry internal well. But I've just realized that sometimes it's not that at all — this isn't emptiness I'm feeling; it's fullness. Fullness looking for an outlet. Love wishing for expression and the reciprocal gift of open reception. Compassion looking for a home to rest its full baskets of heartfelt caring. A heart beating with the strength of God and looking for a sky to play its rhythms through the colors of a sunrise or the whispering harmonies of a sunset. Love looking for a way to give. Give Love.

BRING IT TO LIFE!

What do you feel when you are emotionally full?
What fullness of love might you have inside today that you can express?
Go express it.

JULY

"Perhaps if we remember that it's in the intimate balance between lightness and weight
that we find our inner peace, we can be more willing to embrace
both ends of that spectrum together."

SJK

ZERO GRAVITY

I recently watched a video demonstration of an astronaut wringing out a wet washcloth in zero gravity space. I fully expected the water droplets to form and float lazily away from the washcloth, but I was quite wrong. Due to the surface tension of the water, it clings to the twisted washcloth, encasing the material (and the astronaut's hands) like a wobbly sheath of gel liquid. ✑ It seems this is how we often live our lives: we wring out our internal excesses, yet, when they finally reach the surface, we cling to them, not allowing the old to leave and clear a space to bring fresh water into our thirsty souls. ✑ It takes some emotional weight to counteract the surface tension so we can let go of our old wounds — a little scraping off of old emotional scabs, or some external pressure of a situation that requires us to release our old way of thinking for a new way of behaving. ✑ Perhaps if we remember that it's in the intimate balance between lightness and weight that we find our inner peace, we can be more willing to embrace both ends of that spectrum together.

BRING IT TO LIFE!

Is there something in your life right now that you are ready to let go of?
If so, what would it take to find the courage to apply enough "surface tension"
(emotional strength) to allow you to release that thing?
Take one step toward that today.

JULY 2

"We could all use a delicate sign that we're noticed,
cared about, and supported."

SJK

A KISS ON THE SHOULDER

The evening was nothing special, just our usual small chunk of TV-watching time on the couch before heading upstairs to read in bed. I was fast-forwarding through commercials when I felt a feather-light kiss on my shoulder and turned to see my wife grinning at me. "I just love you, is all," she said, as my heart melted. We could all use a few more kisses on the shoulder. We could all use some light touch on the place where we hold all our stress, carry our burdens, and muscle our way through the hard stuff. We could all use a delicate sign that we're noticed, cared about, and supported. Whether it's an intimate kiss on the shoulder of a lover or a fingertip brush across the shoulder of a loved one, a colleague, a friend, or some other a co-habitant of your life, they could probably use it.

BRING IT TO LIFE!

Today, stay open to the opportunity to provide a light kiss or — if more appropriate —
a touch on a shoulder of someone in your life.
If the chance is there, act on it,
and notice how it felt to provide that connection.

"In all the things that make up the museum of our everyday lives,
that's where art lives. Make sure you write down the address."

SJK

WHERE ART LIVES

I used to think art needed to be a framed painting hanging in a museum with a guard watching, or a huge sculpture roped off from crowds, or other untouchable expressions of talent housed only in locked, barricaded, or guarded areas. Now I'm certain that art lives in every inch of our accessible life spaces.

An email from a friend that says, "It's Friday — the day we miss each other out loud."
A moment of self-discovery during a conversation.
The wavy lines of gravel in the wake of a bulldozer's busy rearrangements.
Music that stops you in your tracks and gently breaks your heart wide open.
A full moon protectively watching over a bustling city after the rest of us turn our lights out.
Sharing of breath in a lingering kiss.
Clack of the letters on the keyboard as thoughts become visible.
A gasp for air after a laugh hijacks your stress.
Paw-sized indentations telling of earlier feline travels across the bed.
In these things that make up the museum of our everyday lives, art lives.

BRING IT TO LIFE!

Today, all day, notice where art lives. At the end of the day, write down all the art experiences you can remember. *How did your art-based perspective impact your experience today?*

*"We believe in the unseen wind, so maybe it's not such a stretch
to believe in an unseen God."*

SJK

FAITH IN THINGS UNSEEN

Sitting in the park on a breezy spring afternoon, I watch tree branches heavy with blossoms sway as if moved by invisible hands, and flowers dancing in unison as if carried by an invisible ocean wave. There's movement all around me, and a clear touch of air blowing along the bare skin on my neck from a source I can't see, yet I feel no fear. "Oh, it's just wind," I automatically tell myself, quickly applying the logical explanation for this force I can only "see" through its impact. ✎ That's also how we know the divine (some call it God, spirit, the universe, a higher power): as a feeling, through evidence of impact, and through each of the experiences and incidents some of us call miracles. ✎ We believe in the unseen wind, so maybe it's not such a stretch to believe in an unseen God?

BRING IT TO LIFE!

Next time a breeze blows, stop and pay attention to how you know it's the wind.
Feel it on your skin and in your hair. See the things it moves, hear the sound as it whispers in your ear, and remind yourself that you aren't seeing wind itself — just the evidence thereof.
*If you can believe in the wind, what else might you believe in
to support you in your life's journey?*

"Some days, we simply need to rest within the loving protection
of someone or something else."

SJK

PLACE OF REST

Hold me
here in your arms oh God
tight to your breast
to suckle your nectar,
feel your heart beat
with mine and fall
asleep
in the sacred cover of your
breath.

Some days, we simply need to rest within the loving protection of someone or something else. For some it's a divine force, for others a human, for still others it's nature, animals, or any activity that deeply engages the heart while the mind can rest. May you find your place of rest today.

BRING IT TO LIFE!

What is your place of rest? Take five minutes to write a description of it,
then schedule 10 minutes at some point today for time in that place.
How might you more regularly spend time in your place of rest?

"Perhaps there's a deep peace in the possibility
that we can let go so completely into our experience
that even the outline of ourselves fades."

SJK

NO TRACE

Buddhist teachings encourage us to step fully into everything we do: watering a garden, peeling carrots, playing, working, meditating, everything. I've appreciated that teaching, thinking of it often and feeling that focus as a loving filling of my heart and soul. I'm recently realizing, however, that perhaps this full attention to a task is not so much a filling as a sort of purifying emptying. Zen master Shunryu Suzuki encourages us to do activities with such focus that we completely burn away, leaving no trace of ourselves. The thought of having no trace of ourselves can be incredibly frightening, yet, on the other hand, perhaps there's a deep, deep peace in the possibility that we can let go so completely into our experience that even the outline of ourselves fades.

BRING IT TO LIFE!

As you go through your day today, practice giving yourself fully to each task with a full focus on the experience of each of your senses, losing yourself in scents, sights, sounds, smells, and tastes. If you feel unable to do this in public, practice burning away into an experience at home while preparing or eating a meal, washing dishes, interacting with a pet, or any activity.
What do you notice as you complete each activity? Is this a practice you might continue?

*"Awake breeds awake, exponentially increasing the chances
of positive impact from generation to generation."*

SJK

SEA STARS AND MUSSELS

Crouched near the water's edge last year, my adult niece and I listened in awe to the Rice Krispie popping sound of barnacles opening and closing their tiny shell doors with the tide, then spent another hour thoroughly engrossed in exploring the Olympia, Washington, docks for sea stars among the pillars bejeweled with mussels. ➵ Yesterday, that same niece sent me a picture of her eight-month-old son, at the same dock, with his chubby little hand exploring the ridges of a multitude of mussels as carefully as if by braille, reading each bump for the magical biological story they each held. His grandfather, barely visible in the photo as the backpack transporter for the precious little explorer, reports his own sense of awe as the baby hands moved on to tracing wood knots with a wonder-filled index finger. ➵ Awareness and awe, carried through the generations in an ever-renewing cycle. ➵ Awake breeds awake, exponentially increasing the chances of positive impact from generation to generation. Today, enthralled by barnacles, sea stars, and mussels; tomorrow, advocating passionately for marine life or natural art or infusing compassion into something well beyond our imagination.

➵

BRING IT TO LIFE!

Today, share your enthusiasm for a particular detail of life with someone in a different generation, and engage in conversation with them about it. Ask them what catches their eye in their environment, or about memories of a time they shared a discovery of awe.

"For a few minutes of bravery in facing our obstacles,
we can gain hours of peace."

SJK

FACE IT

Avoidance is not the answer. I learned this the hard way on the day I hid my ankle weights from my physical trainer, and was then required to wear them for the entire hour workout as penance. Because I had tried to avoid a few minutes of angst in my quest for growth and strength, I got about six times the pain and 12 times the effort. ✎ That's how it works with most things we try to avoid. It sits in the back of our mind, partially hidden, until it gets out in the open and we discover it has grown to (at least) six times its weight and 12 times its effort. ✎ It might be that grudge we've held, putting off forgiveness until we one day might feel particularly loving, or the restorative quiet time that we bury in "too busy" and "don't deserve" and "[fill in name] needs my time more." ✎ These things sit in the background, plugged quietly into our energy stores, draining the juice from everything else we're doing, until one day they come to the forefront, stronger than ever, scarier than ever, and so much more difficult to deal with. ✎ For a few minutes of bravery in facing our obstacles, we can gain hours of peace. Isn't that reward worth the initial effort?

BRING IT TO LIFE!

Is there something in your life you're currently avoiding: a relationship conversation,
doctor's appointment, phone call, bookkeeping, or filing? Take action on that thing today,
then describe in writing how it feels to have faced that obstacle head on.
How might it impact your life to quickly face challenges as they show up?

"I want to hear the angels singing
and touch their faces
only to open my eyes and see my hands
on my own face."
ANGEL N. SULLIVAN

ON THE FACE OF AN ANGEL

I imagine the face of an angel holds a beauty so intense that it would bring me to tears, even as I'd hold the gaze of the soul of God shining through.   I imagine gender would be erased by the features of pure compassion and exuberant joy, and that the form would come from a 3D (or 4D? 5D?) version of light not known to this world.   I imagine ethereal and solid and shimmery and smooth, all showing at once in way that can't quite be visually understood.   But most of all, I imagine what would surprise me in the face of an angel is my slightly crooked grin, paired with that same tiny red spot I have on the tip of my nose.

BRING IT TO LIFE!

Take a few minutes to imagine an angel's face (whether you believe in them or not),
and write a quick list of descriptors you notice in your mind's eye.
At the end of your list, add two distinctive features of your own.
How might you view yourself differently if you believed for even a few seconds
that you share the qualities of a divine benevolent being?
Write down your thoughts, and refer back to them frequently.

"Where have you stood up for your authentic self,
instead of who you thought you should be?"

REBEKAH J. STEELE

BE THE RED PETUNIA

In a world that tends to favor similarity and conformity, I am drawn to — and thrive on — difference. Sure, at times it's uncomfortable (try being an openly gay woman of Mennonite upbringing), but is it really any easier to figure out what's acceptable to the majority and squeeze ourselves into that mold? Artist Andy Warhol suggests there's great beauty in the difference, like a red petunia standing out in full glory in contrast to a window box full of white ones. Let's dare to trade blending in for a brave display of our stunning beauty. Let's dare to be the red petunia (or zinnia or tulip or weed) in a sea of white.

BRING IT TO LIFE!

Be on the lookout for anything and everything red today,
to remind you of the red petunia standing out against a flock of white.
Look for your individuality in the world today: when you're getting dressed,
notice if it's your style, or someone else's. *When you speak, are they your words*
or others' opinions and perspectives you've squeezed yourself into?
Find one small thing that you can be more of yourself with, and make that change today.

"The potential for the distance between heaven and earth to collapse is constant."

SJK

THIN PLACES

It was over 20 years ago on a hillside in France that I felt the separation between heaven and earth melt away. I was alone that evening, propped up against a tree as I watched the stars twinkle through the quiet darkness, and my heart melted into tears. I wished I could feel this — this expansiveness, depth, absolute lack of fear coupled with an overwhelming fullness of love — forever. Eric Weiner calls these places *thin places*, "the locales where the distance between heaven and earth collapses" and we catch a glimpse of the divine. I found more of those thin places in European cathedrals and in the space of my journal as I'd sit writing, overlooking my host family's yard at sunrise or sunset in the magic of France. But we don't have to go to another country to experience this. Those thin places are created by the way the sunlight falls across a sidewalk near home, or the contrast of nature peeking out from a crumbling brick wall, or the smile of a stranger as we share the coffee shop's WiFi password for the day. Thin places are everywhere. The potential for the distance between heaven and earth to collapse is constant. We just need to be willing to see it, feel it, and experience it.

BRING IT TO LIFE!

Think of a time when you felt at peace, deeply safe, and gently or powerfully infused with love. *Where were you? Was that possibly a thin place for you? Where might you find "day-to-day" thin spaces around you?*

"Faith needs no religious affiliation."

SJK

ON FAITH

Taking an early morning walk, I was struck by the majesty of an immense, gold cross adorning the top of a local cathedral spire, raised high into the heavenly blue sky. Then a glint caught my eye, and I noticed the curls of barbed and razor wire in the foreground, evoking whispers of the crown of thorns so often shown on depictions of Christ's crucifixion. Not an image that usually stirs me, but this time it did. It seemed that stunning contrast of the gently beckoning church spire against the sharp warning of razor-studded barriers had a message for me, for us. A reminder, perhaps, that no matter what we personally believe (or don't), there are enough people out there believing in some higher power that sanctuaries of worship are built as places to soothe the cuts from some harsh realities of life. Maybe, even on our days of little faith, we can be sheltered by this knowledge that others are gathered in worship, offering their beliefs to the world around them; in essence, believing on our behalf until we regain our faith.

BRING IT TO LIFE!

As you go through your day today, carry this question with you:
What do you believe in?
At the end of your day, write a list of all you believe in.
Keep it close for days when your faith fades.

"If you really want to get to know yourself, pick up your pen and let your heart-ink flow.
Unplug from your computer; plug into yourself."

SJK

UNPLUGGED

Due to a packing oversight, my sister-in-law went on a week-long trip without a power cord for her laptop. Our initial reaction was great concern about how she would survive without access to her computer.   She reported resorting to a pen and paper as her writing implements, calling it an "interesting experience" ... which fed right into her having a breakthrough of internal understanding. Yes, a breakthrough, without a computer.   A breakthrough came from a few sentences written in pen, on paper, from her hand, from (I dare venture) her heart.   If you really want to get to know yourself, pick up your pen and let your heart-ink flow. No filters, no keyboard intermediary, just you, your pen, and paper — an open receptacle for your inside-out expression.   Unplug from your computer; plug into yourself.

BRING IT TO LIFE!

Set aside 15 minutes today for uninterrupted writing time.
Set a timer, pick up your pen (or pencil) and notebook, and write anything
that comes to mind. Write it all down, ignoring grammar, spelling, and punctuation,
and not bothering with complete thoughts. Just keep writing until the timer goes off.
When your writing time is complete, notice how you feel.
Did you learn anything new about yourself?
Is this an exercise you'd like to repeat more often?

"In tears, we find the parts of ourselves that hold such precious, powerful answers
– tiny, damp messages rolling down our cheeks
as they whisper their secrets."

SJK

IN TEARS

I recently told my wife that it had been such a long time since I last cried that I actually missed it. I should have known better — of course, the next day I was in tears, crying through several Kleenex on a coaching call as my professional and life coach asked those dig-deep questions that bring up all the necessary emotional junk. I was going to just sniff them back and move on, but she encouraged me to "stay with the tears" to see what wisdom they carried. So I cried, and I kept crying quietly until I recognized what I was actually feeling, and we talked through it, and I found answers. Actually, answers, relief, and sunshine (literally — the sun broke through the rain as I dried my tears). In tears, we find the parts of ourselves that hold such precious, powerful answers — tiny, damp messages rolling down our cheeks as they whisper their secrets.

BRING IT TO LIFE!

How do you typically react to your own tears?
What if you saw them as gentle messages — how might you hear them?

"Play with life wherever play presents itself."

SJK

PERIPATETIC

A friend used the word "peripatetic" in an email. I had no idea what the word meant, but I immediately loved it because it sounded so pleasing in my head, and sounded even better when I stumbled through it out loud. Email replies from others soon followed, each of them tossing "peripatetic" around like a beach ball in a filled auditorium. ➥ Peripatetic. Say it out loud: pare .. uh ... puh ... TEH ... tic. Peripatetic. I can hardly resist saying it three times in a row, every time! ➥ The point here actually has nothing to do with the meaning of peripatetic (peripatetic. say it again: peripatetic); I just want to remind us to not take life too seriously. To play with it wherever play presents itself. To take a big ole word that sounds delicious and throw it around willy-nilly, no matter whether we know the meaning of it or not. ➥ And in case you must know, peripatetic means (Oxford Dictionary) "traveling from place to place, especially working or based in various places for relatively short periods."

BRING IT TO LIFE!

Use peripatetic (or an equally delightful big word) in a sentence today three times.
And laugh to yourself (or out loud) each time you do.
Toss it around like you've used it comfortably and correctly for years.
How might you apply this playful attitude to other actions
in a way that would enhance your life and the life of those around you?

"There's energy maintenance, and there's energy infusion,
and what often stands between the two is a state of mind."

SJK

AMAZE ME

There's interesting ... and then there's amazing. There's "Hmm, wonder how that happened? ... and then there's "OMG ARE YOU KIDDING ME?!?" There's the usual and customary things that catch a corner of our attention ... and then there's "WHOAAAAA, YOU HAVE GOT TO SEE THIS!" There's energy maintenance ... and then there's energy infusion. And what often stands between the two is a state of mind; a choice to step so deeply into this experience of life that the ordinary becomes the extra-ordinary, and interesting becomes amazing. What would it take to move your interesting to amazing?

BRING IT TO LIFE!

Set aside 10 minutes. On a piece of paper, make two columns:
the first one labeled "Interesting" and the other labeled "Amazing."
Write a list of things or experiences in your life that you currently find interesting.
Then go back through that list, and beside each item,
write its "kicked up a notch" counterpart in the Amazing column

"Maybe what we really need is to fill ourselves so full with the sensory offerings around us
that we sink easily into an inner quiet
like a kitten with a belly full of warm milk."

SJK

EXPAND INTO STILLNESS

Walking through a Philadelphia neighborhood on a spring morning, I luxuriated in the sensory richness of nature's new growth exploding into life. The environment was full of deep and bright colors, textures of every imagining, scents filling my lungs with pure, exhilarating joy, and the newly-awake vibe of spunky, caffeinated urbanites anticipating the weekend. I eagerly soaked it all in, filling up every cell until there was simply no more room for anything more. So filled, in fact, that suddenly all I wanted was stillness, silence, quiet, and an inner, gentle, open space to give my senses a place to rest after the indulgent sensory feast of the morning. We so often try to approach our inner stillness with an empty plate and wonder why we don't feel fed and nurtured when we come from a place of lack and reaching. Maybe what we really need is to fill ourselves so full with the sensory offerings around us that we sink easily into an inner quiet like a kitten with a belly full of warm milk.

BRING IT TO LIFE!

Take 15 minutes today to walk outside and take in as much as possible
with each of your senses. Notice everything, then look even closer, and touch, smell,
and even taste what is available around you.
At the end of this focused sensory feast, sit for five minutes in a quiet, comfortable spot
and breathe deeply. *Do you find your senses are grateful for the rest?*

"We could use a little internal etching
to remind us of what's important."

SJK

TATTOO TEACHINGS

My niece has the word "breathe" tattooed on the inside of her wrist in white ink — a gentle reminder to herself to relax into her breath and into life.   My wife has the word "laugh" tattooed on her shoulder to remind her to keep laughter in her life — permanently. And it's in a simple Andalus font to keep it, well, simple. I have a fountain pen nib tattooed on the inside of my wrist, aligned to look like it's coming from my vein, with a line of ink flowing to my hand. It's there to remind me to always write ... and to always write from my heart. We certainly don't all need (or want!) tattoos, but we could maybe use a little internal etching to remind us of what's important. What's the teaching you want to keep etched on your heart?

BRING IT TO LIFE!

Write possible answers to the question of what you want
to keep etched on your heart.
Keep that list in mind (and/or near you) through the day for reference.
At the end of the day, select the teaching you'd like to stay aware of, write it down,
and put it where you will see it every morning and evening.

"Through the heat we get to the sweet ... Let's get caramelized."

SJK

CARAMELIZED

I'm fascinated by the process of caramelizing onions. With just heat, oil, water (optional), and a bit of patience and attention, the brash taste of raw onions turns to a decidedly sweet flavor enhanced by a tantalizing, savory undertone.  The scientific goings-on have something to do with the breakdown of onion cells, which release their various components (sugars, proteins, scent-makers), and after evaporation of all that, more things happen to the sugars to break them apart further and miraculously (well, to me at least) increase their sweetness.  Through the heat we get to the sweet. Through the times that try us and break us open, with patience and caring attention to the process, we burn off our bitterness and evaporate the emotional harshness.  Let's get caramelized.

BRING IT TO LIFE!

Is there an area of your life that could use some caramelizing?
What are you ready to burn off, and what sweetness might be waiting
to be discovered through the process?
Take one step today toward a more caramelized life.

"Just because we can't see something doesn't mean it's not there."

SJK

JUST BECAUSE WE CAN'T SEE IT

Just because we can't see something doesn't mean it's not there. Some things are easier to believe (like the sun still shines even when it's cloudy), but other things (like the existence of a benevolent universal energy) might require a larger leap of faith. For those larger leaps, we may need to go through incremental "training" of noticing our faith in the smaller things and working our way up to larger leaps. For example: Our hearts beat in our chest even though we don't see them. A seed holds life even before it sprouts, even though we don't see it. Human potential is stored in each of us, even though it's not readily visible. Just because we can't see it doesn't mean it's not there. Start small.

BRING IT TO LIFE!

Write a list of things that you can't see but still believe are there.

Then write one thing that you want to believe but aren't sure you have enough faith.

Today, even if just for a day, choose to believe in it, even though you can't see it.

WIDE AWAKE   211   EVERY DAY

*"It can take great courage to open ourselves
to healing, compassion, and love."*

SJK

SUNSET

Orange
melts its way down evening's peak
daring me to feel
so I gingerly touch the edge
of color and find the warmth
doesn't scald me after all.

It can take great courage to open ourselves to healing, compassion, and love. Perhaps that's why sunsets intensify gradually, to show us that we can ease ourselves into the intensity of life and gather courage with each minute of unwavering beauty.

BRING IT TO LIFE!

Imagine watching a sunset over the ocean, city skyline, mountain, or meadow,
focusing on the gradual increase and fade of intensity.
Take that image with you today, and consider how you might apply the "sunset approach"
to aspects of your day. At the end of the day, take time to watch the sun set. If the sunset is not
visible where you are, watch a video of the sun setting — a quick Internet search will serve
up a bunch of sunsets for you!
How does sunset's gradual approach impact your perspective?

*"Consider the possibility of your body as a vehicle
for greater expression."*

SJK

THE GIFT OF YOUR BODY

Some believe that the divine, spirit, universal wisdom, magic — whatever you wish to call it — has a voice, and it's (quite literally) yours. Some believe that spirit and energy rely on us, in our human form, to give expression to their messages of light and love through our physical bodies and everything else tangible about our human selves. Consider the possibility of your body as a vehicle for greater expression: Your inner knowing could be a poem placed on your lips by a divine energy that relies on your vocal cords to speak words for others to hear. The empathy you give through a hug could be placed in your heart by a divine energy that relies on your arms to give physical comfort. The soul you gave birth to could be an angel placed into the soft miracle of a baby by a divine energy that relies on your creative capacity to sculpt a physical example of what we are truly capable of. Such a valued vessel, this body we have. Why would we not be invested in caring for it and keeping it in pristine, working condition? Our bodies are a gift; let's treat them as such.

BRING IT TO LIFE!

Consider for a moment the possibility of your body as a vehicle for divine expression.
How does that impact the way you view your body?
What is one thing you can do, starting today, to deeply honor the gift and value of your body?

"Let's remove the chasm between our bitters and our sweets
and choose to live a rich, full, dark chocolate life."

SJK

A DARK CHOCOLATE LIFE: BITTERSWEET

That two-toned experience of loss and anticipation that often comes
just before or after a big change.
The conflicting feeling we get at the end of an old year
as it melts into the beginning of a new year.
The mix of gratitude and sadness near the end of a luscious vacation time.
The perfect blend of bitter and sweet that make connoisseurs of chocolate swoon
at the taste of an exquisite, dark chocolate masterpiece.
We tend to polarize our lives into either bitter or sweet, and in doing so miss the beauty of the
blend that makes up so many of our experiences. Let's remove the chasm between our bitters
and our sweets and choose instead to live a rich, full, dark chocolate life.

BRING IT TO LIFE!

Draw a line down the middle of a blank piece of paper to separate it into two columns.
Label the left column "Bitter" and the right column "Sweet." In the "Bitter" column, list things
in your life that you consider bitter, and in the Sweet column, list things in your life
that you consider sweet. On a separate sheet of paper, make a "Bittersweet" list
by combining words from the Bitter and Sweet columns.
Do the Bittersweet combinations allow for a deeper experience than just bitter or sweet?

"The integration of prayer with other life activities is a powerful way
to connect with the deepest part of ourselves and our world."

SJK

PRAY AND

As a child, I quickly learned the "correct" way to pray: formatted appropriately by beginning with "Dear God" and ending with "In Jesus' name, Amen," offered while sitting or kneeling with full attention on the supplication of the moment. Yes, we kids picked at the coveted macaroni casserole crust while my father "gave thanks" before a meal, but we knew in no uncertain terms that was against the rules. Real prayer was a solemn, singularly focused activity. ⟋ I've recently discovered, however, the joy and freedom of "pray and ... " Pray and listen to music. Pray and write. Pray and run or walk or stroll. Pray and take photos. Even pray and meditate (is it still meditation then? I'm not certain. But I'm sure it's still prayer.) ⟋ The integration of prayer with other activities of our lives seems to me a powerful way to connect with the deepest part of ourselves and our world. ⟋ Maybe it's time to loosen a few more restrictions around the right way to do this whole God thing?

BRING IT TO LIFE!

Whether you call it prayer or something else, what is your "restriction"
around that way of connecting with yourself or a broader consciousness?
How might your "prayer" experience change if you put an "and"
in place of that restriction?

"Practice having the small things matter."

SJK

WHY THE SMALL THINGS MATTER

The wildflower that fights up through the muck of a flood.

The horse softly nuzzling your hand.

The joke told in the midst of grief.

The snore of a loved one beside you.

The split-second flash of hope in a seemingly hopeless situation.

These small things matter — all small things matter — because in a catastrophe, or depression, or great loss, or even the usual stresses of everyday life, the small things might be all you have to hold onto.

Practice having the small things matter.

BRING IT TO LIFE!

At three different times today, pay attention to the smallest detail you can see or think of, such as a vein pattern on a leaf, a genuine smile from someone you pass in the hallway or street, the split-second chirp of a bird, and so on.

What happens to you in those moments of attention?

"Turns out full-focus moments are less about limits
and more about expansion."

SJK

EXPANSION THROUGH FOCUS

Back when music CDs were just becoming popular, my brother treated us to a CD player. Well, he treated himself, but he so generously included me in the listening experience that it felt like a gift to me just as much.   I remember those evenings at dusk — the deep gold of the setting sun climbing over the windowsill into the room as we listened to the magical clarity of the music. "Okay, now listen for the cymbals here!" he'd say, and I'd focus every ounce of energy on hearing that cymbal. Then, "Do you hear the piano in the background?" and sure enough, it was there, playing my heart, although I'd never noticed it before.   To this day, every song is richer and fuller because I hear the individual instruments and the nuances I learned to notice in those music focus hours with my brother.   Turns out full-focus moments are less about limits and more about expansion.

BRING IT TO LIFE!

Take 10 minutes to completely focus on listening to one of your favorite songs, through headphones, earbuds, or lying on the floor in front of your stereo speakers.
Pick an instrument and listen for it, then pick another and listen specifically for it.
Notice each detail you can focus on. Listen to the same song again, this time hearing the interplay of instruments, voices, rhythm, and volumes as a whole.
Notice how this focused time allows you to expand your experience of the music.
What do you notice? How is listening different after the initial focused-listening session?

JULY 27

*"What if we lived more of our lives on dolphin watch,
always on the lookout for beauty and the elusive glimpses of grace?"*

SJK

DOLPHIN WATCH

The Delaware beaches are a popular spot for dolphins, so during a beach visit, my friends and I were on a constant dolphin watch. At dusk one day, we were relaxing just off the ocean, easily sharing conversation and the gentle slowing of the day. 🐬 Until, that is, all at the same time, we saw the dolphins jump. 🐬 "OMG THERE LOOK LOOK LOOOOK!!" we shouted as we all jumped up, pointing. Three dolphins jumped out of the water together in a magical, graceful arch, then slipped gently back into the water as we celebrated the gift of that sighting. 🐬 What if we lived more of our lives on dolphin watch, always on the look-out for beauty and the glimpses of grace?

BRING IT TO LIFE!

Put yourself on dolphin watch today, and see what beauty and grace shows up for you
in your regular day-to-day activities.
At the end of the day, make a list of your dolphin sighting experiences.
Is this an approach you'd like to take more often?

"We don't need to take a tropical vacation to find that relief;
we simply need to dissolve ourselves right where we are."

SJK

DISSOLVE YOURSELF

Sometimes we just need to get away from it all, to take a break from the relentless pursuit of success by physically going to a different location that facilitates relaxation (think sunshine, beaches, rippling waters). We don't need to take a tropical vacation to find that relief, however. We simply need to dissolve ourselves right where we are. Dissolve yourself into detailed examination of a leaf, a flower petal, a brick, your skin, the stitching on your sweatshirt or suit, the fur on a dog's paw, the intricacies of your hand. Dissolve yourself into drawing tiny, colored squares next to each other and coloring them in with a pen or paint, or shading with a pencil. Dissolve yourself in any activity that grabs your deep attention, and the you who re-appears will be changed.

BRING IT TO LIFE!

Give yourself 10 minutes or more today to dissolve yourself in an activity
that appeals to you (see above for examples, or make up your own).
Note how you feel at the beginning of the activity vs. the end.
How might you share this activity with others?

"Connectwork. Your business, your calling, depends on it."

SJK

CONNECTWORKING

Business relationships can be wonderful examples of the power of intentional connection. I was going to include some vignette here from my corporate employee days, then my sister-in-law told me about the connectworking relationship between clownfish and sea anemone — which sounds much more interesting, right? Clownfish tend to hang out in long-term pairs, and as if that's not delightful enough, they choose a sea anemone to live with as well. The clownfish, with its hilarious "wiggle dance," helps keep the anemone aerated, while the anemone provides shelter and safety for the clownfish. Networking: good for our business. Connecting: good for our relationships. Connectworking: good for our business relationships. With connectworking, we get to form relationships with people we enjoy, who share our values, and who get the work we do. The resulting business alliances are simple, natural side-effects. Networking: me. Connecting: us. Connectworking: everyone. Everyone is connected in some way — call it universal energy, one mind, spiritual connection — everyone is connected to you, your business, your goals, and your dreams. Infinite resources. Infinite possibility. Connectwork. Your business, your calling, depends on it.

BRING IT TO LIFE!

Carry this "connectworking" concept with you at work and play today.
How might you act differently if you are feeling and expressing that interconnectedness?

"If it's not about you, you get to let it go, whatever it is."

SJK

IT'S NOT ABOUT YOU

I admit, my automatic reaction to that phrase "It's not about you," is a feeling of rejection. I hear it as a refusal to consider my needs, and as proof that my impact and value is negligible at best. ✎   In reality, though, "It's not about you" is one of the most freeing phrases we can be offered. If it's not about you, then you're not responsible to "fix" it, or figure it out, or carry "it" as an ongoing burden. ✎   If it's not about you, you get to let it go, whatever it is.

BRING IT TO LIFE!

What have you taken on in your life that, in reality, is not about you?
Visualize gently grasping that burden (is it on your back? on your desk? on your doorstep?)
and lovingly setting it away from your realm of responsibility.
How much more space might you have for what is about you
if you let go of more of what is not about you?

"What do you want to propagate in your world?"

SJK

WHAT WE SHARE

"You brought a beautiful sunrise with you this morning," our gym owner said as I stumbled into the gym at 6:00 in the morning, the sun nipping playfully at my ankles. "I already took two pictures. I like to send them to my wife." ✎ It reminded me of the gorgeous, above-the-clouds sunset photo my wife texted to me on her recent travels, captioned with a gleeful "I shared my sunset with you!" ✎ And now, here I am, writing this piece to share the experiences, again, with each of you. ✎ What do you want to propagate in your world? What do you share?

✎

BRING IT TO LIFE!

Write down what you want to propagate (breed) in your world.
Then notice as you go through your day:
What do you share with those around you — and yourself,
in the form of what you pay attention to?
Does your sharing facilitate the growth of what you wrote down this morning?

AUGUST

*"A small symbol of significance and a willingness to interact
in respectful play, and meaning is made."*

SJK

GOOD MORNING, MARY

On our walk to the gym each morning, we pass a house with a small garden statue of Mary standing watch in a perpetual Our Lady of Grace pose: arms slightly raised and open to both receive and bless simultaneously, head tilted in welcoming gentleness, with light blue and softly flowing white robes. The statue is housed in an open wooden box standing on one end with vines and flowers surrounding it. Some days Mary is almost covered in foliage, but after a day or two, the leaves have been cut down to her feet and trimmed around her arms and head. I'm not a Catholic, and have distanced myself from potential heartfelt responses to statues due to warnings in my Mennonite youth against worship of graven images, but I've become fond of this Mary. It started with greeting her each morning with a mischievous "Good morning, Mary" to add levity to the six o'clock hour. Then I started meaning it. Then one morning, she answered back in a deep, loving voice: "Good morning, Starla. May you have a blessed day." It was the voice of my wife, but the exchange brought the statue to life. A small symbol of significance and willingness to interact in respectful play, and meaning is made.

BRING IT TO LIFE!

What can be a "Good morning, Mary" scenario in your life — some small, connecting ritual that you carry out each day? Maybe it's a gentle good morning offered each day to your local barista, or a joyful good morning offered to a symbolic object in your home each morning. Try that new connecting ritual today, and notice its impact.

"Sometimes our inner words are more awake than the rest of us."

SJK

WORDS

At times they come
and pile on my tongue gentle at first then insistent
like the kiss of a lover tasting my soul's sweet savory salty mysteries
Tell us they say, Tell us of you through the heart you express when we leave
and we'll tell you back
words.
So wordless I show them the place where I love and flames lick at my heart and
the place where I fear and its dance taunts my mind and
the place where I dream and fierce hope obliterates doubt.
Silently I hand them my pen with the places I can't speak
telling them Please, please write me
so tonight they gave me these
words.

BRING IT TO LIFE!

Sometimes our inner words are more awake than the rest of us and offer a path to inner discoveries. For 10 minutes, write (with pen and paper) anything that comes to your mind — no matter what sense it does or doesn't make. Just let the words come through your pen and sit on your page. After 10 minutes, read what you wrote, and see what you discover.

"Why use a mere period,
when your life can be an exclamation point of surrender?"

SJK

SURRENDER

What happens on the third cloudy day at the beach when the sun finally comes out? We gasp with glee, throw our arms open wide, and lift our faces to the sun: a pose of worship and pure surrender to the full, joyful experience of the moment. More moments in our lives deserve this all-out welcome, this surrender to our senses and the vibrant experience of the moment. In this mode of surrender, our entire life becomes a potential for exclamation points: The sun's out! Thank you! I'm honored! I believe! I love you! Why use a mere period, when your life can be an exclamation point of surrender?

BRING IT TO LIFE!

Imagine that feeling of opening your heart, chest, arms, and face to the warmth of the sun
after a cold, gray spell ... then feel it one level deeper, one breath longer.
Find three more times today to experience that feeling of surrender.
How did it impact the way you approached your day?
How did others around you respond?

"What if we lived as though who we are and what we love
is worthy of our own approval and bold affirmation?"

SJK

YOUR GIFT(S)

"What do you like about yourself?" my colleague, Nona, asks her seven-year-old daughter, who easily lists off her positive qualities and talents. "What do you want to be when you grow up?" Nona asks, and her daughter quickly answers, "A dolphin trainer or an art teacher." "Are you going to let anything get in the way of doing those things?" Nona asks. "NO!" the child responds, rolling her eyes, as though the consideration of dream derailment is the most ridiculous thing she's ever heard. "I love those things!" What if we all lived as though who we are and what we love is worthy of our own approval and bold affirmation? What an incredible gift to give yourself and this world.

BRING IT TO LIFE!

Write a list of what you like about yourself.
Then write down what you want to be when you grow up.
How close are you to that goal?
Read back over the list of what you like about yourself,
and, armed with that strength, do something that takes you
one step further in that quest.

"Come to OM as you are, and let it do the work."

SJK

THE ANXIOUS OM

My wife and I are not cut from the same cloth. I need to soak in as much of my world as possible, while she only needs little sips. I need to emote deeply, turning myself inside out daily, while her emotional maintenance is much less complicated. I need to spend regular time in quiet contemplation or meditation, which might kill her from boredom. I say, "Oh we'll figure it out, it'll be fine" in pretty much any situation, and she mitigates risk. At night while she's trying to sleep. ✎ It survives, this relationship of difference, because we laugh about it. When I started meditating several years ago, she called it my "OM Time." And when I need to go write (aka "emote"), she grins while motioning wildly with her hands digging into her chest, then throwing wide, imaginary handfuls of feeling. ✎ Then there's my new favorite, the anxious OM, something she came up with that we can both share. When a stress moment builds, we look at each other, take a deep breath, reach our arms out with thumb and forefinger in the "O" of *chin mudra* ... and stretch all our other fingers out rigidly, squeeze our hand and arm muscles tight, clench our teeth, and say with fierce determination, "Ommmm!" ✎ With the Anxious OM, stress turns to laughter, laughter turns to relaxation and coping clarity, and we find our centers again. ✎ Come to OM as you are, and let it do the work.

BRING IT TO LIFE!

Next time you notice the stress building, try a moment of the Anxious Om.
Remember two things: approach it respectfully, even as you play with it, and finish
with a deep breath in, deep breath out, and a whisper of "Thank you."

"Cultivate beauty, and that's what we will grow."

SJK

CULTIVATE BEAUTY

Gangly, bright yellow flowers in an old, wooden planter barrel caught my eye, looking as though they were waving me over to come play a while. Always ready for an interaction with nature, I answered their call and stepped on over with camera ready. Only then did I notice the dead boxwood shrub, mostly hidden in the center of the towering flowers. I felt a pang of sadness for the lifeless shrub, but otherwise, that glitch in the beauty of the flower arrangement barely dampened my enthusiasm. It's like that in our lives: we all have some unseemly bits present in ourselves and our situations, but if we cultivate beauty, the significance of those other parts dwindles. Not that we should ultimately ignore those bits, but first we cultivate beauty to shore up our hearts and souls: literally plant more flowers, or practice more self-compassion, or spend more time opening our hearts to the divine. Cultivate beauty, and that's what we will grow.

BRING IT TO LIFE!

What is a beautiful part of yourself or your life? Write it down.
How might you cultivate more of that beauty? Write that down too.
Take steps to cultivate that beauty today.
Notice how this impacts your ability to handle the parts of yourself
or your parts of your situation that you find less appealing than others.

"Perhaps we could all learn from the innocently intuitive technique
of nine little kids looking for inspiration.
Meditation + Anticipation = Mediticipation."

SJK

MEDITICIPATION

When we were kids, my siblings and I would ask Mom for ideas when we ran out of things to do. She'd get a gleam in her eye and say, "Oh, I can find things for you to do!" We quickly realized that her "things" were chores, so we came up with our own way of generating ideas. Some combination of brothers, sisters, and I (there were nine of us) would lie on our backs, side-by-side on a bed, and share ideas that came to us. When we heard one we all liked, we'd jump up and do it; make tunnels in the hay bales, play Ping-Pong in the springhouse, or build forts beside the willow tree down by the stream. ≈ It strikes me now that the idea-generating pose we used was the *Shavasana* of yoga — the corpse pose where we let our bodies rejuvenate through integration of the energy created from the prior activity (yoga, meditation, still time). As kids, we sensed the value of lying flat on our backs, letting go of the work of thinking, and waiting in anticipation of the next great idea showing up. ≈ Perhaps we could all learn from the innocently intuitive technique of nine little kids looking for inspiration. Meditation + Anticipation = Mediticipation.

≈

BRING IT TO LIFE!

Take 10 minutes for mediticipation. Set a timer, lie flat on your back, legs and arms extended and relaxed, and eyes closed. Anticipate ideas coming as you relax your body and mind. Record the ideas that came to you. *Is this a technique you'd like to continue to practice?*

"What I had forgotten was the value of seeing someone
look me in the eye."

SJK

LOOK THEM IN THE EYE

I recently had the delight of meeting one of my writing coaching clients face-to-face in real life — a significant occurrence since most of my clients I know only through telephone and email communication. Those phone conversations are rich, multi-faceted, open, deep, and absolutely enjoyable, so I expected the face-to-face meeting to simply be a continuation of that connection. What I had forgotten was the value of seeing someone look me in the eye. It's a heart-warming gift to have an eye-to-eye connection, an honoring of each other's inner workings through the expressions of our eyes. Hours later, I could still feel the energy in my eyes from an hour of interacting over breakfast with this person; I still carried with me the feeling of love and gratitude that our eyes had offered each other. Such a simple action, this looking another in the eye, with such profound lasting effects.

BRING IT TO LIFE!

Today, concentrate on intentionally looking people in the eye — gently, openly –
honoring the inner workings of each person you interact with today.
At the end of the day, spend five quiet minutes noticing how your eyes
feel from the inside out.
Then notice how your heart feels.
How was your experience different today as a result of connecting to people eye-to-eye?

AUGUST 9

"This micro view of our everyday objects opens up a whole new world of intrigue."

SJK

MICRO VIEW

It looked like a set of miniature museum pieces: a tiny chunk of yellow swirl, a luminescent green rod, and blue, mauve, purple sculpturettes with stripes and spots painted throughout. Much to my surprise, these multiple pieces of art were actually a microscopic view of sand, shown by photographer and scientist Gary Greenberg in his TED talk about the beauty of the microscopic world. ✎ Up closer than the naked eye can see, a flower's pollen consists of tiny, brightly-colored spheres resembling perfect fish eggs; petals look like a furry blanket, and the central pistil and stamen resemble sticky raspberry preserves. ✎ This micro view of our everyday objects opens up a whole new world of intrigue, a chance to wrap ourselves in the inspiring energy of possibility, curiosity, and maybe even an awareness of the miracles hiding in plain sight around us. ✎ Let's look beyond the surface of our experiences to find the deeper beauties there — in others and in ourselves.

BRING IT TO LIFE!

Today, look closely at the objects around you.
Notice the intricate patterns of your place mat, the texture of a weed, the different colors
that blend to make up the color of bricks, the crisscross pattern
of skin on your knuckles, etc.
What do you notice?
How does this exercise impact your day?

AUGUST 10

IT'S OUR TIME

I was talking with a friend, via email, about time. She finally had a vacation break, and right from the beginning, her time started filling with obligations, appointments, and activities for others. It wasn't the act of helping that was frustrating her; it was the amount of time dedicated to that during her vacation. ⮒ Well, she consoled herself, at least tomorrow is ALL MINE. ⮒ The next day, she followed up that thought with one simple, profound statement, "And you know, really, it's ALL my time, isn't it?" ⮒ Oh wow. Yes. It really is all our time — all of it, every moment. Even when our options seem slim and the path seems clear in a direction we don't want to go, we still get to choose what to do with our time. ⮒ It all starts out as our time; our task is simply (ha!) to decide to whom and how much to give away.

⮒

BRING IT TO LIFE!

Today, claim your time, very intentionally deciding who and what gets your time.
How does it feel to take charge of your time?
Is this something you might want to practice more often?

"Don't let perfect give your fears a place to hang out and eat Cheetos."

SJK

DON'T LET PERFECT

I told a friend that her encouragement just might finally get me to finish a long-standing item on my To-Do list; that I might actually just do it, for heaven's sake. She responded, "Do? It's did! Copy –> Paste –> Bow to the round of applause." Thirty minutes later, and I had completed a task that I had hung onto for over a year! How? By no longer letting "perfect" run the show. Don't let perfect make any project bigger than it really is. Don't let perfect lure you in with the deadly message of "all or nothing." Don't let perfect give your fears a place to hang out and eat Cheetos. Don't let perfect open your storage shed full of debilitating comparisons. Don't let perfect tease you, demean you, promise you salvation, or even offer you candy. Don't let perfection get in the way … so you can make your "To-Do" a "To-Did."

BRING IT TO LIFE!

Where in your life is your quest for perfection holding you up?
Take one step of imperfection toward making progress on that task today.

"When we take the time to connect with our surroundings in new ways,
we open our hearts to the chance of new forms of love."

SJK

BUTTERFLY PAWS

One year I "borrowed" several Eastern Swallowtail butterfly eggs I found on parsley in our garden, and tended them carefully in a small glass aquarium through their metamorphosis stages. One morning, I found a freshly-emerged butterfly perched on a stick near its now-empty chrysalis shell, drying its shimmery, wet wings in the warm sun. ✎ Soon, the butterfly began fluttering and walking up the stick, so I put my finger in its path. To my delight, the butterfly climbed right onto my finger and sat there for several minutes before flitting off across the yard. ✎ The butterfly's deep blue-black wings and the white markings across his body were gorgeous, but what really stunned me was the feel of the little butterfly feet on the tip of my finger; feet so soft they felt like precious miniature paws. So magical it brought tears to my eyes. ✎ When we take the time to connect with our surroundings in new ways, we open our hearts to the chance of new forms of love, and the possibility of butterfly paws.

BRING IT TO LIFE!

Today, touch some part of nature you have never touched before:
perhaps the veins on a leaf, the "fur" on a caterpillar, the underside of a flower petal.
Notice the new sensations as you pay attention to your environment in a new way.

"Fun can be as simple as adding an orange to a pile of children
and shouting, 'Go!'"

SJK

SIMPLE FUN

In one of the deliveries from our gift subscription to the Fruit of the Month Club, we received a type of orange — HoneyBell — proclaiming to be so juicy that they came with a bib and eating instructions to wear the bib while eating orange. ⌣ I mentioned these delights to our gym owner, and we decided his (six) kids needed to experience the purported juice phenomenon. The next day he went home with two juice bombs (aka HoneyBells) and a handful of bibs. ⌣ How did the juice fest go? He reported a no-bib scene ("I figured I'd just let them have a free for all"), several juice squirts in various eyes, giggling, laughter, and a downright fun time. ⌣ We don't need an extravagant arrangement to tap into the pure, sweet energy of fun; it can even be as simple as adding an orange to a pile of children and shouting, "Go!"

⌣

BRING IT TO LIFE!

What simple activities did you call fun when you were a child?
Is there some element of that activity that you can do — simply — in your life now, today?
What other ways can you think of to have simple fun?
Do one of those today, and share your experience with a friend,
encouraging them to "play it forward."

"Sometimes we need to step out from behind the lens
and participate fully in our experience."

SJK

BEHIND THE LENS

You can often find me behind the lens of my camera. I'll race outside to capture a sliver of light kissing the golden throat of a Calla Lily at dusk or peeking through leaves of a giant Red Maple at dawn. Hoping to document a unique moment, I'll crouch at the Honeysuckle vine midday to wait for the buzz of hummingbird wings, and flatten myself out on a sidewalk to get face-to-face with a crawly creature. ⤻ It's no surprise, then, that at the beach recently, I crawled out of bed at 5:30 in the morning to capture pictures of the sunrise. About 100 pictures and a sunrise later, I put down my camera and realized I had missed the sunrise. Yes, I saw it through the lens, but I missed the heart experience of the sleepy sky waking in vibrant ribbons over the ocean, because my mind was so engaged with questions of photographic consideration. ⤻ Sometimes we need to step out from behind the lens and participate fully in our experience — of a sunrise, of a conversation, of the stillness of a quiet-minded moment.

BRING IT TO LIFE!

Next time you reach for your camera, leave it right where it is.
Use your mind's eye instead, and engage fully in the experience of committing
every sense and nuance to memory.
Then write out a recap of the experience from memory,
and notice how much richness you were still able to reconstruct.

"The animals around us can point our attention to things we would otherwise not notice,
or even things we otherwise might not believe."

SJK

SHAKTI SOAKERS

I was sitting for meditation this morning, my mind totally wandering, when I heard an unfamiliar noise. I opened my eyes to see one of my cats reaching way up, pawing at the string of *mala* beads sitting on the desk in front of me—something she's never done before. She looked at me, meowed, and left the room, so I closed my eyes and settled back into quiet stillness for the rest of my meditation time. The second I stood up, my other cat waltzed over to my meditation mat and sacked out, purring up a storm. ⋍ I've heard that cats are quite sensitive to *shakti*, the life-force, or spiritual energy of the universe, that some believe builds and collects around the areas in which we meditate. As surprised as I am to say this, I'm starting to believe that's true. ⋍ As I told my life coach in an email exchange around the feline events of the morning, "I so appreciate these two furry shakti-soakers providing a visual for an energy I otherwise wouldn't see." ⋍ It just might be possible that the animals around us can point our attention to things we would otherwise not notice, or even things we otherwise might not believe.

BRING IT TO LIFE!

Pay attention to the animals in your life
(a great book about animal meaning is *Animal Speak* by Ted Andrews),
and get curious about their behaviors.
What are the possible messages there for you?

AUGUST 16

"In our lives full of searching for completion, arrival, and resolution,
perhaps the greatest experience is actually our sweet yearning."

SJK

SWEET YEARNING

My soul
ravenous for the touch of God.
Tongue
longing for words, taste,
the deep kiss of Divine.
Tears
embracing the ache in the core
of my being
So wet
yet unable to quench the fire
of my sweet yearning.

In our lives full of searching for completion, arrival, and resolution, perhaps the greatest experience is actually our sweet yearning.

BRING IT TO LIFE!

What do you long for and yearn for? Is there even deeper longing or yearning underneath that?
Take five minutes to write about this. Connect with your deep longings and sweet yearnings
today, and notice the impact it has on your thoughts, feelings, and interactions.

"We don't have to impossibly revert back to childhood to regain our sense of wonder; it's still in us."

SJK

THE WOOD KNOT

We were hiking in Canada with dear friends, romping through the woods beside a canal, with curiosity and cameras at the ready. A tree had fallen across the trail, at a perfect height for me to examine its bark and trunk structure. Running my hand along the smooth surface, I was surprised to see a knot that looked exactly like an "outie" belly button! I'm a tactile person, so I spent the next several minutes exploring that odd little swirling bump with my fingertips. I never did take a picture of it, but the look and feel of that fascinating wood knot stuck clearly in my mind. ✎ Soon after our return from the trip, my brother was relaying to me the most poignant moments of his recent visit with his grandson (my great-nephew), and what stuck out in his mind? The way the dear eight-month-old was captivated by a wood knot, spending minutes exploring it with his fingers ... just as (unbeknownst to anyone else), I had done a few days earlier. ✎ We don't have to impossibly revert back to childhood to regain our sense of wonder; it's still in us — each of us — if we simply take the time and attention to re-engage with it. Touch the knots. Always touch the knots.

BRING IT TO LIFE!

Today, engage your childlike sense of wonder. If feasible, find a wood knot and explore it with your fingers, noticing and wondering about every little whorl, bump, and nick. If you don't find a wood knot, use touch to instead explore skin, a plant leaf, a paw, stone, or anything.
Ask yourself the "how and why" questions today that a child might ask.
At the end of the day, reflect on how this perspective impacted your day.

"Nature suggests there's a gentler way."

SJK

SLOW FADE

Many of us start our days abruptly waking with an alarm, and end our days sharply stopping whatever we were doing and dropping exhausted into bed. Nature suggests there's a gentler way. The day fades in with a slowly building sunrise, and the day fades out with slowly lowering sunset. What if we mirrored that rhythm?

BRING IT TO LIFE!

Picture "fading" into and out of each day.
What would that look like and feel like?
What simple changes can you make this week to experiment
with a "slow fade" way of starting and ending each day?

"We can focus on the bitter tastes of self-doubt and fear,
or we can focus on the sweet evidence of our capabilities."

SJK

WHERE WE FOCUS

I gained 2,500 "likes" on my business Facebook page, and I lost two of those followers the next week. Guess what I focused on? The two people who stepped out of the new pack of 2,500.  Over 2,000 (thousand!) people showed an interest in my work, yet I let two (two!) walk-outs kick my confidence to the curb.  We can focus on those bitter tastes of self-doubt and fear, or we can focus on the sweet evidence of our capabilities, the voices that show their support, and the sparks that light our most meaningful passions into fires of inspiration.  What do you choose?

BRING IT TO LIFE!

Today, notice where your focus most often turns.
Are you focusing on things that uplift and support you,
or on things that crumble your confidence?
If your focus isn't where you want it to be, choose a different focus.
Then choose it again.
And choose it again in each moment.

"Some days nothing hands me a taste of the divine like the incredible details of science."

SJK

DIVINE SCIENCE

In seventh grade, I used to beg my incredibly patient science teacher to let us spend class periods watching films about underwater ocean life. On other days, I'd wield a scalpel with fascinated horror as I opened the skin of a formaldehyde-drenched frog in order to explore its tiny insides ✎ In high school, this intrigue carried me through the initial distaste of dissecting a mink, which quickly turned to amazement at each muscle layer, tendon, and ligament. Then, in college, I stepped into a new level of reverence and awe as I studied the muscles of an actual human body, seeing firsthand the mysteries under the skin, particularly the various layers that comprise our musculoskeletal system. ✎   Now, it's not unusual to find me poring over books about the structure and purpose of plant parts as if I were studying a stunning sculpture or prized painting, and quantum theory happily blows my mental doors of possibility wide open. ✎   I find great comfort and strength from my mediation mat, daily mindfulness, and deeply still moments of worshipful space, but some days nothing hands me a taste of the divine like the incredible details of science. ✎   Whether in a garden, a temple, an office, or a lab, inspiration — and a taste of the divine — awaits our discovery.

BRING IT TO LIFE!

Take 10 minutes today to read about some aspect of science that might
be interesting to you: rock formations; how trees grow; natural springs;
how cement hardens; how chameleons change color.
Follow your curiosity, and notice the possibly magical and/or mystical parts of your discovery.

"The relationship between writer and reader is a sacred one."

SJK

THE POET

Steeped in the juice
of a thousands words
I soak my cells in her story
the one I make up
between her lines of poetry
and it's not until I reach the end
with my request for happily every after
that I see the story is mine
draped through the arms of her letters
as we walk through the poem again
together.

The relationship between writer and reader is a sacred one, for in the reading of others' words, and the writing of words to be read by others, we often find ourselves. Perhaps we're not so alone after all.

BRING IT TO LIFE!

Read some poetry today, whether or not you typically enjoy reading poetry.
Look for recognition of your own story in the poets' words,
and see what you learn about yourself.
(Need recommendations? Try Rumi, Hafiz, Ushi, or Mary Oliver)

AUGUST 22

"What if we all do indeed share the same root system, so to speak?"

SJK

LIKE AN ASPEN GROVE

I recently learned that all the trees in an aspen grove are connected to the same root system, so they all share the same genetics. This technically makes the entire colony an individual organism. One seedling produces the whole grove by sending up determined little shoots from the root system, and, in time, those shoots each become a full-fledged tree, expanding the size of the colony but not altering the genetic makeup. As if this isn't amazing enough, in Utah there's an aspen grove of 47,000 (yes, thousand) trees, the whole colony covering over 100 acres, and the root system estimated to be somewhere around 80,000 years old! When you touch one tree in an aspen grove, you are in essence touching all of them, as they are all part of one organism. When you touch a young tree, you are also touching the full lineage extending through time to the very first seedling that created the first roots — the heartbeat of the grove. What if we saw each other in that same aspen grove context of interconnection? I touch you, and I touch your ancestors, your history, your connections to lives loved and lost, and all living matter. What if we all do indeed share the same root system, so to speak?

BRING IT TO LIFE!

Today, notice all possible interconnections in your world.
Act for today as though every living (and non-living) being is part of the same organism,
connected by a shared root system that sustains us all.
How does this impact your day and your perspective?

"Whether we see it or not, we are connected to each other
in many ways, so let's aim to be more aware, conscientious,
and respectful of lives outside our own sphere of daily interaction."

SJK

KEEP OUT OF SOYBEAN FIELDS

We have a sign hanging in our foyer; bold black letters make their point easily against a fluorescent orange and yellow background:

HUNTERS KEEP OUT
OF SOYBEAN FIELDS
HELP PROTECT THE FARMERS' CROPS

Although we initially bought the sign to add a splash of humor to our urban home's entryway, it has actually become meaningful to me. "Help protect the farmers' crops." I live in the city, a far cry from any farmers' crops, yet that sign reminds me to be conscious of the farms, the farmers, those dear soybean fields, and how my actions — even as a non-hunter — could impact them. That sign reminds me that whether we see it or not, we are connected to each other in so many ways, so let's aim to be more aware, conscientious, and respectful of lives outside our own sphere of daily interaction.

BRING IT TO LIFE!

Today, consider a vocational group different than yours and think of ways your life intersects with theirs. Carry that awareness with you today, and provide them the gift of respectfully "keeping out of their soybean fields" while helping to "protect their farmer's crops."

"Apparently, meaning sometimes needs for us to just let it happen."

SJK

LET MEANING HAPPEN

I was agitated and restless. I had been looking for meaning all day long and had come up short. I had flipped through five different inspirational books, and nothing lit a spark for me. I had written in my journal and scratched out a line or two of poetry trying to conjure up meaning through my muse, but she was silent. I had taken photographs of nature, but the images didn't live up to my hopes. ⬱ So I finally flopped down on our back patio love-seat, lay down flat on my back, and gave up. ⬱ Only then did I see the breathtaking view of the finch sitting high on a wire above me, the clouds behind him magically shaped like huge angel's wings perfectly centered with his little body. The sky was a clearer blue than it had been in days, and the glow from the setting sun glinted off the golden church steeple in the distance. In that instant, my heart opened, my mind relaxed, and it suddenly felt as though somehow life really, truly mattered. ⬱ Apparently, meaning sometimes needs for us to just let it happen.

BRING IT TO LIFE!

Take five minutes to sit quietly and take a few slow, deep breaths,
picturing your heart relaxing and opening.
Today, allow for the possibility of meaningful experiences —
no striving, no pushing or pulling, just allowing.
At the end of the day, note the ways meaning showed up for you.

"What if we took that energy we expend on trying to understand,
and instead apply it to paying attention to each new moment?"

SJK

TRADEOFF

It's human nature to continuously want to understand, to feel a sense of security in having our minds chew endlessly on the experiences of our past. We replay our memories time and time again, viewing all the different camera angles, guessing at the motives of each character, feeding the lingering pains, and pulling at the corners of emotional scabs in the hope that we might someday, somehow, understand. What if we took that energy we expend on trying to understand, and instead apply it to paying attention to each new moment? Is it possible that the past would lose power and the present would gain peace? Seems like a valuable tradeoff.

BRING IT TO LIFE!

Today, when you find yourself mulling over something in an attempt to understand it,
step back (literally, if feasible), take a deep breath in, and on your breath out,
tell yourself "tradeoff."
See if you are able to let go of the need to understand — even if only for a moment —
and in focusing on each present moment,
notice the presence of peace that steps in.

"Who's to say what's right? Who's to say what works?
Who's to say what's best?"

SJK

WHO'S TO SAY?

We can study a doctrine and hone a practice and follow the rules and learn the right way and follow the right path and say the right things and act the right way, but ... who's to say what's right? Who's to say what works? Who's to say what's best? You are. In every moment of every day, you get to decide what's your right way, your way that works, your best whatever for you. Who's to say about [anything]? You are.

BRING IT TO LIFE!

Today, pay close attention to your thoughts, actions, and behaviors.
Are you intentionally choosing on your own behalf, or are you simply
following someone else's prescribed path?
Give yourself a say. All day.

"You, my dear, you taste like truth."

SJK

THE TASTE OF TRUTH

I want sometimes
to get lost in you
engulfed in your words or maybe your lips
tongues-tied speaking to each other
through taste buds
touched gently together as if to say
Yes, Oh Yes I agree
with whatever you say
because you, my dear, you

taste

like

truth.

Spirituality, sensuality, and sexuality — so often separated, yet maybe it's in their full integration that we can truly come together to touch the divine?

BRING IT TO LIFE!

Notice your reaction to today's reading. *What message might be in that reaction for you?*
How might you more consciously integrate spirituality, sexuality, and sensuality?
Take one step toward that integration today.

AUGUST 28

"The way we care for the smallest of things is just as important as the way we care for what we consider to be the grandest, most important of things."

SJK

FOR THE LEAST OF THESE

Picking my way carefully along a breaking-up, city sidewalk in my neighborhood, I was curious to figure out what an intricate contraption of small wires, poles, and clips was doing in a neighbor's tiny front planter area. Closer inspection revealed a small, green stalk lightly clipped to each of several poles strung together evenly with a wire frame. Some of the stalks were vibrant, with others either in the process of dying or reviving; it wasn't clear. ✎ But what was clear was the care that someone took as they fashioned an intricate support structure for a handful of nondescript plants. Given the delicate nature of their plant support setup, I'm guessing the builder's care extends well beyond plants to many other living (and non-living?) beings and things. ✎ I was immediately reminded of a well-worn Bible verse (Matthew 25:40) that I know from my early years, in which Jesus points out, "Whatever you did for the least of these, you did for me." ✎ In other words, the way we care for the smallest of things is just as important as the way we care for what we consider to be the grandest, most important of things. And in that caring itself is where we have a chance to touch the divine.

BRING IT TO LIFE!

Intentionally care for something small today, giving greater importance to the recipient of your caring than you normally would. Whether it's picking up a piece of trash, giving a granola bar to the person carrying the cardboard "HUNGRY. PLEASE HELP" sign, or any number of caring acts, care deeply about it. *How does this act impact your perspective?*

"Our senses are each their own miracle,
yet they seem thrilled to have any chance to intermingle."

SJK

THE SMELL OF GREEN

Walking around a lake one morning, I was stopped in my tracks by the delicious smell of green: the heady sweetness of fresh-mown grass laced with a few deeper notes of wild clover and pleasantly pungent, crushed weeds. Even now, remembering that moment, I see the whole scene (the lake, the fading garden phlox, even the wooden docks) in green. ✒ Our senses are each their own miracle, yet they seem thrilled to have any chance to intermingle. Sometimes we're aware of their collaboration — as in my overwhelming sense of the smell of green — but often the sensory mingling is a blissful experience that we overlook, simply because we're not paying attention. ✒ How does blue taste? ✒ What color is softness? ✒ What does royal purple sound like? ✒ Our bodies, hearts, souls, and minds delight in our senses, so why not give them a fully integrated, sensory playground?

BRING IT TO LIFE!

Today, pay close attention to your senses, and when you become aware of one,
intentionally notice another at the same time.
Then start putting together random senses in your own imagination.
What flavor is maroon? What does silky taste like?
Do you feel more awake and aware?

"Touch your world, touch your life."

SJK

IN TOUCH

Touch is one of our most powerful senses, yet possibly one of our least noticed. ✎ Our skin, which houses our touch receptors, is our largest organ at about 16 percent of our body weight, but because it is constantly in touch with something outside of ourselves (our clothes, a book, the air, another person, jewelry, etc.), it quickly gets used to these ongoing sensations, and we soon overlook them in deference to our other senses like sight or smell. ✎ Consider how much more present we can be if we bring touch back into our awareness: a buttery-yellow flower can be experienced as a miraculous living piece of velvet; a cat's fur seems to caress us back with its plush softness; a hand on our arm ignites a brief heart connection; the slightly rough tree bark reminds us that strong and gentle can coexist in a living being. ✎ Touch your world, touch your life.

BRING IT TO LIFE!

Write "in touch" on your palm (or a small piece of paper that you can carry with you)
to remind you to pay attention to your sense of touch throughout your day.
Notice each sensation of touch, and expand your experience today
by using touch as an auxiliary sense as much as possible.
At the end of the day, reflect on how an increased focus on touch impacted your day.

"When we are named, we are recognized, acknowledged, and gently set
on this incredible path of discovering and becoming our unique, individual selves."

SJK

THE GIFT OF OUR NAMES

When my mother was still alive, I used to call her each year on my birthday and thank her for naming me Starla. ⤙ Not only do I love the sound of my name, it has also been a ongoing rich source of positive interactions with otherwise strangers, like this email I recently received from our financial advisor's assistant: "One more thing ... after speaking with you a while back, I went home to my nine-year-old daughter and said, 'I just heard the most wonderful name — Starla.' She agreed and has now named her beloved Barbie after you. She said the name has 'star power.'" ⤙ Aside from the thrill of having a beloved child's Barbie namesake, I was flooded anew with gratitude for the gift we have in our names. When we are named, we are given a part of the one(s) who named us — a fact so dear to me, especially since both my parents have died. But even more importantly, when we are named, we are recognized, acknowledged, and gently set on this incredible path of discovering and becoming our unique, individual selves.

⤙

BRING IT TO LIFE!

How do you feel about your name? Do you like it or not — and why?
If you like or love your name, have you expressed gratitude for it?
If you don't like your name, what name would you absolutely love to have, and why?
Consider your answers. Is there some hidden part of your truest, beautiful self
that is asking to be named and brought into the forefront of your life?

SEPTEMBER

"The seamless blending of notes seems to remove my usual perceptual barriers,
and the possibility that somehow we are all One seems quite likely."

SJK

IN HARMONY

As I listen to hymns from my growing-up years, I am transported by the intertwining eight-part harmonies back to the church auditorium filled with a community of voices, all offering their part to the beauty of the whole. Although I've not attended church in years, musical harmony still brings me almost instantly to that sense of interconnection with everything and everyone around me. Whether it be the hymns my early cells were nourished by or the harmonies in my current, broad range of secular music, the seamless blending of notes seems to remove my usual perceptual barriers, and the possibility that somehow we are all One seems quite likely. We have so many chances to experience deep harmony running through the song of our lives; we simply need to listen and let the music carry us.

BRING IT TO LIFE!

Set aside 10 minutes. Select a song you love that includes some rich harmonies,
and focus completely on listening to how the harmonies intertwine with each other.
Use headphones or earbuds, if possible, to bring the music even closer to you.
Listen to the song a second time, this time simply noticing how you feel.
Can you find an openness to the possibility of a deeper and broader
connection with the world around you?

"Any one of us can make any part of any day a Special Edition."

SJK

SPECIAL EDITION

"There's a Special Edition of Love Dollars on the kitchen table for you," my wife said as I packed my work backpack for my trek to the local coffee shop. "Special Edition" because it was only Thursday, and Love Dollars are typically reserved for Friday — the day when a few dollars magically appear near my wallet to foot the bill for my end-of-week coffee shop treat. Love Dollars because they signify my wife's understanding of how I cherish my little Friday morning celebratory scone ritual, and because the money comes from our shared bank account yet is still offered as a gift to me. Special Edition because we were shaking up the routine a bit. But, most importantly, Special Edition simply because she designated it as special. Any one of us can make any part of any day a Special Edition.

BRING IT TO LIFE!

Designate today as a Special Edition, and act accordingly.
At the end of today, note how your day was impacted
by the Special Edition designation.
Is this something you want to do more often?

"Doing something 'from the floor up' gives us access to the full physical,
emotional, and spiritual length of our bodies."

SJK

FROM THE FLOOR UP

In his book, *The Art Spirit*, painter Robert Henri suggests "painting should be done from the floor up," not from a comfortable sitting position on a chair. ✍ As I sit here writing from my comfortable chair, I quickly see — rather, feel — his point: with this seated crimp in my body, the words start only just above my waist, the lower half of my body not involved in this expression. ✍ Doing something "from the floor up," however, gives us access to the full physical, emotional, and spiritual length of our bodies, all standing firm on the grounding (quite literally!) foundation below our feet. Our energy can flow up and back down without rounding the constricting corner of a seated position. Fascinating! ✍ So, physically, our foundation is the floor, the ground ... and what then is our internal foundation, that something that allows us to do our best work from the ground up, living our most solid lives with the most free flow of vibrant energy?

✍

BRING IT TO LIFE!

Set aside 10 minutes. Find a quiet, somewhat private place (indoors or out) where you can stand quietly without interruption. Stand with your feet planted firmly on the ground, apart just enough for easy, steady balance. Notice how solid your feet feel, and imagine that same strength in your legs, your joints, your waist, your core, your neck, your head, and beyond.
Carry that image with you as you go through your day today.
How does it impact your day and the experience of those around you?

"That thrill of the hunt gives us an extra shot of energy,
a boost of enthusiasm, and a perspective of possibility."

SJK

THE THRILL OF THE HUNT

One of my clearest childhood memories is of spending hours looking for fool's gold, or pyrite — a mineral that, when it catches the sunlight, looks like it could be actual gold. Those rocks with little chunks of pyrite in them had no monetary value, and I was well aware that it was not actual gold, but that didn't dampen my enthusiasm one iota. ✑ I was in it for the thrill of the hunt. I loved the anticipation of knowing there were hidden bits of something unusual among the blah, normal stones of our driveway. ✑ That thrill of the hunt — whether we're kids or grown-ups, whether it's fool's gold or fulfillment we're hunting for — gives us an extra shot of energy, a boost of enthusiasm, and a perspective of possibility. ✑ To this day, my body remembers that thrill of the childhood hunt, and all it takes to bring the feeling and energy back is to spend five minutes hunting for a wildflower in the city, 12 positive words on Facebook, or three somethings unusual anywhere else. ✑ Give yourself the thrill of the hunt.

BRING IT TO LIFE!

What is something discoverable in your area or life that you'd be excited to find?
Hunt for that today, and allow yourself to feel the thrill of the hunt.

"Not every pain requires a complete overhaul of ourselves or routine;
often, it only takes a slight adjustment."

SJK

SLIGHT ADJUSTMENTS

Exercise is a nearly daily ritual for me, regularly honoring the capacity of my body and appreciating its ability to wake up my mind and heart. One day, after several days of morning exercise on our stationary spin bike, my left knee got cranky, and I winced in pain going up or down stairs. I sadly pondered the need to give up cycling as a form of exercise, ready to choose my knee's comfort over my preference for the spin bike exercise. Then it occurred to me that my left leg felt a bit out of alignment when I was on the bike. Maybe, just maybe, could I make a slight adjustment to the clip on my left shoe and relieve the strain on my knee? So I shifted the clip about a centimeter, and to my great relief and joy, the next spin bike session left me with zero knee pain. Not every pain requires a complete overhaul of ourselves or routine; often, it only takes a slight adjustment.

BRING IT TO LIFE!

As you go through your day today, notice if anything feels out of alignment —
physically, spiritually, emotionally, or in any other way.
What slight adjustment might you make to possibly put yourself back in alignment?
Do that.

"Those exquisite times of inspiration don't easily come at our call;
there needs to be some sort of tipping point to step us from the edge of enthused
to a deep dive into the clear, azure ocean of inspiration."

SJK

THE TIPPING POINT OF INSPIRATION

We've probably all experienced them — those moments when life shines like a precious diamond and every facet seems to offer us a different gift of delicious experience. ✎ Those moments are my holy grail as a writer. Much of my day, every day, is spent in activities that make the way for and beckon to that elusive inspiration. I tend my tiny, backyard urban garden looking for the face of God in the grinning pansies, and sit in public spaces watching for the divine among the human, and ride the waves of life hoping to catch The Big One and ride it all the way to inspiration. ✎ One of the reasons those exquisite times of inspiration are so rich is because they don't easily come at our call; there needs to be some sort of tipping point to step us from the edge of enthused and excited to a deep dive into the clear, azure ocean of inspiration. ✎ That tipping point? I'm pretty sure it's BELIEF. Belief that our ideas have value, that our lives have meaning, that someone or something cares for us and wants us to also care for them. Belief added to hope, to pain, to confusion, to happiness, to anything tips the scale to inspiration — the feeling we have and the infinite possibility we are when we sit in the lap of the divine.

BRING IT TO LIFE!

What inspires you? Jot down a list of everything you can think of, large and small. *What role does belief have in each of these?* Can you add the impact of belief to even more moments?

SEPTEMBER 7

*"What you don't see might just be
where the most profound information waits."*

SJK

WHAT YOU DON'T SEE

I have worked by phone with the same business and life coach for over six years, yet have been in the same room with her only once. I have profound conversations with writing coaching clients, yet most of them I have not met (and likely never will meet) face-to-face in person. Isn't it limiting to not be able to see the other person? Isn't the visual essential for creating a context for these incredibly important conversations? I say no. That what you don't see is a mystical communication that may only be available when the visuals are removed. What you don't see is the energy that sends chills of cellular-level understanding through the listener; and the tears that flow freely from client or coach because there's no "how I look" embarrassment; and the profound images that appear in our minds simultaneously because our vision is turned inward, free from the distractions of outward sight. What you don't see might just be where the most profound information waits.

BRING IT TO LIFE!

In phone conversations today, pay close attention to what you don't see.
What do you hear in voice tones? What do you feel in the energy exchange?
What images pop into your mind?
What parts of you are engaged in the conversation when you can't see the other person?
Now think about paying this close attention in the conversations you have face-to-face, with
the other person visible. *How might what you don't see enrich even those conversations?*

"No, thank you. I'm waiting for my YES."

SJK

NO, THANK YOU

When was the last time you said, "No, thank you" to something big enough that the choice made your knees shake? When was the last time you said, "No, thank you" to something important enough that the choice made you cry? When was the last time you said, "No, thank you" to something gripping you tight enough that the choice took your breath away? In this yes-awarded society, let's not forget that it's our "No, thank you" that carves out space for a soul-bursting "YES!!" to show up, take root, and expand throughout our entire lives.

BRING IT TO LIFE!

Write a note to yourself,
"No, thank you. I'm waiting for my YES."
Carry it with you today.
Commit to saying NO to two things today that are (or would be)
taking time and space away from a more important YES.
What would it take for you to make this a habit?

"Makes me wonder how many of us really live life
with telephone pole vision — missing the magic."

NANCY J. DUNCAN

TELEPHONE POLE VISION

My brother sent an email to our family, and all it included was a photo, with the subject line "Telephone Pole."   As I expected, the photo did include a telephone pole ... beside a gorgeous rainbow reigning over a verdant crop of rain-drenched trees, and sunlight so magical it seemed digitally altered.   All that stunning beauty, and the caption pointed us simply to the Telephone Pole.   Although my brother supplied that caption in jest, it was such a powerful reminder of how much we can overlook if we don't intentionally pay attention to our lives and the world around us.   In the words of my coach, I too wonder, "How many of us live life with telephone pole vision — missing the magic?"

BRING IT TO LIFE!

Each time you see a telephone pole today, let it remind you to look for the magic
(whatever that means to you) in the environment or in that moment.
At the end of your day, write a list of the day's magic moments.
Is this a practice you'd like to continue?
How might you share the experience with those around you?

"Interest, excitement, imagination, and deep play;
that's what curiosity sounds like."

SJK

WHAT CURIOSITY SOUNDS LIKE

During a recent visit, our six-year-old twin niece and nephew discovered the small, self-contained water fountain on our patio. Within seconds, they were crouched down in front of it, spouting out questions as they watched water splash down the different levels. ⤳ "What makes it go on?" ⤳ "Do you ever make it stop?" ⤳ "When does it get empty?" ⤳ "Where does the water come from?" ⤳ "How does it [the water] get up to the top?" ⤳ So we had a brief lesson on how pumps work, with my little scholars repeating the process to me, wanting to make sure they understood every detail. Then things got really good. ⤳ "I wish I were really little, then I could stand right there (points to four-inch top ledge) and slide down the waterfall." ⤳ "Do you think if we'd be really little, we'd get stuck in the pump? We would have to build a ladder to hang onto." ⤳ "And then we could build a ladder here (points to middle six-inch ledge) so we could climb up to the sunny spot!" ⤳ This went on for 30 minutes, all three of us completely engrossed in our fountain world until we had to leave for a baseball game. ⤳ Interest, excitement, imagination, and deep play: that's what curiosity sounds like.

BRING IT TO LIFE!

Today, get as curious as a set of six-year-old twins in everything you do.
How does that perspective impact your day?

"With my attention all over the place, I felt that familiar inner knot
start to form as my focus couldn't find a safe place to land."

SJK

UNI-TASKING

As I sat down to write this morning, I had my computer open (social media, email), my phone at hand (texting), two books and two notebooks open, and a To-Do list in plain, unavoidable view ... while I ate my breakfast. Attention all over the place, I felt that familiar inner knot start to form as my focus couldn't find a safe place to land. ✎ Then I was reminded of something Zen master Shunryu Suzuki said: "When you eat, eat." Not work, read, play, talk, AND eat. Just eat. ✎ Single focus. ✎ When you read, read. When you listen, listen. When you write, write. When you love, love. ✎ All my notebooks are now shut. My phone is set aside. My To-Do list is out of view. And I'm writing one page, totally focused on you. ✎ In our worlds full of multi-tasking, we could all use a good dose of uni-tasking.

✎

BRING IT TO LIFE!

Today, pay attention to your multi-tasking habits,
and turn as much of those multi-tasks into uni-tasks.
Notice the impact of focusing your energy and attention.
Is uni-tasking something you would like to do more often?

"We can decide to take our hearts to work every day,
giving our soul a chance to dance with our intellect and accomplish far more
than with our brains alone."

SJK

TAKE YOUR HEART TO WORK

Our hearts don't ask to be left at home when we go to the office, yet somewhere along the way, we started believing that our hearts don't belong at or in our work. Each morning on the way out the door, we grab our car keys, brains, and go-cup of coffee … and toss our hearts onto the kitchen counter. ✍ Then at the end of the work day, we bring our sore brain and tired body home, toss the car keys on the counter, and spend the evening trying to revive the dried-out heart we left out on the counter all day. ✍ It doesn't have to be that way. ✍ We can instead decide to take our hearts to work every day, giving our soul a chance to dance with our intellect and accomplish far more than with our brains alone. We can engage with our co-workers and our clients on a level that facilitates greater collaboration, greater sharing of wisdom, and greater acknowledgement of each other's talents as we become co-creators instead of co-workers. ✍ Our hearts are powerful business tools — let's be brave enough to bring them to our work. Every day.

BRING IT TO LIFE!

Take a few minutes to picture how your day might play out and how it would feel
if you intentionally took your heart to work today.
Then do it.

"Choice = empowerment = possibility."

SJK

AS IF YOU HAD CHOSEN IT

Eckhart Tolle encourages us to respond to any moment "as if [we] had chosen it." If I had actually chosen to have that client contract dissolve, maybe I could see that it leaves room for a new client more matched to my work. If I had actually chosen to have that house-for-sale not pass inspection, maybe I could see that we talked ourselves into liking it in the first place and that the next, perfect place was already waiting for us. If I had actually chosen for a long-term relationship to break apart, maybe I could see that the pain was burning off an old part of me that no longer served my current path. Choice = empowerment = possibility. What if we lived more of our lives as if we had chosen it?

BRING IT TO LIFE!

Look at something today that you are unhappy or dissatisfied with.
How would you think, feel, or act differently
if you had actually chosen the situation exactly as it is?
Take one step toward that change today.

"When your inner wisdom needs a vehicle to show itself, consider your pen."

SJK

HEALING WRITING

Words

Bits

Falling so smoothly onto paper though

really it's all

frag

ments

waiting for tomorrow

to piece together today

while the pen takes over and

writes me again.

Writing down our words can be healing, no matter whether we consider ourselves to be writers or not. Poetry in particular gives us total freedom to express everything from fragmented thoughts to a seamless, rhythmic flow, often giving us new understanding of what is "going on" with us. When your inner wisdom needs a vehicle to show itself, consider your pen.

BRING IT TO LIFE!

Take five minutes to write any words or phrases that come to mind, in any structure.
When the time is up, re-read what you've written.
What did you discover? How might you use freeform writing to learn more about yourself?

SEPTEMBER 15

*"What if, when life gets too big, we allow ourselves to only occupy
the space we have energy to fill?"*

SJK

WHEN LIFE GETS TOO BIG

Sometimes life simply gets too big. We can't quite get grounded in who we are, what we believe, or what we truly want, and too many ongoing decisions overwhelm us as each option feels too difficult and the obstacles insurmountable. ⮑ Our life gets too big, so we push ourselves to expand and fill the huge space our life has become, until one day we hit our expansion limit and, like an over-filled balloon, we break. We break, and in those smaller pieces we've become, we begin to heal. ⮑ Yes, we do heal ... but might we heal more quickly if we give ourselves permission to skip the middle, breaking part of that process from time to time? What if, when life gets too big, we allow ourselves to become (or stay) smaller – to only occupy the space we have energy to fill — so we don't need to break?

⮑

BRING IT TO LIFE!

How big is your life right now?
Are you expanding beyond your healthy limits to try to fill that space,
or are you allowing yourself to be the size you need to be?
What would it take for you to change the size of your life to match you,
rather than the other way around?
Write down three possible action steps, and today take the first step.

"Some days it's time to simply welcome life exactly as it is."

SJK

AS IT IS

I look for beauty daily, hoping to stumble across some magical, sensory experience that moves me beyond my standard anxieties of living. I will go out of my way to walk through the park in search of nature's transcendent gifts, listen to song after song that might inspire me to new insights, and lose myself in imagining that beach vacation planned for the end of next month. ⟳ Some days those tactics are exactly what I need ... but other days it's time to drop the searching, the hoping, and the reaching. Some days it's time to simply welcome life exactly as it is. To look at what's here, now, and simply pay full attention to it. To drop the need to assess or judge. ⟳ Some days we need to simply relax into faith that this day, this moment, is meant to be exactly as it is.

⟳

BRING IT TO LIFE!

Write "as it is" on a small sticky-note, and keep it with you today.
As you observe your environment and experience the various facets of your life today,
melt any labels of good or bad or beautiful or not
with a deep breath and a quiet whisper to yourself of "as it is."
As you fall asleep tonight, take a deep breath,
and wrap yourself in the strength of that phrase "as it is."

"In my concern for others, I was losing my own breath."

SJK

FULL BREATHS

Going for a run on the boardwalk during a beach writing retreat, I noticed I quieted my breathing each time I passed a walker. I didn't want to disturb their walk with my runner's panting. After each "passing," I was even more short of breath from holding mine back, and had to gasp a bit to regain my normal, exercise-breathing rhythm. In my concern for others, I was losing my own breath. And in the end, without my own breath, I have no life available — for me or for anyone else. How often do we give up essential parts of ourselves by being overly concerned for others?

BRING IT TO LIFE!

Notice today what you give to and for others.
Is what you're giving enhancing or reducing your capacity to "breathe"
(or work, create, worship, rejoice, thrive, etc.)?
Will you choose yourself, others, or a life-giving equation of both?

"Sometimes we all need a little bit of random."

SJK

THE TIME I ALMOST DIED

I keep a running list in my iPhone of possible writing topics, so this morning I went to that trusty list for ideas and saw "And then there was the time I almost died." ✎ I have no idea what I meant there: no time (that I'm aware of!) that I almost died, no metaphorical or allegorical meaning I could remember, and no connection whatsoever to anything that made sense to me. ✎ But you know what? It made me laugh. The randomness of that sentence and my utter at-a-loss confusion made me laugh. ✎ Sometimes we all need a little bit of random, something that makes us go HUH? stop in our tracks, and maybe even laugh. ✎ So I'm sharing my random "And then there was the time I almost died" with you. Randomly.

BRING IT TO LIFE!

Today, look for "random" — anything that stops you and makes you say, "Huh?!"
Just because.

"I felt your beauty last night in the dark, deep stories hidden in the braille of your leaves."

SJK

TO THE GARDEN AT NIGHT

I call "secondary senses" the senses which are not most natural to me. One night I took a tour of my garden, using my secondary sense of touch instead of sight.

I felt your beauty last night in the dark
deep stories hidden in the braille of your leaves
a new you unread until I touched you
in my garden tour, lights out, stars too dim to offer view
just the gift of (temporary) sight removed
nudging a different sense into action
a finger stroll through your twigs, stalks, the other parts
ignored when sight takes the lead.
Nerve endings reached out grateful to exercise in a new way
sensing green in the ridges buttered orange in the smooth
tactile hues of your natural essence like vapor infusing my heart
with the plea to remember remember this part of me tomorrow when your sight
keeps your hands in your pockets unused in your daylight tour of my being.

BRING IT TO LIFE!

See a tree, flower, or other plant with your sense of touch today, instead of vision.
What do you notice through touch that you didn't notice when using sight?

"We have the power to turn down the world's volume."

SJK

TURN DOWN THE VOLUME

When I was younger, my brother used to turn the stereo volume all the way down at the appropriate times so I wouldn't hear any swear words in the lyrics. We used to laugh with every brother-induced gap in sound, but it became such a habit that I'm still surprised when those words now slip through when I'm listening to the songs he used to censor for me. We don't often have the reinforcement of a creatively caring brother to help us turn down this world's volume — whether it's filtering out a word or two, or turning the pace and noise of life down a few notches — but we do have the power to turn down the volume ourselves. Is there too much social media noise tromping on the quiet voice of your inner wisdom? Are you turning up the volume on resentment when it needs to be turned down so compassion can be heard? Is the sound of life's delicate notes getting drowned out by the shouts of your To-Do list? Choose today to monitor your own healthy volume.

BRING IT TO LIFE!

Pay attention closely today to the volume of your life, both literally and figuratively.
Notice how many sounds you take in at any given time
and which ones you choose to turn up or turn down.
Are there any volume changes you'd like to make?
If so, take one step in that direction today.

"Perhaps the gray of the external world
allows us to see our own internal sunshine more clearly."

SJK

RAINY DAY SUNSHINE

Woken gently by the soft sound of steady rain, my heart expands hopefully as my spirit wakes into joy. My usual morning lethargy is quickly washed away by the rain, and I immediately feel the pull of my writing space, knowing the words will be there waiting for me as the raindrops water the world around me. ✎ What is it that takes the gray dampness of a rainy day and turns it to gold in my veins and wraps its comfort similarly around others who engage in mindful and creative activities? ✎ Perhaps the gray of the external world allows us to see our own internal sunshine more clearly. Perhaps the outside shadows prompt us to find and bathe in our own glow. Perhaps the sky-produced waters become a conduit that allows us to touch the divine electricity within.

BRING IT TO LIFE!

The next time it rains, pause to turn your attention inward and notice your own qualities
of warmth and light. If you already have a comforting relationship with the rain,
express your gratitude, either verbally or in writing.
If you have a contentious relationship with rain, set aside 10 minutes of after-dark time,
and from a darkened room, watch the rain slide down a window for five minutes. Notice each
raindrop, and allow your breathing to deepen as you watch. After five minutes of focusing
on rain, take five more minutes to write a list of your qualities of "internal sunshine."
Repeat this exercise each time it rains, and notice any impact on your relationship with rain.

"Let's instead let it be simple: let us believe, think, and act in love."

SJK

LET IT BE SIMPLE

During the early stages of my coming out process as a lesbian, I participated in email discussions on a listserv for gay and lesbian Brethren Mennonites. I've since chosen a different spiritual path, but back then we wrestled with our understanding of scriptural guidance in light of our homosexuality. ✍ One particular discussion stands out clearly in my mind — the debate of what our role as followers of Christ called us to do regarding judgment, particularly now as people who were quickly judged and condemned as sinners ourselves. I suggested that perhaps the only job we had was to follow the example of love, without judgment or labeling of sin. One participant pushed back, "But isn't that too simple?" ✍ We complicate so many things in our lives, especially when it comes to religion, with interpretation of doctrine tying our brains (and eventually our hearts) into knots. ✍ Let's instead let it be simple: let us believe, think, and act in love — simply.

BRING IT TO LIFE!

Write "Let it be simple — let it be love" on a sticky-note,
and keep it where you will see it throughout the day.
Notice moments where your thinking or feeling gets complicated,
and remind yourself to "Let it be simple," asking, simply, "What would love do?"
Then do that.
How does this impact your experience today?

"It's not a rush; it's the pace of art."

SJK

THE PACE OF ART

One morning while writing in a coffee shop, I had the treat of overhearing the shop owner training a new barista on how to create latte art. "It's not a rush; it's controlled. It's not a rush!" There, like a little calm island in the midst of the morning rush, they stood, carefully teasing swirls of rich, chestnut-brown espresso through the white-capped latte foam. Perhaps we could all benefit from applying this approach to our lives. It's not a rush; it's the pace of art.

BRING IT TO LIFE!

Today, when you find yourself rushing through any activity,
stop, tell yourself, "It's not a rush," and slow your speed to the pace of art.
How does that change of pace impact your experience?

"In the confusion, there is grace."

PAMELA SLIM

IN FAVOR OF FALLING APART

Creative and life blocks happen: a mix of emotional complexities puts kinks in our flow, and inspiration, forward movement, and even hope come to a screeching, burning-rubber scented halt. ⤳ Maybe some days we just need to fall apart. ⤳ Maybe in the falling apart, we will find the grace to let go, followed by the strength to rebuild and a new storehouse of courage, faith, and trust.

BRING IT TO LIFE!

What does "falling apart" look like for you?
Do you allow yourself this freedom?
Tuck that possibility in the back of your mind for the next time you are at a loss,
blocked, or utterly confused.

"We can choose to pause life, even if only for a moment,
to get some water, then hop back into our storyline."

SJK

PAUSE THE BOOK

Although my twin niece and nephew are growing up in the digital age, they still enjoy old-fashioned, hard-copy books, printed on real paper, with real pages that make a shuffling noise when you turn them. ⟿ One evening I was savoring being part of their four-year-old, bedtime story reading routine, when Jared pushed himself off my lap, saying, "Pause the book! Pause the book — I need some water!" It took a few seconds for his request to sink in as I made the connection between this physical book and the digital command ... and then we burst out laughing. Of course it made sense to him to say pause the book! ⟿ We now use that phrase in our household like a magic button. If we need to take a break from any activity, we say, "Pause the book!" If we want the other person to pay attention, we say, "Pause the book!" If there's just too much going on and we need a rest, we say, "Pause the book!" ⟿ Because in reality, we can choose to pause life, even if only for a moment, to get some water, then hop back into our storyline.

BRING IT TO LIFE!

Today, when you find you need a break, say to yourself (or out loud),
"Pause the book!" and then simply pause.
No excuses, no justifications, just "Pause the book," and give yourself what you need.
When you're ready, the "resume" button will be right there.

"Some might call this all coincidence, but to me,
each of those butterfly moments is a divine kiss."

SJK

BUTTERFLY BLESSING

We planted new window boxes at the front of our city home, and as I finished watering them, a butterfly flitted over, rested for a moment on a deep red, geranium petal, then moved on. This butterfly blessing used to happen frequently during my years as a suburban landscaper — I'd finish a new planting, and a single butterfly would alight on a flower near me for a moment as if to say, "Yes, this is good, this is good," then fly off. I've been thrilled to see the same butterfly blessing here in our urban environment: even though butterflies are less frequent day-to-day visitors, one has stopped by after each of our planting sprees to christen the setting as a nature-approved environment. Some might call this all coincidence, but to me, each of those butterfly moments is a divine kiss, a reminder that as we put energy into our life-affirming intentions and attentions, Someone/Something's got our back.

BRING IT TO LIFE!

Go through your day today looking for a "divine kiss" — evidence that you're supported
in this world, even if you're not sure you even believe it.
At the end of the day, reflect on your "divine kiss" experience(s)
by writing down notes.
What did you notice?

"We can see something else, something deeper,
through the eyes of our heart."

SJK

THROUGH THE EYES OF YOUR HEART

At our friends' home during a vacation trip to Canada, I sit with the cool breeze dancing around my bare ankles, a lacy warmth of sunshine kissing my calves as Ambre McLean adds a musical frame to the picturesque morning scene — and my heart opens like a time-lapse video of a flower in bloom. As I look up from my notebook, I realize I no longer see only the surface of my surroundings; I'm now seeing something else, something deeper, through the eyes of my heart: my wife checking her iPhone is love personified, the garden phlox is a purple-gowned princess reverently holding court, the woven rug is an offering of comfort, the clouds a gentle protection from the vastness of infinity, and my pen waits to write a letter from God. Open the eyes of your heart, and waken your soul.

BRING IT TO LIFE!

Set a timer and take five minutes to sit quietly. Close your eyes and breathe deeply.
On the first in-breath, silently say the word "love" to yourself. On the out-breath, say,
"compassion." Repeat, with "love" on the in-breath, then "compassion" on the out-breath.
After five minutes of breathing love and compassion, open your eyes. With this renewed
awareness of your heart, continue with your day, and notice how deeply you are able to see.
Can you see a deeper green in the leaves? A gentler heart in the brusque stranger?
A modern marvel in the golden-domed architecture of a nearby church?
What do you notice when you are able to see through the eyes of your heart?

"When we fill a space of love with love,
we give grace an irresistible home."

SJK

THE SPACE OF LOVE

I spend exercise, meditation, and writing time most mornings clearing the gunk and cobwebs from my internal space to make way for those divine elements that carry me though each day: things like patience, faith, joy, trust, and love. I know deep down that those rituals are essential to my overall health and wellbeing, yet I still at times neglect them, figuring I'll just push through the day and be totally fine. Then the anxiety starts building, and my focus scatters to the whims of any moment as I attempt to add some balancing force against the knots and doubts and gremlins moving into my inner world. It plays out just as Gurumayi Chidvilasananda reminds us, that if we don't fill the space of love with love, that space will be filled by something else. When we fill a space of love with love, we give grace an irresistible home. What will you choose to fill your space with?

BRING IT TO LIFE!

Set aside 10 minutes. Clear a physical space (small or large, you choose) in your home, and, in that space, put the word LOVE. It can be a simple sticky-note, an index card with LOVE drawn out in some way, or any other way you choose to display the word LOVE.
Commit today to keeping that physical space clear and filled with LOVE.
Note how this perspective impacts your day.

*"Our inner life remains incomplete unless we are willing to exuberantly honor
the external evidence of the divine in the world around us."*

SJK

DIVINE DISTRACTION

In Madeleine L'Engle's book *Love Letters*, we spend time in a convent watching the interactions of the nuns. One of the younger nuns is unsettled by an older nun's tendency to indulge in sensory experiences, like savoring the juicy pulp of an orange or allowing the colors of a sunset to move her heart. The younger nun's concern was that these would be distractions from the "true" spiritual work of inner contemplation. The older nun responds that being able to experience the varied beauty of the external world through our senses also counts as an experience of God.   Yes, internal focus, contemplation, the study of various spiritual texts, and times of deep, inner quiet are important parts of a conscious life, but our inner life remains incomplete unless we are willing to exuberantly honor the external evidence of the divine in the world around us.

BRING IT TO LIFE!

Set aside five minutes to eat a peach when you don't need to worry about the mess or how you appear. Experience eating that peach with as many senses as possible: see and feel the juice flow, listen to the slurp, taste the sweet nectar and bitter peel, feel the fuzzy skin and soft, sticky, inner juiciness. Lick the rough pit, and carefully feel the sharp point on its end as you inhale the deep, fruity scent. When finished, notice how you feel. *What is your heart doing? Breathing? How aware of your senses are you? If those five minutes were a distraction, is it possible that they were a divine distraction of value to your day and inner experience?*

"At a time when our standard resources fail us,
and nothing tangible nudges us toward the side of life,
we can grab onto a morsel of faith."

SJK

WHAT DOESN'T KILL YOU

Depression is very real, very serious, and, in some cases, even deadly. ✎ Perhaps it's the severity of this disease that makes surviving it one of my most hopeful situations ever, and gives me such a profound appreciation of the saving power of faith. ✎ When we experience the excruciating depths of darkness (whether in ourself or someone near us), we can choose to give up and stop life ... or we somehow find the faith to believe — even if just for a moment — that things can change and that the next breath might bring relief. ✎ At a time when our standard resources fail us, and nothing tangible nudges us toward the side of life, we can grab onto a morsel of faith, as small as a mustard seed, and hold on through one more minute, just long enough to choose life. ✎ What doesn't kill us does indeed make us stronger, for it gives us faith — the bedrock of hope, and ultimately, life.

BRING IT TO LIFE!

Where in your life might applying a grain of faith help strengthen you?
What would it take for you to give that situation one more dose of faith,
a few more minutes of believing?
Do that today.

OCTOBER

"Every moment is a little death, and every next moment a little life.
In this way, we create our lives by choice."

SJK

RESURRECTION

It doesn't matter so much whether you believe the biblical resurrection story as a literal happening or as a metaphor (or neither); the truth within it is the same: we have the capacity to start anew. ⮑ In any moment we can choose to start again. It might take time to get the logistics of life in alignment with that new start, but the very moment we decide to start again, the resurrection process has begun. ⮑ We must also remember that the resurrection process isn't all sunshine and sandalwood — that death of the current situation is often required in order to make way for the new infusion of life. ⮑ No wonder we balk at change, hang back from transformation, and choose (consciously or not) to tolerate less-than-meaningful living: in doing so, we don't have to put anything to death. ⮑ But in doing so, we also miss out on Life. ⮑ Every moment is a resurrection — what will you bring to life?

BRING IT TO LIFE!

Think about what you want to bring to life, then what needs to "die"
in order for that to happen.
Take 10 minutes to write a description of what you want to bring to life,
then choose one step (as small or large as you wish) that you can do today
to give that new situation life.
What would it take for you to take one more step each day toward your new situation?

"From within a broken heart, we have access
to the light of self-compassion, new understanding,
and a tenderness borne from the wound."

SJK

FROM WITHIN A BROKEN HEART

I, like many of us, spend plenty of time trying to avoid experiencing a broken heart. I've been there before, and it almost killed me (literally), so I'm not keen to spend time there again. It occurs to me, though, that I actually live little versions of a broken heart almost daily: expectations not met, judgments I make against myself, assumptions I make of others' negative impressions of me, or even an experience of beauty too intense to contain within my heart. I try to avoid that breaking, yet, when I'm looking out though a heart crack, I remember it's from within that broken heart that I have access to the light of self-compassion, new understanding, and a tenderness borne from the wound. At our deepest level, from within a broken heart is a way we can see God.

BRING IT TO LIFE!

Next time you feel that crack in your heart (is there one there now?),
step inside and take a look out.
What are you able to see from within that broken heart?
Write it down, and keep it nearby
to remind you that even a broken heart holds great gifts.

"Some would have sacrificed the tree to get the fence they wanted,
but these folks instead saw the potential in the current situation
and created a work of art with nature."

SJK

WORK FROM WHAT IS

Each time I passed a particular tree on my neighborhood walks, I would stop to stroke its trunk and whisper, "Hello my dear!" The answering tingle in my fingertips pulled at my heart as I'd see this gorgeous pear tree straining against a way-too-close fence that rubbed the tender bark with each breeze. ➛ Then one day the fence was new, with a framed cut-out carefully designed to allow the tree its natural growth — a unique feature that also made the fence exquisitely beautiful. Some would have sacrificed the tree to get the fence they wanted, but these folks instead saw the potential in the current situation and created a work of art with nature. ➛ When we work from the current reality of "what is," we give ourselves the chance to engage creatively with a situation and find even more beautiful solutions than we thought possible.

BRING IT TO LIFE!

If you come across a situation today that seems hopeless or even just less than ideal,
look closely at what is available to you in that moment.
What can you do when you work from "what is" instead of "what I wish it was"?

"If we believed that every part of our lives is divine,
how would that change us?"

SJK

DISGUISED AS YOUR LIFE

Paula D'Arcy suggests that God comes to us disguised as our lives. If we believed that every part of our lives is divine (in whatever form or concept resonates with us), how would that change us? Might we love everyone and everything more fully? Might we care for each blade of grass and every weed, and kiss the limb of every tree we meet? Might we learn tenderness and strength, and use them both with a gentleness we've never felt before? If God is our lives, how does that change us?

BRING IT TO LIFE!

Approach today as though every part of your life is divine.
At the end of the day, reflect on how this perspective impacted your actions,
thoughts, feelings, and interactions with others.

"Those pains and restless confusion are our internal request
for a pause to allow our inner goo to gain strength."

SJK

GROWTH SPURTS

I was acutely aware of my growth spurts as a kid because they usually involved pain. Bone-deep aches woke me at night, and in high school, leg pain from microscopic bone fractures kept me off my beloved basketball court for a couple weeks. Apparently I was growing too fast, and my body needed time to catch up to itself. Now, fully grown (and beyond), I'm recognizing those growth spurts in my emotional and spiritual self: they hurt, and they sometimes sideline me, leaving me weak and vulnerable, tiptoeing around inside myself until I can put emotional weight back on my heart and soul. That vague, emotionally foggy feeling and a scale heavy on the side of questions but light on answers is often just our growth spurts: cracks, fissures, and joints beautifully weakened to allow a fuller expansion of our inner growth. Those pains and restless confusion are our internal request for a pause to allow our inner goo to gain strength — so it can solidify into a more firmly developed version of ourselves. It's just a growth spurt; give yourself some time to catch up.

BRING IT TO LIFE!

Next time you experience a general restlessness, or the frustration of not enough answers
to your questions, or the pain of any sort of emotional cracks, consider the possibility
that it's a growth spurt symptom.
What are you in the midst of learning? What transition are you in?
What extra strength will you have when this growth spurt is complete?

"We can choose. We can take back time."

SJK

TAKE BACK TIME

It's an odd little creature, this thing we call "time." Many days we're just trying to "find time" to get everything done — hurrying scurrying racing from one thing to the next, exhausting ourselves, and lamenting our lack of time. Yet, as children, time stood still, like the days I lost track of time for hours with my friend Becky while floating sticks down a rainwater stream, or looking for fool's gold in the driveway stones, or making teeny bows and arrows from twigs and rubber bands. What makes the difference in our view of time? The activities we are doing, the mood we are in, and the amount of things we have scheduled into our day; all things which we actually have control of. We can choose. We can take back time.

BRING IT TO LIFE!

What did you do as a kid that made time seem to stand still?
How can you bring that same feeling back into your life today?
Do that activity today.

"Those morning rituals, when poured full of gratitude,
can make all the difference in any day."

SJK

FRESH GROUND GRATITUDE

It almost makes me cry
the scent swirls of fresh ground coffee
so sweet the crush
as I smell the deep brown
from their little roasted bodies happily
sacrificed
to my morning
energy.

One of my morning rituals is a fresh cup (or two) of coffee, savored, appreciated, and even, (dare I say it?) loved. Those morning rituals, when poured full of gratitude, can make all the difference in any day. Honor them.

BRING IT TO LIFE!

Do you have a morning ritual that starts your day with gratitude?
If so, pay special attention to it today, appreciating its place in your life.
If not, what is one thing you can add to your morning that would boost your
gratitude quotient for the morning? Start that today.

OCTOBER 8

"Let's honor our inherent connection to the natural world
with more regular face-to-face interaction with nature,
not just the chemical replications thereof."

SJK

YOUR LIVING ROOM ORCHARD

According to Diane Ackerman in her book *A Natural History of the Senses*, people of almost all nationalities have a need to surround themselves in their homes with the scent of pine or lemon on their floors and walls. What does that say about our inherent connection to nature? And our longing to keep that connection close? Let's honor that connection more often in our lives with regular face-to-face interaction with nature, not just the chemical replications thereof.

BRING IT TO LIFE!

Buy a lemon today, cut it open, and gently inhale the fresh lemony scent.
Repeat throughout the day as feasible.
What do you notice when you breathe in the natural lemony fragrance?

"You can go anywhere on a stream of music."

SJK

ON A STREAM OF MUSIC

Sitting at a local hipster coffee shop, I was captivated by their cello music soundtrack: first because it connected me to my cello-playing sister, then because I was carried away on the stream of music.   Without even noticing it at first, I started feeling the rich cello notes as liquid emotion, hearing the sound of water in each vibrant stanza, following the current of music swirling around my heart. The plucked notes appeared in my mind's eye as crystal clear droplets of water breaking gently free as the water in the music stream splashed over rocks in a sun-dappled forest stream. ✎ Those few minutes of instrumental music took me away from my immediate environment and sat me down by a forest stream, complete with the sound of trickling waters and the scent of pine and new leaves, filling me with the easy energy of a summer afternoon in the woods. ✎ You can go anywhere on a stream of music.

✎

BRING IT TO LIFE!

Set aside 15 minutes today to listen to instrumental music,
and let it transport you to wherever it wants to take you.
After you "return," write a description of what you experienced while listening to the music.
Include anything you imagined or felt during that time.
How might this practice positively impact the areas of your life
where you most need a positive change?

"Truth transcends."

SJK

TRUTH AND TRANSCENDENCE

I've always hated practical jokes, and believe me, I seldom hate anything. If you want to see a furious me, play a practical joke on me. I admit, I could stand to lighten up there in the spirit of good fun, but this goes deep.  My parents always told the truth. In fact, they didn't play practical jokes because that was too close to lying. They didn't often communicate with me deeply or intimately, but they told the truth, and I knew without a doubt I could trust their words — completely and always. Practical jokes, then, are to me a betrayal of trust. In those painfully imperfect relationships, trust offered a deep, healing connection that transcended the gaps. Lies, of any perceived size or severity, diminish a relationship. Truth, on the other hand, transcends.

BRING IT TO LIFE!

Today, notice every word you say, and ask yourself, "Is this truth?"
At the end of the day, note your observations.

OCTOBER 11

"Mutually beneficial acts are the best!"
TINA BURKHOLDER

50 PERCENT

Up early at a beach writing retreat, watching the sun rise with four other women friends, our quiet conversation brought up a bit of WIDE AWAKE wisdom that I needed to capture for this book. I mumbled that I needed my notebook but didn't want to have to go get it, so my friend jumped up, saying, "Where is it?" as she went to retrieve it from my night-stand. ✍ When she returned, I thanked her profusely, noting how kind it was of her to sacrifice a few moments of the sunrise to retrieve my notebook. "Well," she admitted, "it was only 50 percent for you — I also needed to get my journal, so it was also 50 percent for me." ✍ Mutually beneficial acts: conscious caring for our self and another. Consider the possibilities.

✍

BRING IT TO LIFE!

Pay close attention your actions today.
What percentage of self-care vs. other-care do you notice?
Is that the percentage that most generously serves both you and the other?
If not, what is one step you can take to shift that percentage closer to where you want it?
Do that TODAY.

"Turns out that struggle and explicit understanding
aren't requirements for wisdom and growth; we can get that in the letting go."

SJK

DETANGLING

I've long been an intellectual grappler. I've loved pouring out evidence into my journals and engaging with analysis of my inner-goings-on, yanking the end of a feeling thread until it knots ... then pulling even more by applying additional analysis and intellectual reasoning. ✎ Then I'll pull the next thread until it knots, study every angle, and get even more tied up. I repeat this process until frustration gets high enough that I give up the "figuring out" and just stop, still holding onto that tangled mess of intellect and emotion. ✎ I've discovered, however, that life detangles much more easily if I start with the letting go instead of ending with it. When the analysis starts to get knotted? Say, "You know what? Nothing to figure out here; it just is," and breathe into release. ✎ Turns out that struggle and explicit understanding aren't requirements for wisdom and growth; we can get that in the letting go.

BRING IT TO LIFE!

Pay attention to the thoughts and issues that you keep thinking about
and analyzing in your life. Practice taking a deep breath and letting go
of the need to understand and struggle. Then practice again. And keep practicing.
What happens over time as you are able to let go more easily?

"What's your inspiration equation?"

SJK

INSPIRATION EQUATION

On Friday mornings, I wander my urban neighborhood, keeping an eye out for a random inspirational place to do some writing. This morning I was drawn to the edge of a nearby public park: partially tended plantings clustered around a low stone bench made of deconstructed brewery pillars, and a wall mural, stop signs, and structures covered in climbing ivy sprawled behind me.   It wasn't a standard representation of beauty, yet to me it was a perfect spot for gathering energy and expressing it through writing. For me, outside + natural elements + real life = inspiration. What's your inspiration equation?

BRING IT TO LIFE!

Take five minutes to write a list of elements that help provide
an environment of inspiration for you.
As you go through your day today, keep the list with you, and notice
any other things that add a feeling of inspiration to a space, nudging you
to soak in the energy and express it in some way.
How might you use this list at times when you're feeling uninspired or lack energy?

"When we learn that our own discomfort is bearable,
we eventually realize that the discomfort of others is also bearable."

SJK

(DIS)COMFORT

I used to think meditation was meant to put us in a zenned-out state to give us a place to rest. Bliss. The thrill of nothingness. A singular, individual experience of pleasure, paradise, and peace. That's all part of why I meditate, yes, but there's another incredibly important reason — to practice tolerating discomfort. Sitting quietly when my mind wants to race over my To-Do list? Discomfort. Paying attention to what's going on in my body when the meditation mat brings tears? Discomfort. Staying put when I'd rather pace restlessly around grief or fear? Discomfort. Something amazing happens when we "sit with" the discomfort: it fades. Discomfort somehow dissolves into the silence, dispersing throughout the space we create through the still time of meditation, soon fading also even in our "off the mat" life experiences. But there's more. When we learn that our own discomfort is bearable, we realize that the discomfort of others is also bearable. We can hear their pain and feel their confusion, fear, and sorrow and still be able to really listen, because we know we can handle discomfort. In that space of togetherness, our discomfort fades and we exchange a gift of peace.

BRING IT TO LIFE!

Think about something uncomfortable, and willingly feel it. Set a timer for 10 minutes and sit quietly. Notice what you feel, taking in deep breaths and breathing out into your discomfort. Continue to notice with as little thinking as possible. Notice how this impacts your discomfort. *How might you use this when in the presence of another person's discomfort?*

OCTOBER 15

"When we care fully — pay attention on behalf of one another —
the mundane gains meaning, apart comes together, and it all starts to matter."

SJK

CARE FULLY

"They just came out of the oven," the barista said, pointing to the scones in the midst of what looked like a stressful morning behind the coffee shop counter. She didn't have to tell me that, and I didn't have to care, but she did ... and I did ... and the connection of that moment made the morning matter. When we care fully — pay attention on behalf of one another — the mundane gains meaning, apart comes together, and it all starts to matter. Care fully. Love fully. Live fully.

BRING IT TO LIFE!

Bring your full caring to everything you do, say, think, and feel today.
How does this impact your day?

"The way we see our world impacts the way we respond to it."

SJK

ORDER

The more time I spend in the city, the more I find myself tuned into the geometry in the world around me: straight-line shadows intersect at right angles as sunshine pours through a wrought iron fence; the corner angle of a rooftop edge slices through soft blue sky; the diamond patterns of a chain-link fence keep me a protective distance from the tender tulips bravely standing amid the urban noise and bustle.   We humans tend to find comfort in order, in things being in line and in a row (ducks or other), and in patterns. Perhaps that's why in a hectic environment the visual geometry stands out: our eyes are searching for order to reassure us that we have some level of control and can know what to expect next based on certain patterns. The way we see our world impacts the way we respond to it, so next time you're feeling uncertain, fearful, or nervous about next steps, look for the visual order in your world, and drink it in until your cells relax.

BRING IT TO LIFE!

Look for geometry in your environment throughout the day today,
anywhere and everywhere you are.
Notice how you feel when you've been paying attention to visual order all day.
*How might you integrate this focus into your daily life
to help sustain a healthy level of calm?*

"Each moment of an open heart is a risk,
and a potential for deep, life-changing healing."

SJK

OPEN-HEART SURGERY

My father, my aunt, and my father-in-law have all had open-heart surgery, and they all reported that the experience shook their foundation. This surgery puts a person face-to-face with their own mortality, apparently a deeply profound experience of full-being (physical, emotional, and spiritual) vulnerability. 🖎 Although certainly a difficult procedure, this open-heart surgery also had a beautiful side effect in the healing: the vulnerability included in the rebuilding process incorporated a new combination of strength and tenderness in their approach to life and relationships. 🖎 Open-hearted living works the same way: deep vulnerability opens our chest and shakes our core at times, yet, each time we rebuild, we get a little braver in allowing ourselves to heal with strong threads of tenderness safely reinforcing any new wounds. 🖎 Each moment of an open heart is a risk ... and a potential for deep, life-changing healing.

BRING IT TO LIFE!

Think of a situation in your life that could benefit from you showing up
with a more open heart.
What are the risks (real and perceived)?
What are the rewards (real and perceived)?
What one step do you want to take today to change that situation?
Do that.

"We can touch the divine if we are simply willing to open our souls
to the possibility of mystical interconnections
of the world around and within us."

SJK

SHAMS TABRIZ

Jalaluddin Rumi, a teacher at a divinity college in the early 1200s, met a wandering mystic, Shams Tabriz, and his life was changed forever. From the deeply devoted love he experienced for and with Shams, Rumi poured out ecstatic poems showing the incredible depth and breadth of divinity woven inseparably into his very human experience. ⸎ Rumi surrendered his entire being to union with Shams, a longing which many Eastern religions identify as our longing for union with God, the divine, ourselves. ⸎ If only we all had a Shams Tabriz to open our door to God. But, actually, we can be our own Shams if we are simply willing to open our souls to the possibility of mystical interconnections of the world around and within us.

BRING IT TO LIFE!

Find and read some Rumi poems (in a bookstore, library, on the Internet).
As you read, don't concern yourself with intellectual understanding;
notice instead any shift in your body or feelings as you read.
Those are the shifts of your interconnection with Rumi and his words and his divine spirit.
Is it possible that we truly are all connected through our inner God?

"If you hear a voice within you saying, 'You are not a painter,'
then by all means paint ... and that voice will be silenced."
VINCENT VAN GOGH

JUST PAINT

We all get stuck. Stuck in a general lack of action even in our areas of most frequent enjoyment and inspiration. Stuck in a crippling mix of Doubt + Fear. ⤙ We doubt the value of our work and fear the possibility it won't be notable, so we do nothing. We doubt the importance of creating something new, and we fear the reactions to what we make public, so we do nothing. ⤙ Yet, when we finally just do the work, something shifts within us. Longings become sweet beliefs, and pain becomes the fire of exquisite beauty while our senses lose their heavy fog and become an endless supply of fuel for our soul. ⤙ What is your "painting" — that activity (as poet Rilke notes) that can give you purpose in the still of the night and the glare of the day? ⤙ One action is all it takes to get moving, so take that step, and just "paint."

⤙

BRING IT TO LIFE!

What activity of yours comes to mind as you read van Gogh's quote?
Take 10 non-negotiable minutes today to just do that activity.
Notice the effects.

"In the presence of sun after a rain, everything becomes diamonds."

SJK

LOOKING FOR DIAMONDS

They're not the ones in the jewelry store, those diamonds I always look for; they're the ones that appear outside: the priceless gems of light glinting richly off the raindrops kissed by sunlight after a light rain. ✑ On the tongue of a purple iris, the sun laughs against a water-drop and the wink catches my eye, spreading my grin as I join the festivities. ✑ Sliding smoothly down a fence wire, another drop catches the flash of the sun's spotlight like an escaping diamond thief, barely making it to safety in the ground's greedy recesses. ✑ The rose wears a raindrop crown, proudly reflecting the sun's majesty along the edge of its delicate forehead. ✑ In the presence of sun after a rain, everything becomes diamonds — we just need to look.

BRING IT TO LIFE!

Next time the sun shines after a rain (or in the morning dew), step outside
and look for "diamonds" for five minutes.
Notice every glimmer and sparkle, and try to pinpoint
the exact water drops reflecting the sun.
Notice how you feel after looking for nature's diamonds.

"What if we saw the world around us
as full of potentially trophy-worthy treasures?

SJK

EVERYDAY TROPHIES

She was the cutest little thing, bumping happily along in her stroller, her dad (I assume) pushing her along the rocky garden path. She had the most interesting look on her face — something between excitement and intense concentration — so I looked more closely, and realized she was carefully holding a clump of blooms. She was staring hard at that little bouquet while holding it out in front of her like she was showcasing a precious trophy. ✎ What if we approached life with that same appreciative fervor? What if we saw the world around us as full of potential trophy-worthy treasures?

✎

BRING IT TO LIFE!

Look for "everyday trophies" in your day today,
and when possible, showcase your findings.
How does this impact your view of your life and your environment?

"We all are part of life, together."

SJK

RELATIONSHIPS WITH EVERYTHING

Writer Natalie Goldberg tells of a friend who commented that Natalie has "relationships with everything" — people, objects, nature, you name it. It's because we are all part of everything, Natalie responds, and I absolutely agree. As I walk through a park, my soul greets everything in grateful connection: the blades of grass softening my step; the weathered picnic table waiting, with its deep purple strips of peeling paint, to host my morning writing session; the crumbling stone wall shoring up a flowerbed spilling over with wildflowers; the swing set playing hard with kids in the cool morning air — we all are part of life, together. Some might scoff at the notion that we humans can have a relationship with rock, for example, or the razor wire around the parking lots in the city. To that, I simply respond, try it and see.

BRING IT TO LIFE!

Today, pay close attention to your relationship with anything and everything.
Affirm your relationship with the tree on the corner by silently saying,
"Thank you for adding oxygen to our air."
Appreciate how the sidewalk offers a clear path for you to walk.
Admire the way rubber mulch on the playground pads the falls of our little ones.
Notice how this approach impacts your day.

"Giving doesn't work without a receiver."

SJK

RECEIVING

They were sharing a café breakfast, plus a cappuccino for him and an espresso for her, welcoming the day al fresco as the sun nudged the shadows into the alley. He stood up as she gathered her things and handed him a $10 bill. He made no move to accept it, shaking his head, "No," and anchoring his hands on his hips as he took a step backward. She reached out further, saying something I couldn't hear, her hands insisting he take the money as he continued to refuse it. Finally, she won the battle by tucking the money in his belt. He sighed with a small smile, moved the money to his back pocket, and they walked off into their day. Giving doesn't work without a receiver. Allow someone to tuck that gift into your heart right away so they don't have to resort to your waistband.

BRING IT TO LIFE!

The next time someone gives you something (a compliment, a smile, a wildflower from the woods, a gift of any sort), receive it with an open heart and full gratitude.
How does this impact your experience (and theirs)?
How might you apply this act of open receiving to your own self as giver and receiver?

"When the act of caring seems too big, just start small."

SJK

WAYS TO CARE

It was a grumbly sort of morning. For no apparent reason, I was having trouble finding the caring tone in my inner voice as I pushed my way reluctantly through my morning's work. "Your writing is bunk," my gremlins whispered, tossing out additional zingers like, "Why bother? It's no good anyway," and, "You don't matter to [fill in the blank] anyway, you know." Ouch. ✎ They say the way to feel something in particular is to offer it to someone else, but, honestly, I didn't have the energy to offer caring to some other person. ✎ Since work wasn't, well, working, I took a break to water the flowers out back. It was horribly hot and dreadfully humid, but as I gave each plant a cool drink, my heart expanded. My attention turned to their prolific display of brilliant blooms, and as water dripped on my bare toes, I realized what I felt was caring. Caring for the flowers that rely on me to keep them alive between rain storms. Caring for the natural artwork I've borrowed from nature's divine museum for my back patio "gallery." ✎ As soon as I realized the "I care!" feeling, I wrapped it lightly around me and dashed back inside to apply it to my work ... where it came out in my writing, then filtered easily into my client interactions. ✎ When the act of caring seems too big, just start small.

BRING IT TO LIFE!

Write a list of small acts of care — ones that take little energy
and help open your caring heart. Choose two acts of care and do them today.
How does this impact your interactions today?

*"What if we step to those outskirts and use that area
to applaud, collaborate with, question, grapple with,
and appreciate who and what we find there?"*

SJK

IN THE MARGINS

You can tell which books on my bookshelf mean the most to me by the number of markings in the margins: exclamations of agreement, questions, asterisks and stars, and names of people I'm reminded of or want to share a particular snippet with. The margins are where I laugh, question, applaud, collaborate, and appreciate — where my experience of the book goes beyond a mere reading of text and becomes a relationship. It's disturbing to me that margins can be such an important place in a book, yet, in our larger world the word denotes the place we push people and things to, that we deem unimportant, unworthy, or too different for acceptance and inclusion. What if we take our treatment of book margins and apply that to social margins? What if we step to those outskirts and use that area to applaud, collaborate with, question, grapple with, and appreciate who and what we find there — thereby enriching the whole scenario? What if the margins — outside of the main text – is where the real beauty and value awaits?

BRING IT TO LIFE!

Take five minutes to write about your treatment of the margins in books,
then another five minutes to write your thoughts about your treatment of social margins.
What do you notice?
Commit to having a brief conversation about margins today with a friend or colleague.

"We can offer molten love to this world and turn gray
from a lifeless blah to a soft, sweet comfort,
rumbling with the energy of compassion."

SJK

THE SOFT, SWEET GRAY

Writing on a cozy, rainy, summer morning, I was joined as usual by my precious, all-gray cat. She brought her sweet gentleness over to me in one big, fluffy ball of purring fur and a light meow of greeting, then flopped down to stretch her full, silken, rumbling self against my leg. ➳ As usual, my heart melted in the energy of her gentle oh so gentle soft sweet gray, and once again, I was reminded of the incredible power of deep gentleness — in our dear pets, yes, and also in humans. ➳ We can melt our own hearts when we cultivate a deep gentleness in ourselves. We can offer that molten love to this world and turn gray from a lifeless blah to a soft, sweet comfort, rumbling with the energy of compassion. ➳ Be the soft, sweet gray, the vibration of a rich purr that shakes the dust and brokenness from the incredible experience of the essence of life.

BRING IT TO LIFE!

If you have a chance to spend time with a gentle animal today, do so.
If not, simply imagine the experience of gentleness.
What does gentleness feel like to you? What does it look like? Act like?
Commit to sharing a few moments of gentleness today with yourself — in either action or intention, or both — and do the same in interaction with someone else.
How does this impact your day?

"We expect all this from the ocean,
so that's precisely what it gives us."

SJK

EXPECTATION

Watching people at the beach, I noticed something. As each person stepped off the walkway onto the sand, they stopped, scanned the ocean horizon, and took a deep breath before slowly walking toward the water. Many of us carry an expectation for our interaction with the ocean. We expect it will soothe us, transport us, and bring us home to ourselves through the rhythmic splash of waves and pull of the tide. We expect all this from the ocean, so that's precisely what it gives us. What if we expected more — in that same open, trusting way — of the "usual" experiences, places, and situations in our lives? What gifts might they give us?

BRING IT TO LIFE!

Take a moment to think of what you want for your day —
either from a particular situation, or from the whole day in general.
Maybe you want that upcoming meeting to go smoothly, or to be offered much-needed encouragement from the universe in some way or another.
Whatever it is, expect that today. At the end of the day, write down the evidence of your expectations playing out in some way, even if not in the way you expected,
and whisper a "Thank you."

OCTOBER 28

"Divine tenderness is waiting to hold us through every breath of life."

SJK

DIVINE TENDERNESS

I grew up in the hands of an often brusque and judgmental God. Sure, he was kind enough to me within the bounds of my utmost religious obedience to the Bible, but lacking in the deep warmth I longed for then — and still do. The difference these days is that I'm finding that divine tenderness not just in one God-figure but in a variety of ways; in the

touch of a friend,
gentle lick of a cat or dog,
gaze of a baby,
laughter of a colleague,
tears of a worshiper,
and in the evidence of prayers offered on my behalf.

When we can let go of our vision of a harsh and distant God, we can embrace the vision of divine tenderness that's waiting to hold us through every breath of life.

BRING IT TO LIFE!

What was your childhood experience of God, the divine, a higher power, spirituality, the universe, or whatever you call(ed) it? How is that experience different for you today?
Is there anything you still long for in your experience of the divine?
If so, look for evidence in any breath of life that your longing is being heard.

"All of these beings have become a part of my community
simply because we acknowledge each other's existence on a regular basis."

SJK

CREATING COMMUNITY

The workers gutting the house next door have become part of my daily routine: each time I leave the house, they smile and wave, and we genuinely wish each other a good morning or day. ⤸ The cat hanging out in the windowsill on Poplar Street greets me with a calico-faced meow most mornings as I trek to the gym. ⤸ Further down, on the other side of the street, the big, squooshy-looking cat sprawled out lazily on his windowsill usually can't be bothered to acknowledge me, but I still thrill each time I see him. ⤸ The diner employees taking their smoking breaks wave "Good morning, how are you?" through the clouds of smoke. ⤸ At the gym, we all share the zombie-faced, bed-headed look of the way-too-early workout crowd. ⤸ And that's all before 7:00 in the morning. ⤸ All of these beings have become a part of my community, not because we share a huge list of compatible qualities — or even belong to the same species! — but simply because we acknowledge each other's existence on a regular basis. ⤸ It doesn't have to take a huge effort to create community; it can be whatever and whomever we choose to offer a golden thread of connection to.

BRING IT TO LIFE!

Today, notice who you have chosen (or not chosen) as part of your community.
Is there something or someone you'd like to add?
Connect to them in any small way today.

"If you want me to love you now and forever,
learn exactly how I like my coffee."

SJK

CARING THROUGH COFFEE

If you want me to love you now and forever, learn exactly how I like my coffee: strong, with half-and-half plus raw sugar; the color of melted Mexican caramel and a sweetness that holds its own yet succumbs to the bold coffee flavor just as I swallow. Whether you learn my coffee specifics or not, chances are that if I first meet you during any event involving coffee or tea, I'll struggle to remember your name, but three months from now, I'll still know that you like your coffee black and medium-strong, with one packet of artificial sweetener (yellow packet preferred, then pink, then blue as last resort). Why? Because, to me, coffee preparation is a sacred ritual, so I care a lot about those details, and offer that same caring to others by in turn giving attention to one of their possible rituals. Caring through coffee, tenderness through tea?

BRING IT TO LIFE!

What is a detail in your life that you care deeply about?
Is there a way to expand that care to the same detail in others' lives?
What other detail can you consistently pay attention to in others' lives,
to offer them a different taste of caring?

"Honest seeing is what moves us from harmful neglect to active care."

SJK

WHETHER WE WANT
TO ACKNOWLEDGE IT OR NOT

It's easy for me to go out to my garden and look only at the healthiest specimens, drinking in the beauty of flourishing flowers in the most pleasing arrangements. Why bother looking at the slimy calla lily stem drooping brown over the container's edge, eaten off at the base and left to die? Why pay attention to the determined crop of weeds in one corner and the powdery mildew snuffing the health out of the honeysuckle vine? ⤺ Because it gives me practice in gentle and open seeing — a nonjudgmental look at the truth of the situation. It pains me to acknowledge an unhealthy plant in my well-cared-for garden, yet that honest seeing is what moves me from harmful neglect to active care. ⤺ Whether we want to acknowledge it or not, we each have the potential to do harm to those around us — and to ourselves. Practicing compassionate attention through the details of our everyday life teaches us how to look more openly and gently at the truth of our behaviors without defaulting to judgment. ⤺ Less judgment = more self-compassion = less harming = more love.

BRING IT TO LIFE!

Sit quietly for five minutes with eyes closed, and think of someone you love unconditionally. Feel that love as deeply as possible. Let that feeling remind you of your incredible capacity to love. Today, notice each detail of your life, thoughts, and behaviors through this love. Simply notice. No right or wrong, no judgment, no plans for fixing anything — just notice and apply loving compassion. How does this attitude impact your behavior?

NOVEMBER

"Touch is a bridge between our external and internal experience."

SJK

JUST A TOUCH

I wear a cologne called "Touch." I've considered changing scents over the years, but I'm not willing to let go of all that the name means to me and reminds me to be aware of. Touch has an incredible power: to nourish, provide comfort, communicate deeply, and on the darker side, to cause pain. It impacts the giver and receiver at exactly the same time — a shared experience of connection in a world tending toward isolation. It's no coincidence that our English language describes an emotionally impactful moment as "touching." Let's remember, too, that touch isn't just for human-to-human contact; it's for connection to all the textures and temperatures of our life experience: skin touching skin, fur, flower petals, and the invisible kiss of a soft spring breeze. Touch is a bridge between our external and internal experience. No wonder Burberry describes Touch cologne as "the essence of life!"

BRING IT TO LIFE!

Take a moment to become aware of your hands, especially the fingertips and palms.
Can you feel the energy there?
Touch five items around you, noticing for each touch what you feel in your hands,
and even deeper in your heart/emotions.
How is each touch similar? Different?
How might you use touch today to intentionally experience your world
in a more intimate and gentle way?

"When I hear the magical notes of delectable piano music,
my fingers tingle, my heart-beat deepens, and all my dreams seem possible."

SJK

MUSICAL MASSAGE

Piano note fingers
touch my soul's braille
sightless reading through
keys
of my internal sharps, flats
forte turns to
pianissimo
minor, major chords
kneading
a pressure point massage of my emotional knots.

BRING IT TO LIFE!

Take 15 minutes today to listen to music that "massages" your emotions
into relaxation.
Create a playlist of those songs, and label it "Musical Massage,"
so you can use it any time you're tense.

"Kindness is an act of attention as much as effort."

SJK

A DRINK OF WATER

I watched a lanky young man walk up to the coffee shop door, stopping briefly to loop his beagle's worn, green leash to the outdoor bench leg. Starting to open the door, he noticed a bowl of fresh water on the stoop and stepped back down to move it within reachable distance of his dog. A few minutes later, the dog was drinking sloppily from the bowl, his tail wagging appreciatively. The café owner paid attention through a simple bowl of water available for customers' dogs. The dog's owner paid attention by easily moving the bowl within reach of his dog. And I'm paying attention by simply bringing the story to this book, so you can pay attention to something you didn't even witness. That drink of water is such a sweet reminder that kindness is an act of attention as much as (more than?) effort. Consider the possibilities!

BRING IT TO LIFE!

Today, look for "drinks of water" (small acts of kindness born from attention),
and provide three "drinks of water" to the world around you in some way.
At the end of the day, write down the acts of kindness you remember,
including your own.
Which had the greatest impact on you and why?
Is this a practice you might consider doing more often?

"I've long believed that profound beauty and pain
are simply opposing ends of the same spectrum."

SJK

BEAUTIFUL BLUES

Listening to Eva Cassidy's song *Drowning in the Sea of Love,* I'm reminded of the beauty in the contrasts of blues songs. The mournful lyrics add to the deep cries of the instruments, yet the insistent rhythms pull us out to the dance floor of life to sway joyfully with the sorrows. ✎ I've long believed that profound beauty and pain are simply opposing ends of the same spectrum. The powerful interactions of the contrasting blues music components seem to support that theory, and offer us an example for life: in the midst of pain, we can add a drop of beauty to make the situation more palatable, and in the midst of beauty, we can allow a drop of pain to deepen the full experience. ✎ Beautiful blues: the full-spectrum moments in music ... and life.

BRING IT TO LIFE!

Listen to any blues song. Try Eva Cassidy's *Drowning in the Sea of Love*
if you need a suggestion. Note the contrast between the lyrics and the different parts
of the music. Also notice how the song overall impacts the way you feel.
Is it possible that beauty and pain can co-exist in a way that actually expands your life?
How might you experiment with that today?

"Because of that little dash of pleasure,
I remember chicken pox with a smile;
the itching and scratching and skeevieness of it all a distant whisper
to the flavor of the liquid in that little bottle of magic."

SJK

IN PRAISE OF PLEASANT

I, like many of us, had chicken pox as a kid: the full-blown itches and scabs and whole-being unpleasantness for what seemed like for.ev.er. Yet, what do I recall first when I step back to the memories of that time? The delicious nectar they called medicine. My god, it was amazing. It tasted like a liquid version of my most desired candies, and for a kid with quite the sweet tooth, that was outright heavenly! Because of that little dash of pleasure, I remember chicken pox with a smile; the itching and scratching and skeevieness of it all a distant whisper to the flavor of the liquid in that little bottle of magic. Is it a stretch to suggest that even as adults, we can be positively swayed by just a bit of pleasant? Ask my friend who sent me an email yesterday to report that she was carried through an incredibly stressful day by the sight of the photo she had just added to her desk — her young great-niece standing in a tiny swimsuit near the ocean.

BRING IT TO LIFE!

What are things or experiences you consider to be pleasant? Add one to your day.
Choose another of those, and add it to someone else's day.
What impact did those two actions make in your day?

*"A lifetime of practicing laughter may just be
what carries us through not only the moments of life,
but also the moments of death."*

SJK

DEATH IS (NOT) A LAUGHING MATTER

She could no longer speak in her last three days, but she could still laugh. ➤ Mom was never that great at connecting with us on a "let's discuss our deep feelings" level; we tended toward the intimacy of shared laughter instead. I guess it makes sense that's what we held onto then at her deathbed, weaving laughter through even the most painful moments. ➤ Miraculously, in her last days, laughter was one of the only recognizable sounds Mom could make. It was clear that she was cracking jokes even though she couldn't speak and could barely move. ➤ We gathered for three days around her bed, feeling the grief. Then, when it got too strong, we turned to laughter. We each tried to get Mom to finally admit our designation as The Favorite Child (to no avail). We ate ice-cream and drank coffee around her bed, intentionally dropping cookie crumbs on her legs in her last hours to honor her love of sweet treats. We laughed, oh, how we laughed together, even as tears poured. ➤ We certainly didn't build our laughter competency with death in mind, but it strikes me that a lifetime of practicing laughter may just be what carries us through not only the moments of life but also the moments of death.

BRING IT TO LIFE!

Today, simply find reasons to laugh ... and laugh some more!

"The question isn't whether it's necessary to revise,
but are we revising toward a deeper truth?"

SJK

REVISION

Poet Margaret Robison suggests that "the only purpose of revision is to get more deeply to the truth." Although she's speaking here of writing, it seems the same applies to life. ✎ We can revise our own selves time and time again, and if we get no closer to "the truth," maybe it's time to look more closely at our motivations for revision. ✎ Are we revising our outward appearance to squeeze into the style du jour, or to be outwardly more in alignment with our inner selves? ✎ Are we revising our spiritual practices to follow a list of shoulds, or to follow a deep longing for greater connection? ✎ Are we revising our jobs to gain status, or to practice more deeply our purpose? ✎ Revisions are the nature of growth (thank goodness). So the question isn't whether it's necessary to revise, but are we revising toward a deeper truth?

✎

BRING IT TO LIFE!

Think of a revision you might want to make in your own self or your own life.
Is that revision likely to take you toward a deeper truth, a greater understanding
of yourself or those around you?
If not, what revision might you instead make that could open a path
to deeper understanding and truth?

"You've got a looming deadline, commitments pressing,
and you're generally buying into the idea that you don't have time.
This creativity thing ... it makes time. Yeah ... it's that kind of magic."

Ellen Stoune

CREATE TIME

Time spent in creative endeavors tends to fall to the bottom of our priority lists. We don't stop to take photos because we are in a rush to just get somewhere. We don't paint, draw, or color unless some child in our lives insists we join them. We don't journal because we're too busy writing our next To-Do list. We don't sing and play our instruments because of an urgent deadline looming around the corner. ✍   We continue to yearn for time to do these activities that feed our souls, yet it turns out that creative acts actually (as Ellen Stoune notes) make time. Hard to believe, I know, but try it, because, "Yeah ... it's that kind of magic."

BRING IT TO LIFE!

Set aside 15 minutes today that you don't think you can spare.
Do any sort of creative activity, not worrying about skill level or results for even one second.
At the end of those 15 minutes, what has changed for you?
What might happen if you took these 15 minutes EVERY DAY, to feed your soul?

"She must still see with an ever gentle heart."

MARGARET GIBBS MCCAIN

SIGHT SHIFT

I suspect it's no coincidence that my nearly-blind cat is the one who joins me for meditation each morning while the sighted cat is usually off causing a ruckus somewhere else in the house. When her sight was better, this cat didn't show up very often during my meditation time, yet, as her sight deteriorated, her meditation time visits increased. Now, she is often sitting at my meditation mat before I am, waiting to start her purr as soon as I sit down. ⥅ I view this dear cat as my reminder that our inner vision is a powerful version of seeing; that although the gift of physical sight is incredible and valuable, it's the depth of inner sight that most strongly supports our entire lives. As my nearly-blind cat drapes peacefully over my crossed-legged lap, I am reminded to sit with my physical eyes closed and turn my attention inside: to what my body feels, to the space between each breath, and to the tangible feeling of divine energy that vibrates from my core to boost my belief. ⥅ In those moments when our eyes and attention are intentionally closed to the outside, we give ourselves the freedom be more wide awake on the inside.

BRING IT TO LIFE!

Take 10 minutes of quiet solitude today.

Set a timer, then sit with your eyes closed and focus your attention on your internal self.

When time is up, take a few minutes to jot down what you "saw" (felt, experienced) internally.

"Was it a caring act of love on their part? Who knows.
But that's the impression it left to greet all those passing by."

SJK

LEAVE AN IMPRESSION

Some of the sidewalk trees here in the city have little decorative fences around them, lining concrete squares cut out of the sidewalk to give the trees a little space to breathe as they stand guard in our neighborhoods day after day. This morning on my walk back from the coffee shop, a new ankle-height fence caught my eye, the fresh wood standing out on a gray, cloudy day against the cement landscape. If I hadn't stopped to take in the scene, I wouldn't have noticed the butterfly, but there it was: a small silver charm on a leather bracelet, tied loosely to one of the mini posts. There was no fanfare, and no obvious reasoning for that charm, but my heart lifted as I pictured someone gently draping the jewelry there. Was it a caring act of love on their part? Who knows. But that's the impression it left to greet all those passing by. What impression do you leave behind as you move from moment to moment in this life?

BRING IT TO LIFE!

Think for a few minutes about the impression you want to leave as you go through your days.
On a sticky-note, write a phrase that describes that impression.
Take that note with you today, and leave it at a place where others will see it.
Challenge another person in your life to do the same activity.

*"Our bodies naturally turn toward the light when we give them
the space in our busy schedules to reach toward the sun."*

SJK

PHOTOTROPISM

You've seen it in plants, the growth toward light. Put a flower pot on a windowsill, and what happens? The flowers turn their faces toward the sun, their little cheeks soaking in the nourishing light for growth.   Humans aren't all that different. Watch someone step outside after an extended period indoors, and what happens? They turn their face up toward the sunlight, soaking in the warmth, breathing in the oxygen, and expanding in the nourishing light.   Our bodies naturally turn toward the light when we give them the space in our busy schedules to reach toward the sun.   Make room for phototropism. Daily.

BRING IT TO LIFE!

Today, practice phototropism — turning toward the light.
Lift your face to the sun, breathe in the oxygen, and let yourself expand
in the nourishing light.
How does this impact your day?

"For some, it's holding space. For others, prayer. For all, a gift."

SJK

HOLDING SPACE

At the end of a phone call with a dear friend yesterday, she asked me, "What space can I hold for you over these next two weeks?" We coaches at times laugh a bit at ourselves for the "holding space" lingo, but I can tell you in that moment, the only thing I felt was pure love and support. With my heart wide open, I asked that she hold space for me to have confidence in my work and to feel the excitement of knowing I'll soon be finishing a huge project (this book). ✑ I then asked her the same question, "So what space can I hold for you?" She was quiet for a few moments, then explained that just receiving that question felt like such a gift — for someone to offer their energy on her behalf. ✑ I'm still thinking about that conversation today, knowing there's a space being held for me, and knowing too that I'm doing the same for someone else. ✑ For some, it's holding space. For others, prayer. For all, a gift.

BRING IT TO LIFE!

Take five quiet minutes and ask yourself, *"What space can I hold for you?"* Write down your answer to yourself. Commit to asking the same of one person you interact with today, choosing the language that feels most appropriate to you: *"What space can I hold for you? How can I best support you? What prayer might I whisper for you? What thoughts can I think on your behalf?* Write "holding space" on a sticky-note, and carry it with you today.

At the end of the day, reflect on the impact this exercise had on your day.

"Skidding in the damp grass, the dog grabbed the oversized stick, dashed back, and, dropping it at his human's feet, danced eagerly in full anticipation of the next throw."

SJK

EAGER

Although the leash was attached to his collar, the other end dragged freely as the cream-colored yellow lab raced after the stick his human playmate had just thrown. Skidding in the damp grass, the dog grabbed the oversized stick and dashed back, dropping it at his human's feet and dancing eagerly in full anticipation of the next throw. ✎ As I watched this display go on for quite some time, I found myself thinking, "Oh, to have that sort of eagerness in my life!" ✎ What would it take for us to experience that eagerness? Watching that dog, I'd say it takes full focus on full-faith anticipation of delight; full-bodied, full-being involvement in the present moment and meaningful interaction with no holding back. ✎ Let's find that oversized stick today and be the eager yellow lab — fully.

BRING IT TO LIFE!

What is something in your plans or To-Do list for today that you are feeling less than eager about?
How might you tweak your approach to this plan or task to allow you to bring eagerness to it? Do that today.

"As long as someone cares, there's hope
in this great big world of ours."

SJK

AS LONG AS SOMEONE CARES

There are days when almost everything in my world seems to be lined with rough sand-paper. I brush against a missed deadline and get a bright-red welt, or my words catch the rough patch of someone else's mood and we both feel the sting, or a life-changing loss leaves a burning scrape across my heart. It can all seem pretty useless at times, this living thing we do. ✍ And then someone cares. Someone sends a "thinking of you" note, or brings you cinnamon buns and coffee (and themselves), or offers some other perfect application of support ... and suddenly there's a salve to soothe our stings, scrapes, and burns long enough for us to heal. ✍ As long as someone cares, there's hope in this great big world of ours. ✍ We can practice by caring for the smallest tender flower in nature, or the easiest person to love in our lives ... then expand that caring to the more difficult areas of our city streets, the overwhelming disasters in a country so far from our own, and even to ourselves. ✍ As long as someone cares, there's hope.

BRING IT TO LIFE!

What do you care about?
Write it in a list, allowing yourself to feel the caring as you make your list.
What do you want to care about but find too difficult?
Make a separate list for those things, people, and situations. Choose something from this list, and find one step you can take to increase your caring in that area. Do that today.

*"No matter how many layers we add to ourselves over the years,
our divine core still remains. Under the layers, we always shine."*

SJK

UNDER THE LAYERS

Watching a time-lapse video of artist Laurie Maves creating a painting, I was surprised by the number of times she painted, drew, or chalked over what I had assumed was the final product. ⮑ The very first layer was a few words — lyrics from a song chorus — which she quickly drew over ... only to re-write the words on top of the mountain image she had just covered the same words with. She repeated this process numerous times: write, draw/paint over, re-write, draw/paint over, until something in her declared the painting complete. ⮑ No matter how many layers Laurie added to that painting, the initial foundation of meaningful words was still there in its original form (never mind that we could no longer see that first layer). ⮑ No matter how many layers we add to ourselves over the years, our divine core — that initial layer of meaning and value that we were created from, created with — still remains. No matter what, under the layers, we always shine, we always matter.

BRING IT TO LIFE!

Take 10 minutes of quiet writing time alone.
Write about the layers you've added to yourself over the years.
Then write about the purest core of you, that part that exists as your central foundation.
Take that core self image with you today, and note how it impacts your day.

"I pick up the scent of fresh mulch like a bloodhound on a trail."

SJK

BE THE BLOODHOUND

It took me several trips through a particular Philadelphia park over a span of two years to realize it was the same park I had spent several hours in during a pre-move "check out the city" visit. I wasn't confused because the park had changed (it hadn't); I was confused because my experience of the park had changed so significantly. ✎ During my first visit to that park, I was a suburban girl sitting nervously on that park bench, hearing cars more than birds and smelling city more than country, wondering fearfully, "Can I really be happy here?" Yet, two years later, now that I'm comfortable and familiar with the city, I hear birds more often than the background noise of city bustle, and I pick up the scent of fresh mulch like a bloodhound on a trail. The park is the same, but my attention sure is different! ✎ Our inner states (fear and nervousness, security and comfort) highlight things in our environment that confirm those feelings for us, and, thank goodness, vice versa, so we have the power to change our experience by where we put our attention. Be the bloodhound of your own experience — choose your "scent," and follow it to your desired experience.

BRING IT TO LIFE!

Afraid about a new step in your life?
Follow the scent of (pay most attention to) the parts that comfort you.
Bored with your current life?
Follow the scent of what interests you. Notice how this exercise impacts your experience.

"Our bodies allow us to ingest the world and make it a part of us,
securing the interconnected feeling that in some way we all long for."

SJK

FULL-BODIED EXPERIENCE

The older I get, the less I take my body for granted. I expected this change of perspective, but not the particular flavor that awareness has taken. Yes, I'm grateful that I can move freely (except for that shoulder issue I've had for years), and that I am in good health, but lately I'm becoming just as grateful for the miracle of how our bodies allow us to experience life through our senses. Our senses give us a physical way to interact intimately with our external worlds. Our bodies absorb scent molecules, stimulate nerve endings, manipulate light rays, vibrate those little drums in our ears, and gather information into receptor cells on our tongues — allowing us to smell, feel, see, hear, and taste our world. Our bodies, the physical representation of our individual human being, are what allow us to ingest the world and make it a part of us, securing the interconnected feeling that in some way we all long for. Yes, for all that, I bow down to my body, with my body, in deep gratitude for its invaluable gifts and service.

BRING IT TO LIFE!

Take five minutes to sit quietly and experience each of your senses, one at a time.
If you are missing one of your senses, experience whatever sense has become strengthened in its place. And with each sense, offer a whisper of thanks to your body: "I thank you for the sense of smell, for the sense of touch, for the sense of sight, for the sense of hearing, for the sense of taste." Make today a feast of sensory awareness.

"How we heal emotional wounds is not that different from healing our physical wounds."

SJK

HOW WE HEAL

I recently put a deep, sharp slice in that tender spot between my thumb and forefinger, learning the hard way that broken ceramic has wicked cutting power! It was an "Uh-oh, do I need stitches?" situation, but after applying every bandaging option in our medicine cabinet, I decided I could do this on my own. ✎ I learned quickly about wound care. It only took one time of grabbing something with that hand to realize that I needed to protect this wound at all times. And one time of opening that gap too far to realize I needed to avoid stretching that area. And one time of peeking under the bandage and poking gingerly at the wound edges to realize that testing the healing process too quickly was not a good idea. ✎ Plenty of learning, care, and gentle attention, and four days later, there's barely any sign of the cut, just a slight tenderness at the slice site. ✎ How we heal our emotional wounds is not that different from healing our physical wounds:

Protection: surround our selves with gentle caring.

Patience: stop picking at the edges.

Limits: don't stretch too far and ask too much of our sore spots.

Part miracle, part mindfulness, healing is a collaborative effort between us and our bodies; us and our spirits; and us and — as some might say — God.

BRING IT TO LIFE!

Do you or someone close to you have a physical or emotional cut?
How might you apply your collaborative effort to the healing process (your own or theirs)?

"We know we've heard our song from within when we're filled with surprise,
amazement, and a deep desire for more of that same experience."

SJK

SONG FROM WITHIN

The artist Robert Henri (1865-1929) suggests that at rare times we are given the gift of hearing "the song within us." Those are the moments, he says, when we manage to keep our intellect at bay and protect a safe space for our extremely sensitive internal song to play. ✎ We know we've heard our song from within when we're filled with surprise, amazement, and a deep desire for more of that same experience. It's a combination of feeling that begs for expression, and it's that feeling, says Henri, that compels artists to keep returning to their work and keep finding continued means for expressing that inner song. ✎ We call that "song" by different names (inspiration, God, inner wisdom, purpose, bliss, flow), and we create a protected space for it by engaging in moments of stillness, intense focus, or activities that spark a deep love in us. ✎ Let's stay awake to our song from within.

BRING IT TO LIFE!

Have you experienced what Robert Henri calls the song within you?
If so, write a description of that experience, touching on each of your senses: sight, touch, hearing, smell, taste, and intuition. If not, imagine your song within, and write a description of what you imagine. Today, as you go through your day, keep your attention open to hearing moments of the song within you.
How does this impact your day?

"Soft focus brings the unexpected into view."

SJK

SOFT FOCUS

Sharp focus

cuts

slices

separates

so soften it, smooth

out the edges and let it flow

while gentle light shines to center

mellow energy brimming

over from the core

connected vibrant inspired

gently contained

focus soft focus.

BRING IT TO LIFE!

Looking around you, stop at the first thing that catches your attention, and focus intently
on the smallest center of the object. Keeping your gaze on that center spot, take a deep breath
and relax your focus, looking instead at the periphery of the center spot.

What are you able to see when you relax your focus?

How might you apply soft focus to a current challenge in your life?

"Miscellany gives us a way to refer to that which we can't categorize ...
and in doing so, gives us permission not to categorize and not to label.

SJK

MISCELLANY

I sent an email recently to my sister, thanking her for paying such close attention to the details of our ridiculously large family: important dates, milestones, acknowledgements, and other miscellany. When she reported chuckling at the word "miscellany," I realized what a not only delightful, but also incredibly important word it is. Miscellany gives us a way to refer to that which we can't categorize ... and in doing so, gives us permission not to categorize, not to label, not to put everything in a neat little bucket that lumps similar things together in an indistinguishable mass. Miscellany allows us to look at an individual something and appreciate it for simply what it is, all by itself on its own, not by how it compares to something, or how it does or does not belong to a certain group, or how it relates to anything else. Miscellany allows for the treasures of individuality. Oh, what a breath of fresh air!

BRING IT TO LIFE!

Today, give your day the gift of appreciating miscellany —
those one-off items and experiences that just refuse to be categorized,
homogenized, or melded in with something else.
What do you notice?

"We can use our abundance to strengthen our souls to the point where we can
wrap our arms around anything, anyone, anytime,
and offer a moment of unconditional love, peace, and hope."

SJK

PLANT THE SEEDS

How can we swallow our own dinners when others are starving?
How can we cash our paycheck when others earn only what they beg?
How can we decorate our home when others live on the streets?
How can we tend our own lush gardens when others have only dry clay?
How can we give ourselves health, care for our souls, and play from our spirits,
when others have only hardship and survival on their minds?

We can plant the seeds of hope in our own lives, the seeds of love, of compassion, of empathy, and of deep, deep love. We can practice self-love so we can offer others love without needing anything in return. We can use our abundance to strengthen our souls to the point where we can wrap our arms around anything, anyone, anytime, and offer a moment of unconditional love, peace, and hope.

BRING IT TO LIFE!

What seeds are you longing to plant in your life?
What is one thing you can do to plant that seed?
Do it. Today. No guilt, no doubt, nothing but pure, determined hope.
Plant. Just Plant.

*"Amazing grace: the most of you, amplified,
and returned to you a thousandfold."*

SJK

AMAZING GRACE

Although I've always loved the music of the hymn *Amazing Grace*, I've equally cringed at its lyrics of "saved a wretch like me." A wretch was someone, I felt, who is an absolute mess and somehow unworthy at the core. So, although I felt the redeeming power of the four-part harmony singing to "We've no less days to sing God's praise," the feeling that stuck with me in relation to grace was, unfortunately, "wretch." ⤳ Years later, after hearing other people of various religious, spiritual, and ethnic backgrounds use the term "grace" enough times in a different way, I've realized a shift in my perspective on "grace." ⤳ Instead of grace being some barely-deserved fix to my deep, human shortcomings, it's become the light that shines on my wholeness. It's the kiss of the divine, the offering of strength from the universe, and the deep compassion that comes through those I work with, love beside, and live among. ⤳ Amazing grace: the most of you, amplified, and returned to you a thousand-fold. Amazing indeed.

BRING IT TO LIFE!

What is your understanding of "grace"?
Does it shore you up or tear you down?
If it's not what you want it to be, consider choosing a different perspective.

"It wasn't until later that I realized that 'impatience' and 'I'm patience'
have the same letters in the same order."

SJK

(IM)PATIENCE

Just before I was going to blow impatiently past a woman standing in the middle of the stairs leading down to the subway, she turned around, glanced at me, then turned her face to the sunshine, saying with a smile, "I'm not sure where to go ... It's just so nice out!" Turns out it was, indeed, so nice out. It wasn't until later that I realized that "impatience" and "I'm patience" have the same letters in the same order.

BRING IT TO LIFE!

When something slows you down today (as it most likely will!),
allow yourself to slow with it, even if only for a literal minute.
What happens for you, in your body and your thoughts, in that moment?

"It's in the pure stillness I find myself."

SJK

IN THE STILLNESS

February 15, 2011, excerpt from my spiritual journal

It's in the pure stillness I find myself.
Tears, heart, joy — missing. No, I have it ALL. Already there.
All it needs is my attention.

What if we do have it all? What if the only thing missing is our attention? Go to the stillness and find out.

BRING IT TO LIFE!

What part of you needs your attention today?
Give it 10 minutes of attention through stillness in whatever way works for you.
Go. Find yourself there.

"When routine starts to feel more like bored or lazy
or oh-dear-God-give me-something-different, it's time
to upset the proverbial apple cart and shake it up."

SJK

SNOW GLOBE IT

Routines are my friend. They provide security, comfort, familiarity, and forward momentum without wasting important brain power. But, my goodness, some days I just have to switch things up. When routine starts to feel more like bored, or lazy, or oh-dear-God-give-me-something-different, it's time to upset the proverbial apple cart and shake it up. Take that snow globe of life, and shake it just enough to let those beautiful little flakes swirl around and shift your attention. Take a different route to work. Swap your morning and evening routines. Walk by the river instead of the treadmill. Pull any book off your bookshelf and read a chapter. Listen to someone else's iPod. We need routine ... and we can thrive on change. Shake it up, and let it settle where it will. Like a snow globe.

BRING IT TO LIFE!

Choose one part of your routine today, and change it in some way
that seems interesting and/or exciting to you.
Notice how that change feels.
Is this something you might want to do more often?

"Maybe laughter is God."

SJK

WHEN GOD LAUGHS

I grew up with a rather somber God. I mean, he seemed a nice enough guy and all, but I couldn't quite shake the image of a wizened old man in a cascading white beard and white, glowing robe. I simply couldn't picture laughing it up with my buddy God. The older I get, however, the more I'm thinking that those deep-laughter moments between humans are what happen when God laughs. You know, those laughing fits when two or more of you are doubled over, laughing so hard you've got tears running down your cheeks, and even though the immediate humor passes, you're still rendered helpless with ongoing guffaws? Could be that we're just riding that wave of God's own laughter. That sure would explain the incredible power that laughter has for healing, connection, cleansing, and reinvigorating. Or maybe it's even more than that. Maybe laughter *is* God.

BRING IT TO LIFE!

As you step into laughter in any situation today,
notice how laughter impacts your mood and the way your body feels inside and out.
Is it possible that laughter is a way to transcend the "stuff" of life for a few moments?
How might you bring even more laughter into your days?

*"When we live in this place of NOW, we live in
a constantly renewing place of possibility."*

SJK

THE PRESENT MOMENT

Deepak Chopra talks extensively in his book *The Power of Now*, about the positive power of the present moment. In fact, he suggests we cannot be unhappy when fully engaged in the present.   Consider this: the present moment includes neither past nor future, either of which evokes the greatest stress, sadness, and fear in our lives. When we live in this place of NOW, we live in a constantly renewing place of possibility.   As soon as we are aware of this present moment, it has already turned into a new present moment, encouraging us to engage with a manageable reality instead of an over-blown, fear-inducing fantasy.   Notice the present moment, and live there.

BRING IT TO LIFE!

For the next minute, focus on each second as a "new now."
Practice letting each moment arise, then immediately fade as a new moment replaces it.
Practice letting each old moment go, completely.
*If you learned how to expand this awareness of the present moment
into ongoing chunks of time, how might that change your approach to the past,
the future, and to each present moment?*

"Oh, what a balm it is to be given loving visibility
in this blur we call life."

SJK

BEING SEEN

We had recently returned from a visit to friends in Canada. When another friend asked me about the trip, I reported a delightful time of fun, enjoyment, and connection. Then, surprised by my grateful tears, I found the real answer: "I felt seen. For those three rich days, I was SEEN through shared laughter, full-ranging conversations over coffee and meals, and time spent paying attention to each other." (It's likely no coincidence that this set of friends include a couple who in their wedding vows pledged to "be a witness" to each other's lives.) Oh, what a balm it is to be given loving visibility in this blur we call life.

BRING IT TO LIFE!

Think of a time you recently felt seen. *Who was with you?*
What was it that helped you feel seen?
Write a description of how it felt.
Today, offer that gift of "being seen" to yourself and to others you interact with.
Notice how it impacts your day.

"I wonder now how often my own judgments of others' actions
are so far off base, so deeply mistaken?"

SJK

DEEPLY MISTAKEN

Gentle morning sunlight splashed across the gray-blue door of a city row house, highlighting the silver house number and framing it with a shadow stencil of leaf patterns, while the silver gleam of doorknob and door frame completed the stunning visual. Captivated, I crossed the street and squatted down to get the perfect up-angled composition, and took a photo. ➥ Within seconds, that door opened quickly, and a man in a crisp pink shirt appeared, demanding to know, "Why are you taking pictures of my address?" ➥ Totally surprised, I reacted with truth ... and a frightened tone of defiance: "Because it's beautiful!" ➥ The man's face relaxed, and he smiled in relief. "Oh, I thought you were a terrorist or something!" ➥ I assured him, with several apologies, that I simply found the combination of the metal, the colors, and the shadows lovely and wanted to capture that beauty. ➥ I left that interchange deeply shaken, and I realized it was because my actions had been so misunderstood, and the homeowner's judgment of my intent had been so deeply mistaken. I wonder now how often my own judgments of others' actions are so far off base, so deeply mistaken?

BRING IT TO LIFE!

Today, allow for the possibility that your assumptions of others' actions
could be mistaken (even deeply mistaken), then act accordingly: pause before reacting,
ask direct questions, add empathy, then reassess and adjust your response if necessary.

DECEMBER

"Allow the softness of dusk to soothe your day."

SJK

DUSK

You ask me,

Dusk,

As you gently wring the light from day

Dripping with gold of tomorrow's promise,

Do you believe

in magic my child?

Do you believe?

And I nod, melted, speechless,

wishing I had the words to say

Yes

oh God

yes.

BRING IT TO LIFE!

Today, set aside time to notice the sweet light of dusk.

Watch and feel how it kisses everything with a glow of gold and puts

a hint of magic in the air.

Allow the softness of dusk to soothe your day.

"If I could bottle it, I'd fill warehouse after warehouse
with tiny containers of my wife's laugh."

SJK

IF I COULD BOTTLE IT

If I could bottle it, I'd fill warehouse after warehouse with tiny containers of my wife's laugh, and label them each with a tiny photo of her eyes squeezed shut with tears streaming from them as she laughs herself practically inside out. Many people have echoed this sentiment about her laugh, so I know I'd have plenty of buyers for this product. If you could bottle some delightful part of yourself, what would it be?

BRING IT TO LIFE!

Take five minutes to think about the question:
If you could bottle some delightful part of yourself, what would it be?
Write down your answers.
As you go through your day today, ask yourself the same thing
about others you come in contact with.
Share the question with one person today for their own reflection.
How does this exercise impact your day?

DECEMBER 3

"In paying close attention to our actions,
we get a glimpse of our desires."

SJK

DESIRE

Daniel Ladinsky suggests in his book *The Purity of Desire: 100 Poems of Rumi*, that every human external action can be traced back to an internal spiritual need. ✑ It would stand to reason, then, that our deepest desires and the actions we take to satisfy those desires are actually signposts to our spiritual needs. ✑ I don't know what each desire-based action correlates to spiritually; I just know that in paying close attention to our actions, we get a glimpse of our desires, and it's quite possible that from there we can open a door of understanding to our truest spiritual needs. ✑ If our actions point to our desires, which point to our spiritual needs, the reverse would be that meeting our spiritual needs addresses our desires, which then changes our actions. ✑ Think what actions will show up as we honor those spiritual needs with regular time and attention!

BRING IT TO LIFE!

Ask yourself deeply, *"What do I want? What do I deep down, really, truly want?"*
Without much thought, write down the answers that come to you.
What spiritual needs are asking for attention?
Take one step toward meeting one of those needs TODAY.

"What if our deepest, most transformational moments
are beyond understanding?"

SJK

BEYOND UNDERSTANDING

Wrestling with some inner knots, I write into them to shine a spotlight, hoping desperately to understand what's there so I can release the tension. Journal pages fill, and still my angst remains. "If I could just understand what I'm feeling, I could let go," I think. "If I analyze long enough, apply enough 'figure it out' pressure to my mind, I could break through, understand, and finally move forward." I try to convince myself. But what if the way forward is to set our understanding aside and breathe so deeply into those knotted feelings that they begin to melt from the inside out? What if our deepest, most transformational moments are beyond understanding?

BRING IT TO LIFE!

Today, when you find yourself mulling over something in an attempt to understand it,
take a deep breath, and on your breath out, say to yourself, "Beyond understanding."
Picture the tightness inside you melting with each breath as you gradually let go
of the need to understand (even if only for a moment).
Carry the phrase "beyond understanding" with you today,
along with that feeling of a warm, inner melting.
How does this exercise impact your day?

"Notice the way many children so easily and naturally give love;
tiny arms have big hearts."

SJK

TINY ARMS, BIG HEARTS

My office overlooks the playground of a city charter school. At regular intervals through-out the day, the kids pour onto the gated, fenced-in playground like a stream of ants on a focused mission, dispersing to all corners once inside the fence. This morning in the swing set area there is just a handful of children, outnumbered by parents and caretakers who are sitting along the fence, watching. A few minutes ago, an adorable child in bright pink shoes dashed over to one of the grown-ups and threw her arms around her. Immediately, a second child followed suit, throwing his arms around the same woman. Mostly covered by traditional, modest clothing and veil, the only thing showing on this woman was her hands — wrapped around two children (one wearing hot pink tennis shoes) piled on her lap with their sweet little arms around her. Tiny arms, big hearts. What a powerful example these children are, no matter how small or big our arms are!

BRING IT TO LIFE!

Notice today the way many children so easily and naturally give love.
Commit to living with and from a big heart today, just like them.
How does this impact your day?

"Crystal-clear clarity isn't the only beauty in the waters of our lives."

SJK

MURKY WATERS

I didn't notice it until I had arrived back home and was looking at the photos I had just taken; the reflection of the trees and sky on the murky river water shone in such rich blues and deep greens. The original sky and trees held a lovely color, but, in comparison, the intensity of the reflected colors was absolutely breathtaking. ✑ Apparently the shadows and murky depths of the water acted as a boost, amplifying everything in the reflection. ✑ The shadows and murky depths in our lives can have that same effect on our life experience if we take the time to notice: the questions piling up just under our emotional surface level reflect an empathy to those around us who also are questioning, wondering, and searching, while the murkiness and imperfections in the depths of our being reflect a compassion for our shadowy parts. ✑ Crystal-clear clarity isn't the only beauty in the waters of our lives.

BRING IT TO LIFE!

What shadows and inner murky waters are you aware of in yourself?
How might they allow you to open your heart to see
and to be a reflection of compassion and empathy?

"Tears sit quietly on our eyelashes, and for that brief moment
we know, without a doubt, the reality of God."

SJK

DIVINE DETAILS

In college, I wrote a letter to my boyfriend. The details recounted my experience during a trip to Salzburg, Austria, tweaked to become a shared (imaginary) experience.

Dear S., We start from the little inn on the corner of the stone-paved village, toting only crusty bread and tattered paperbacks. Making our way down the narrow street, we're drawn in by a sweet scent and peek into a flower shop in the front of an age-worn home. Grinning, we throw our heads back and breathe deeply, inhaling the very heavens. We wander past candy stands, gift shops, and store after store overflowing with watches and clocks, yet we let time pass without a glance. Salzburg holds nothing but the present moment, replenished as soon as it is used up, only adding ticks of excitement and easing the day deeper into our veins. Around a corner, our world disappears into awe. Directly ahead of us, rubbing the foot of the snow-dusted Alps, stands a magnificent, stone haven. The cathedral's dark doorway promises a cool salve for our hearts, and we walk softly inside, slipping easily into pure, unquestioning peace. The damp air wraps like silk around our souls as we stand in the center of hope and healing, unaware of ourselves. Tears sit quietly on our eyelashes, and for that brief moment we know, without a doubt, the reality of God. And the rest is for you to finish as you wish ...

BRING IT TO LIFE!

Re-read the letter, and finish the experience as you wish, carrying the details with you today.

"They say the way we begin something is the way we continue it,
so let's savor the beginning, the 'first sip' of it all!"

SJK

THAT FIRST SIP

A friend texted me this morning while her first cup of coffee was still brewing, so I soon got the pleasure of sharing that first-sip moment with her. Sure enough, a little smartphone tweet tweet, and there was her text: "Aaaaaah, that first sip ... " I was already two cups in, yet that message still evoked the feeling of luxurious delight I experience with that first sip every morning.

That first sip of morning brew ...
That first bite of evening dinner ...
That first breath of vacation's ocean air ...
That first glimpse of meeting a loved one in person for the first time ...

... all of those "first sip" moments of magnified experience that we often forget to cherish. They say the way we begin something is the way we continue it, so let's savor the beginning, the "first sip" of it all!

BRING IT TO LIFE!

Today, commit to experiencing first sips and savoring each one for an extra few moments.
At the end of the day, take 10 minutes to write notes describing the first sips
that you remember most vividly.
How did this exercise impact the way you feel by the end of the day?

"When we are willing to experience our own lives fully and intentionally,
we can deeply empathize with others, responding to them with compassion
that comes from shared experience."

SJK

I GET IT, I KNOW

As happens from time to time in calls with my professional life coach, I wept through my current frustrations and confusion, and, as also happens (all the time), I left the call with a fresh approach and energizing clarity. ✍ The next day, I had the honor of coaching one of my clients who happened to bring up the same issue that I had worked through the day before. Because of my own inner work, I was able to provide the empathy of "I get it, I know" and offer my client the same questions that had led me to my answers the day before. ✍ It struck me that when we are willing to experience our own lives fully and intentionally, even when it requires stepping through confusion and being with the pain, we can deeply empathize with others, responding to them with compassion that comes from shared experience. ✍ When we brave the unknown, to use a phrase from poet Ushi Patel, and meet our lives with full attention and engagement, we give ourselves the gift of an endless storehouse of "I get it, I know."

BRING IT TO LIFE!

Is there a piece of your life you've been shying away from?
What would it take to step into that experience today, even if just a toe-length in?
Take that action today, and notice how soon you'll have the chance
to say to someone else, "I get it, I know."

"Re-new, to make new again — we can choose it at any time
by letting the old slip through our grasp
as we open our hands to receive the new."

SJK

RE-NEW

On Friday mornings, I regularly use one of my favorite coffee mugs: a pure-white mug adorned only by a simple RENEW near the top, with "RE" and "NEW" in subtlely different colors. ✎ Re-new, to make new again, to start over, to transform the old into something fresh — we can choose it at any time by letting the old slip through our grasp as we open our hands to receive the new. ✎ We can take our tiredness and re-new our energy by changing our schedule for an earlier bedtime, or an afternoon nap, or exchanging acts of obligation for offerings of delight. ✎ We can take our ennui and re-new our verve by replacing our tired old habits with new rituals of meaning, discovery, and self-support. ✎ We can take our anxiously knotted insides and re-new our peace and life force by remembering to give full room to each oxygen-laden breath. ✎ We can take any moment and re-new it with the polish of choice.

BRING IT TO LIFE!

What do you most want and need to re-new today?
What are three actions you can take to let go of the old to make new
for the re-new-al replacement?
Take one of those actions today.

"As it is stated, so shall it be."

SJK

TODAY I AM

Flipping back through my spiritual journal, several days in a row during November 2012 caught my eye. Each one consisted of only one sentence, in all caps, each one starting with the phrase "TODAY I AM"

November 13
TODAY I AM COMPLETE FREEDOM AND TRUST.
November 14
TODAY I AM GRACE AND CONFIDENCE.
November 15
TODAY I AM COMPLETE FREEDOM AND TRUST.

I must have needed some reinforcement on that third one from two days prior! ✎ Notice, it's not "Today I want," or "Today I will be," or "Today I ask for." It's a simple, clear declaration of how I AM, as current truth, whether true or not. ✎ As it is stated, so shall it be.

BRING IT TO LIFE!

What or how do you want to be today?
State it using the "TODAY I AM _____" format.
Write it down and carry it with you through the day.
How does this exercise impact your day?

"Enjoyment doesn't have to come in huge luxuries or top-notch events.
Sometimes all it takes is letting ourselves be touched
by someone else's brief moment of joy."

SJK

GUMBALL

On the way out of the grocery store, I always eye the giant gumball machine, salivating over the prospect of chewy sweetness, never mind the sore jaw from the inevitable staleness. ✍ This time, as I left the grocery store, the woman in front of me stopped just in front of the exit, turned around, and circled back to — you guessed it — the gumball machine! Grinning to myself, I watched her dig in her wallet for a quarter, getting that luscious gumball (it was green), and chewing at it all the way out to the parking lot. ✍ Not only did she enjoy the experience; I did too. And every time I pass that same gumball machine each week, I grin at the memory of the fully grown woman treating herself to a gumball. ✍ Enjoyment doesn't have to come in huge luxuries or top-notch events. Sometimes all it takes is letting ourselves be touched by someone else's brief moment of joy.

BRING IT TO LIFE!

What is a 25-cents-or-less moment of enjoyment (edible or not)
you can treat yourself to today? Do that.
And encourage someone else to do it with you.
How does this impact your day?

"Today, this moment, and every moment,
we stand on the tightrope of time,
and the way to find our 'just right' balance
is to simply Be Here Now."

SJK

THE GOLDILOCKS APPROACH

Every day, we come from a yesterday and will (likely) soon step into a tomorrow. With every moment, we create a new past and step into a new future which quickly becomes the present moment, and the cycle continues. ➥ So what should we do with today — spend it reliving the memories of yesterday, or looking ahead at the promises of tomorrow? ➥ Either. Neither. Both. Whatever is here now: be with it, honor it, and celebrate it! ➥ It's like standing on a beach with a damp pile of sand in our open hand as the overflow sifts gently through our fingers, leaving us with a small gathering of granules. The "too much" parts of yesterday's overflow return from whence they came, leaving us with the "just right" parts for the next moment, the next day: the Goldilocks Approach. ➥ Today, this moment, and every moment, we stand on the tightrope of time … and the way to find our "just right" balance is to simply Be Here Now.

➥

BRING IT TO LIFE!

Right this moment, where are your thoughts taking you? To the day ahead?
To something still hanging on from yesterday?
Look around you at your now. Feel how you feel now.
Today, carry a note that says "Be Here Now." Notice how that awareness impacts your day.

"In the heart of nature, we discover our own heartbeat."

SJK

THE HEART OF NATURE

As I notice the pink, heart-shaped flowers on the miniature begonia glowing in the sunlight on my windowsill, I realize my own heartbeat shifts slightly. It's almost imperceptible — the feeling of my heart expanding, a momentary slowing of its work as it pauses to recognize nature's heartbeat in those heart-shaped flowers. I used to brush those nature-connected experiences off as imaginary moments in my creative mind, but I'm beginning to believe there's much more real there. Imagination isn't what immediately warms the palm of my hand when I place it on one of my favorite trees on an urban side street. Imagination isn't what brings tears to my eyes when I see the tiny, heart-shaped leaves appear each spring from the Forest Pansy Redbud trees. And imagination isn't what consistently quiets a baby's anxious crying when carried outdoors. When we pay attention to the heart of nature, we have the chance to discover our own heartbeat.

BRING IT TO LIFE!

Take 15 minutes today to look for heart shapes in nature.
If you're not near an accessible outdoor area, go to a local store
that includes - or is - a garden center.
Stop and touch the heart shape, and see if you can feel your own heart respond.

"Feel the warmth of the sun through your skin, into your heart."

SJK

SUNLIGHT

Sunlight
warm like the breath
of a lover
kissing my arm
to remind me
I
still
matter.

BRING IT TO LIFE!

The next time the sun shines, find a place where you can sit or stand
with sunshine touching only part of you.
Close your eyes and feel the warmth of the sun-kissed part of your body,
allowing that feeling to seep deeper — through your skin, into your heart.
Carry that feeling with you, and notice how it impacts the rest of your day.

"Moments of full, shared attention
give peace an open doorway to our hearts."

SJK

WATCHING BIRDS

Several mornings a week, my precocious cat, Jazzy, and I pause our busy lives to watch birds together. She sits at the back door, her little body taut as her head follows the movements of the birds having their morning meetings on the wires between houses. This cat doesn't really appreciate being picked up, and being held is on her terms only — except when we watch birds together. I scoop her up and hold her little body against my chest with her sweet, fuzzy belly open to the world and her back facing me, while her little legs dangle over my arms: front legs over my upper arm, hind legs over my lower arm. As I nuzzle the top of her head, we watch the birds together for a few minutes as one combined unit. Such a small thing, but the tenderness of it brings my attention fully to that moment. Those moments of full, shared attention give peace an open doorway to our hearts.

BRING IT TO LIFE!

Think of one small act of shared attention you can participate in.
What is that act?
Who is the person or other being who would appreciate and understand
that moment with you?
Share that act of attention with that person today.

"What if we step away from the backstage position we approach so much of life from and simply leave the theater ... and live."

SJK

OFF STAGE

Performance anxiety; I get it every day.

Will I seem present enough for my clients?

Will I sound wise enough for my coach?

Will I be strong enough for my partner's comfort?

Might this action make me more lovable? Or maybe this one? Or this one?

Does that expression cover enough of my pain? And this one hide my frustration?

Will that behavior be too much? And that other one too little?

Will I seem brilliant enough in my writing? Deep enough in my meditation?

What if we step away from the backstage position we approach so much of life from and simply leave the theater ... and live. Just. Live. As. Ourselves.

BRING IT TO LIFE!

In what ways do you approach life as though it were a performance?
What would it take for you to leave the theatre and step into life
as exactly who you are?
Take one step in that direction today.

"What an incredible gift it is
to have someone reflect us positively back to ourselves."

SJK

THIS SOUNDS LIKE YOU

Every few months, I receive an email from a dear friend, sharing a quote or a link to an article or video, accompanied by her words that "This sounds like you." So far, I've recognized myself in each thing she's sent, but even if I didn't, my heart would still melt a bit with each email, realizing anew what an incredible gift it is to have someone reflect me positively back to myself. Find the beauty of those you love (and don't!) in something that touches your heart, and share it with that person, letting them know that "this sounds like you." You may just learn to do the same for yourself.

BRING IT TO LIFE!

Today, notice things in your world that remind you pleasantly
of other people in your life.
Choose one of those people, and send them a note
with reference to whatever reminded you of them,
and let them know, "This sounds like you."

"Sit with me here and take a deep breath of silence."

SJK

SIT WITH ME HERE

Sit with me here
and take a deep breath of silence
feeling the warmth
of a steaming cup of coffee
a moment alone/shared
in y/our own private café,
a chance to escape/return to every sip of life
to (not) feel.
Sit with(out) me here
for whatever reason
with this mug full of only what you need
and feel the comfort
of moments made
just and only for you.

BRING IT TO LIFE!

At some point today, set aside five minutes to simply enjoy a cup of your favorite
soothing beverage and appreciate that moment, made specially and only for you.
Is this an exercise you'd like to do more often?

"I need to stop and get to know all the details of this rich and precious life
to surround myself with the friendship of beauty."

SJK

STOP AND KNOW THEM

My dear wife has had to learn a great deal of patience in experiencing this world with me. I'm much like a child constantly enamored with whatever catches one of my senses, so a six-block walk to the grocery store, for example, can easily become a 30-minute field trip. ≋ I need to touch things: plants, fence posts, cats, dogs, and the crumbling brick on the corner of a 100-year-old house. ≋ I need to get up close and personal to examine the striations of tree bark, the mandala effect of seedlings arranged meticulously as a flower head, and the sunlight glinting off the silver threads of my wife's hair. ≋ I need to inhale the ancestral scent of sun-roasted stone, hear the innocent singing of someone mistaking their earbuds for privacy, and taste the fresh mint beckoning me from a random window box. ≋ I need to stop and get to know them — all the details of this rich and precious life — to surround myself with the friendship of beauty, shoring myself up for the days when life gets too big, too rough, or too raw. ≋ Today, tomorrow, and the next day, stop and know them — those intricate creative details of life — then introduce them to those who have the gift of being in contact with you.

BRING IT TO LIFE!

Today, stop and get to know the intricate details of life — often.
Share an observation with a friend or colleague (or stranger!).
How does this impact your day?

"See the cares disappearing under a crashing wave,
then surfacing to slowly fade out of view on the horizon."

SJK

AT THE LIP OF THE OCEAN

At the lip of the ocean
I hear her ask
in the whoosh of receding waves
Hello, one of my heart, what do you need?
What can I get you?
Silently, I toss her my cares
weeping as she gently crushes
and pulls them out to the horizon.

BRING IT TO LIFE!

What cares are on your mind or heart today?
Write them down, then close your eyes and reach out your hand with
the list of cares in it, offering it to the ocean in your mind.
See the cares disappearing under a crashing wave, then surfacing
to slowly fade out of view on the horizon.
Notice any difference in your feeling of cares after this exercise.

"Disappointment is the incubator of priority plans."

SJK

THE OTHER SIDE OF DISAPPOINTMENT

Near the end of a mostly-gray, cold, and sunless winter in Philadelphia, my upcoming Florida vacation took on a savior-like quality: if work was frustrating, I imagined the southern sunshine kissing my warm skin as I lay by the pool; if positive emotions were low, I imagined the ocean waves licking my toes and the sand buffing my rough heels. ✎ Unfortunately, mother nature had other plans, giving us three Florida days of clouds, cold, and drizzle, with sunshine an almost unbearable tease when it finally unveiled itself an hour before leaving time. ✎ I was so disappointed I could hardly breathe. ✎ So I made plans — determined, come-hell-or-high-water plans — to get back to the tropical sunshine sooner than later. My soul was so deflated that I couldn't ignore the urgency of my need for a sunshiny travel break from regular life. ✎ I realized then that disappointment is the incubator of priority plans. If you're willing to look your most bone-crushing disappointments in the eye, they become signposts to your divine longings and clear guides on your path.

BRING IT TO LIFE!

Do you have a current disappointment?
If so, what is it — really? What longing has not been met?
Visualize what you were hoping for that didn't come true
(the catalyst for your disappointment),
and take one small or large step toward making it happen. Today.

"What if we allowed ourselves to believe that we rest in the arms
of a divine source that has no options for us other than 'you win'?"

SJK

TWO SIDES TO EACH COIN

Rumi, in his poem *A Coin Toss for Your Soul,* describes a possible scenario at heaven's gates: a soul arrives before God, and God reads some notes from the angels, then suggests that maybe the better way to decide whether the soul gets an ongoing union with God or not is to toss a coin. ✎ So God tosses a coin, saying to the soul, "Heads, you win," union with God. The kicker? Both sides of the coin are heads. ✎ What if we experimented with seeing both sides of any situation as valuable, as preferable? Or even better yet, what if we allowed ourselves to believe that we rest in the arms of a divine source that has no options for us other than win; that both sides of our life coin are heads? ✎ Consider that.

BRING IT TO LIFE!

Spend five minutes picturing a divine coin being tossed in honor of your life,
knowing that heads means "You win."
See the coin landing with heads up (since both sides are heads),
and allow yourself to feel the relief of knowing, even if only for a moment,
that your life is of divine value.
How might this exercise impact your thoughts, feelings, and interactions today?

"Fall into the arms of grace and love."

SJK

IN THE ARMS OF GRACE

In the arms of grace
held
in infinite safety
gentle whisperings
pry open our hearts
Love
my dear ones
Love
through the infinity of the ocean
the constancy of the sunrise
the incomprehensibility of all that we call
Divine
Fall
into the arms of grace
and Love.

BRING IT TO LIFE!

Take a deep, deep breath, and imagine easily falling into the safe arms of grace,
whatever that means to you.
How might you take that feeling into the rest of your day?

"Yeah, they can see you.
And that's exactly why we must dance to the joyous music in our souls."

SJK

LET THEM SEE YOU

It was a particularly enjoyable Saturday at the gym. I had just finished an endorphin-fueled treadmill run and was feeling delightfully healthy and strong. ✍ So, naturally, when a grooving song piped through my earbuds, I stopped everything and danced. Right there in the middle of the gym. ✍ Laughing, the gym owner came over and quietly asked, "Um, you know we can see you, right???" ✍ Oh yes, I knew. And it didn't really matter, because I was just that happy. ✍ Yeah, they can see you. And that's exactly why we must dance to the joyous music in our souls. ✍ Let them see you. Let them dance.

BRING IT TO LIFE!

Today, watch for your own moments of happiness, and magnify them for others to share.
Turn a grin into a chuckle or all-out laugh.
Turn a thought of, "I like this song" to the movement of dance, even in your office chair.
Hug the daylights out of someone in appreciation of who they are.
Let them see your joy. Let them dance.

"There's a time for spirit and a time for skin."

SJK

WITH SKIN ON

There's a precious story of a child who's being tucked into bed for the night. After she says her prayers, she begs her mom to stay with her as she falls asleep. When her mom gently reminds her that God is there to keep her company, the little girl replies that yes, she knows that, but, tonight, she needs someone with skin on! We can get great comfort and companionship from all manner of spiritual connections, and, still, some times we simply need someone with skin on. Let's not forget in the quest for spiritual growth and awareness that we are also human.

BRING IT TO LIFE!

There's a time for spirit and a time for skin.
Today, pay attention to what you offer others
and how well it fits their needs.

"Turn yourself into a living conversation with the divine."

SJK

LOVE, ME

Recently I've been closing my journal entries with "Love, Me" followed by a little heart. I'm not really a little-hearts person — yet there they are. And I'm not writing in those journals to dear anyone in particular, yet there's my signature as if on a letter. It's the unexplained urges like that which continue to point me to the existence of a mystical Connection in this universe. A journal entry, that I think is just a recording of my own thoughts, ends with a clear "Love, Me" closing as though to a quite-familiar, loved one (including, for heaven's sake, a heart??), Or maybe what I really mean is love (no comma) me. Love me. A request. A plea. Either way (with or without the comma), that closing turns my musings and ramblings into a conversation, a chance to be heard fully. Heard by I don't know whom or what, and I'm not sure it even matters. Add a "Love, Me" or "Love me" to your journal entry, your self-talk, your prayer, your quiet moments, and your everything. Turn yourself into a living conversation with the divine.

BRING IT TO LIFE!

Today, see how many times you can add a quiet, whispered (or written) "Love, Me"
or "Love me" (whichever you most naturally express at each moment) to a situation.
How does this impact your day and your feeling of connection?

"Let the beauty we love be what we do.
There are hundreds of ways to kneel and kiss the ground."

RUMI

KNEEL AND KISS THE GROUND

Rumi gets gratitude. You see it threaded through line after line of his poetry, the deep-seated gratitude so intense that it simply has to be expressed. The appreciation so strong that we drop to our knees and kiss the ground. When was the last time you stepped so deeply into your gratitude that it brought you to your knees? You can choose to do that today or any day because the intensity of your gratitude doesn't depend on the size of the "gift" (in the broadest sense of the word); it depends on the flexibility of your heart and your willingness to let the gratitude rise up from the deepest, most purely golden core of you. Let gratitude melt you to your knees … so together we can kneel and kiss this holy ground of life.

BRING IT TO LIFE!

Write three things you are deeply grateful for,
then take five minutes to sit quietly and feel that gratitude.
After those five minutes, kneel gently, put your palms together,
and kiss your hands in a gesture of thanks.
Take that gratitude with you throughout your day today.

"We can stumble sleepily over that threshold into the next year
and carry on with the same burdens and stale dreams,
or we can step wide awake into the new year carrying only that which we choose."

SJK

TAKE IT OR LEAVE IT

I find the threshold of a new calendar year to be a delicious time of reflection and intention-setting. ✑ We can stumble sleepily over that threshold into the next year and carry on with the same burdens and stale dreams, or we can step wide awake into the new year carrying only that which we choose. ✑ We get to honor the past year of life by re-savoring the memories, celebrating our successes, and acknowledging our growth since this time last year, then leaving the past gently as we choose what to take into the next year. ✑ We get to re-select our dreams, revive our hopes, and re-claim our time and our selves as we pack our suitcase of intentions to carry into the next year. ✑ Take it or leave it — the choice is yours, and what better time to choose than at the turn of a year?

BRING IT TO LIFE!

Set aside 10 minutes to pay attention to this threshold time of year.
Write a list titled "Take It" — things you choose to carry with you into the following year.
Then write a list titled "Leave It" — things you choose to leave in the past.
Notice how it feels to be intentional about this transitional time of year.
Is this something you might want to do for other significant transitions, such as birthdays,
relationship changes, project completions and beginnings, and so on?

"Let's honor the endings: let's allow them our time,
offer them our comfort, and give them our attention."

SJK

HONOR THE ENDINGS

As I write this next-to-last page, I notice it's also the next-to-last page in my writing note-book. My heart soars for a moment as I picture the thrill of getting out the fresh new note-book so full of open possibility, immediately followed by a pang of sadness as I feel the ending of the writing stage of this book project. ⤺ Endings are complex happenings in our lives. On one hand, they signal a closing and a completion, and, even in the most desired endings, usually come with a sense of loss. ⤺ On the other hand, endings mark time in meaningful ways as they make room for beginnings and clear space in our spiritual and emotional closets. ⤺ Let's honor the endings: let's allow them our time, offer them our comfort, and give them our attention.

BRING IT TO LIFE!

Write "Honor the endings" on a sticky-note, and put it where you will see it
in the course of each day. Next time you have an ending (big or small) in your life,
take the time to honor the ending. Write a list of acknowledgement for whatever is ending,
then write a list of possibility for what the ending is allowing you.
Notice how this impacts your experience of an "ending."

DECEMBER 31

"Today, as I write this last page, I need to say Thank you!
Thank you, dear reader, for giving these words
the pleasure of your company."

SJK

TO BE COMPLETE

I had a coach who ended phone calls (individual or group) with the question, "What do you need to say to be complete?" Some days "complete" required nothing extra, while other days, it was a mention of gratitude, a quick question, a request, or one last bit of information passed on. ⮌ Today, as I write this last page, I need to say "Thank you!" to be complete. Thank you, dear reader, for giving these words the pleasure of your company. Thank you for giving these pages your attention. And thank you for giving the world your precious, life-giving awake moments of conscious living. ⮌ Today, this page is the final page of your yearlong journey with this book, with yourself. ⮌ What do you need to say or do to be complete with this leg of the journey?

⮌

BRING IT TO LIFE!

Set aside 15 minutes to answer this question:
"What do you need to be complete?"
Then take action on it.
Go. Live.

WIDE AWAKE. EVERY DAY.

ABOUT THE AUTHOR

Starla J. King, author of *Wide Awake. Every Day.*,
lives in Philadelphia, Pennsylvania with her delightful
wife and their feline troublemakers.

Starla is a creative non-fiction
writer, poet, photographer,
and certified Creativity
Coach and Writing Coach.
Through *OutWrite Living*,
Starla promotes and facilitates
the use of creativity as an
essential part of healthy,
productive, peaceful, and
meaningful living.

To explore opportunities to work with Starla and to
sign up for her blog, visit http://outwriteliving.com.

Wide Awake. Every Day. is available on Amazon.com
and at book events announced on outwriteliving.com
and on Starla's blog.

CPSIA information can be obtained at www.ICGtesting.com
Printed in the USA
LVOW03s1230201113

362063LV00001B/1/P